S0-BEH-024

'08

NIM CHIMPSKY

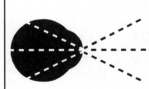 This Large Print Book carries the Seal of Approval of N.A.V.H.

NIM CHIMPSKY

THE CHIMP WHO WOULD BE HUMAN

ELIZABETH HESS

THORNDIKE PRESS
A part of Gale, Cengage Learning

GALE
CENGAGE Learning

Detroit • New York • San Francisco • New Haven, Conn • Waterville, Maine • London

GALE
CENGAGE Learning™

LIBRARY OF CONGRESS CATALOGING-IN-PUBLICATION DATA

Hess, Elizabeth.
    Nim chimpsky : the chimp who would be human / by Elizabeth Hess. — Large print ed.
       p. cm.
    Originally published: New York : Bantam Books, 2008.
    Includes bibliographical references.
    ISBN-13: 978-1-4104-0686-6 (hardcover : alk. paper : lg. print)
    ISBN-10: 1-4104-0686-5 (hardcover : alk. paper : lg. print)
    1. Nim Chimpsky (Chimpanzee) 2. Chimpanzees — Psychology. 3. Human-animal communication. 4. Sign language. 5. Chimpanzees — Biography. I. Title.
    QL737.P96H465 2008b
    636.9885092'9—dc22   2008005385

Published in 2008 by arrangement with The Bantam Dell Publishing Group, a division of Random House, Inc.

Printed in the United States of America
1 2 3 4 5 6 7 12 11 10 09 08

*For Nim, Pete, Kat,
and the other beasts in my life*

what is most unexpected is language
the way it threads us through and through
we the knots tied in the net
our lives the fish we catch in it
                    W. E. R. LaFarge
                    ("how we are connected")

CONTENTS

Nim's mother, Carolyn, in Norman, Oklahoma

PROLOGUE:
THE UNEXPECTED
BIRTH OF
NIM CHIMPSKY

November 19, 1973, began like any other day at the Institute for Primate Studies (IPS) in Norman, Oklahoma. There, on the outskirts of town, where suburbia fades into rolling farmland, a motley group of forty chimpanzees hooted and shrieked in anticipation of their breakfast. Emily Sue Savage (now known as Sue Savage-Rumbaugh), a graduate student at the University of Oklahoma and a regular visitor to the chimp houses at IPS, no longer cringed at the sound of this earsplitting racket. Savage spent most of her days at this research facility, collecting data for her forthcoming dissertation on mother-infant behavior in captive chimpanzees.

The chimps were in two different buildings, one of which was attached almost like an in-law apartment to the house that belonged to Dr. William Burton Lemmon, Savage's mentor and the director of the

Institute. This building was where Lemmon's adult chimps lived and where Savage went to observe mothers and newborns during their first few weeks together. Most graduate students never went near the adult chimps, preferring to spend time with the much more amusing, less hostile adolescents, who were tucked away in a barn located a short distance from Lemmon's house. But Savage had chosen to study the older, bigger females. She had become inured to their odors, their aggressive gestures, and even the jets of water (or feces) they spat at her face; she understood their anxieties and appreciated their sense of humor. The budding young scientist, who would later become world famous for her groundbreaking language research with her own colony of bonobos, had clocked so many hours with these chimps that she identified more with them than with her fellow students.

That afternoon, Savage was observing Carolyn, a wild-born, eighteen-year-old female, when she saw her bend over and pull a small, dark form out of her massive body. There was no mistaking the dripping, writhing package. Trying to blend into the scene as unobtrusively as possible, Savage sat quietly and watched as Carolyn, an experienced mother, began to hug and groom her new baby, her seventh. A few critical seconds ahead of the chimps who shared quarters in the building, Savage closed one of the guillotine doors separating the cages from each other to give Carolyn some privacy and some protection from her mates. After several more minutes of focused observation, Savage went to spread the news.

Savage's teacher, the charismatic and highly unconventional William Lemmon, felt as proud of each newborn delivered by one of his chimps as if he had played a part in their creation. He rarely missed the advent of a pregnancy or, for that matter, any other development in his chimpanzee colony. But he had not known that Carolyn was pregnant, much less that she was about to give birth. She had produced six infants over the past four years (including two sets of twins) and Lemmon felt she needed a rest, so he had put her on birth control pills, the same kind that humans take, in an early experiment in primate population control. Carolyn was one of the first chimps on the pill. But apparently the pill is not foolproof for any species.

As soon as he heard the news from his student, Lemmon rushed to Carolyn's cage and found her cradling the damp, sputtering infant. This baby, as adorable as his older siblings, had protruding ears, saucer eyes the color of maple syrup, and string bean arms and legs. When he cried, Carolyn issued a rhythmic stream of whimpers that had an instant calming effect, almost like a lullaby. She ran her lips over every inch of his skin, gently kissing and grooming him from head to toe.

Grooming, an activity that cements the bond between chimp mother and child, begins at birth. In the wild, mother and child often remain together for three or four years, in constant physical contact with each other, while the youngster receives detailed instruction in the fine art of jungle survival. In captivity, the bonding process and with it the lessons passed along from one generation to the next may not remain intact; chimp mothers frequently reject their infants, refusing even to hold them after giving birth. It's as if their maternal instincts have been switched off, sometimes temporarily, sometimes forever. Like humans, chimpanzees can suffer from severe depression.

But Carolyn was an ideal mother. She held her baby close to her with one arm while she swatted away flies with her other hand. Then she leapt up onto a perch in her cage and turned her back toward her audience to face the wall, preventing Lemmon and the others in the small group that had gathered from seeing her baby. The gesture made a powerful statement, which none of them had any trouble understanding. Carolyn knew the drill. She would not have long to experience the pleasurable thrall of motherhood. This baby, like all her others, would soon be taken from her, destined for one of the research projects to which Lemmon sent most of the chimps born at IPS. As it happened, number 37, as he was listed in Lemmon's primate records, was slated for a prestigious ape language study at Columbia University, which the lead scientist had dubbed Project Nim after its research subject, who was intended to bear the name Nim Chimpsky. Carolyn's baby, known as Nim throughout his life, was taken from his mother ten days later.

Baby Nim in New York City

INTRODUCTION:
CHIMPS ARE US

Chimpanzees were never meant to be born, or live, in captivity. For millions of years they were safely hidden away in the African jungle, far from human eyes, where they hunted and foraged for food, fashioned crude tools out of sticks and stones, organized themselves into tight social groups that functioned like small, warring tribes, and lived by intricately structured codes of behavior that were passed down from generation to generation. In the sixteenth century, however, accounts of their existence made their way back to "civilization," opening their secret world to a public fascinated by reports of exotic, human-like creatures in faraway lands. It was only a matter of time before explorers from Europe would capture some of these creatures and bring them back for display, turning them into spectacles for an awestruck audience. King Kong was just around the corner.

19

Then as now, chimpanzees mesmerized us, precisely because of their resemblance to us.

The word *chimpanzee,* which was introduced into the vernacular of the Western world in 1738, comes from *kivili-chimpenze,* a term in the Tshiluba language, spoken in what is now the Democratic Republic of the Congo. Translated loosely as "mock man," the word suggests that the inhabitants of the Congo who first encountered chimpanzees might have believed them to be the product of couplings between humans and other species. This belief is echoed in the accounts of many writers documenting their own first face-to-face meetings with chimpanzees, back in the days when these "trophies" were still a great novelty. One of the earliest of these accounts, written by diarist Samuel Pepys, seems the most relevant to the life of Nim Chimpsky.

In 1661, Pepys boarded a naval ship just back from Guinea, to see an impressive wild creature of unknown provenance. The captain of the ship, uncertain how to safely unload his dangerous treasure, had invited eager onlookers to come aboard. Astonished, Pepys described the beast as the offspring of "a man and a she-baboone."

While he was no doubt in error about the patrimony of what was almost certainly a chimpanzee, he did have an intuitive sense of the kinship between it and us.

In his writings, Pepys made another prescient comment about chimpanzees. He noted with amazement that the beast he encountered on the ship appeared to understand English. Pepys speculated that the "baboone" could probably be taught to "speak or make signs." To him, the notion that chimps might learn a human language was apparently not a huge leap of faith. In this, he anticipated the research of scientists many centuries later, who were similarly convinced of our fundamental kinship with members of the primate world, and likewise certain that they could be taught language. And therein lies the essence of our longtime fascination with these animals. At some point, most of us have communicated, using a few words and gestures, with a very bright dog. Now, imagine communicating with an even brighter, more intuitive animal who might have the intelligence of a six- or seven-year-old child and look like a (very) distant relative.

Not only do chimpanzees resemble us physically, but as infants they adapt so readily to a human lifestyle that comparisons between us and them are inevitable. These similarities have made them ready candidates for research on subjects going far beyond the medical experiments they've been subjected to since the early twentieth century to the evolution of language and even to the very nature of our humanity. The possibility of interspecies communication, coupled with the notion that chimpanzees might hold, whether in their blood, their brains, or their bodies, the key to the survival of the human race, has turned these animals into invaluable objects not just of wonder but of scientific inquiry.

Nineteenth-century drawing of an encounter with wildlife in East Africa

However, chimpanzees are "hard keepers," a term often used by zoo employees who understand the difficulty of maintaining these high-strung creatures behind bars. During the seventeenth century, the era when Pepys made his observations, few if any of the apes taken from Africa and brought to Europe, often as gifts for royalty or scientists, survived long enough for much scrutiny. Chimpanzees have highly sensitive immune systems, and they are acutely vulnerable to human diseases. Infant chimps, often chosen for export because they were far less menacing as well as easier to snatch — especially after their mothers were shot dead — were even harder to keep alive than adults, since no one understood that they needed the same quality of care and constant attention as human babies; if they are not held close, cuddled, fed constantly, and given affection, they die. All of which helps to explain why it took so long for the scientific community to gain access to the species. It wasn't until 1828, close to two centuries after Pepys described what may have been the first chimpanzee captured in the jungle and successfully kept alive long enough to be transported to another country, that the London Zoological Gardens was able to make available for scientific observation its collection of exotic species, which had been painstakingly garnered over a period of several years. This collection eventually opened to the public in 1847, becoming the first modern zoo. Charles Darwin, among others, spent hours taking notes on the zoo's lone gorilla while working on *The Origin of Species,* published in 1859.

During the nineteenth century, there were still so few wild animals in captivity that one enterprising early American zoologist, Richard Lynch Garner, made a trip to Africa in 1892 to observe the apes in their own habitat. But getting close enough to the chimps and gorillas to be able to see them safely was extremely difficult, so Garner, inverting the usual order of things, decided to build himself an elevated cage in the jungle, from which he proceeded to observe and photograph the animals around him for 112 days. Garner was not a particularly reliable source on primates, nor did he have what a present-day animal rights advocate would consider an enlightened attitude toward them, but he was a pioneer. Like a good imperialist, he eventually captured his own colony of apes and brought it back to England, where, as historian Harriet Ritvo explains, exotic collections of animals imported from faraway lands had become symbols of human domination over the wild and of Britain's global expansion.

As Pepys seems to have intuited, chimpanzees are very close to us, genetically speaking, closer to us than they are even to gorillas. By recent estimates, 98.7 percent of the DNA in humans and chimps is identical. In 2006, Harvard geneticist David Reich discovered evidence that we share a common ancestor, the product of sexual relations between humans and chimpanzees. Reich speculated that over the course of millions of years, "protohumans" and "protochimpanzees" produced numerous hybrids. These so-called missing links emerged briefly approximately five million years ago and then, unable to reproduce successfully (although the females could reproduce with other chimps, the males were sterile), soon disappeared. But the possibility of a hybrid species makes our evolutionary connection to chimpanzees even more concrete, as only species that are closely related can produce any kind of offspring at all.

The study of these connections may have begun in England with Charles Darwin and Alfred Russel Wallace, but it took off in the United States in the years that followed. By the beginning of the twentieth century, psychologist Robert Mearns Yerkes, who had been born in 1876 on a small farm in Pennsylvania, was on his way to becoming the American patriarch of primatology and in particular of chimpanzee research. Yerkes had studied animal behavior and comparative psychology at Harvard, where he received a doctorate and joined the faculty in 1902. Early on, Yerkes became fascinated with chimpanzees, a species ready-made for comparative studies, and searched for opportunities to observe them in the flesh. As a result, he began corresponding with a Cuban woman who had taken over her family's summer estate just outside Havana and used it to house her private collection of animals. Madame Rosalia Abreu was particularly fond of chimpanzees and apparently also enjoyed the attentions they brought her from various scientists. Her chimps were treated more like children than animals, a novel concept to men of science. Madame Abreu called her animals by name, developed personal relationships with them, and fed them high-quality food. Her reward came in 1915, when she announced the birth of a chimpanzee, the first to be born in captivity and the subject of much discussion in the scientific community.

Abreu invited Yerkes to come and see her prize for himself. Accompanied by a team of researchers, he went to Cuba to observe Abreu's colony — a rare opportunity, and one that gave rise to an epiphany: chimpanzees were close enough to humans that they could be used as surrogates in the research laboratory. Since chimps were viewed by the general public as wild animals with no language, culture, or feelings (and certainly no organized advocacy group behind them), subjugating them to the cruelties of vivisection would not create the controversy that would inevitably accrue to research on humans. Yerkes saw them as blank screens, open and available for any research project that might be for the good of humankind.

By this time, Yerkes had made his mark by developing an intelligence test for the army, used to separate the officers from the soldiers, the men from the boys — and ultimately the blacks from the whites. He had rejected Darwin's theory of natural selection and instead became an advocate of eugenics, a surprisingly popular cause which promoted the principle of scientifically manipulated selection. (Endorsed by leading figures of the era including George Bernard Shaw and Winston Churchill, eugenics was eventually thoroughly discredited by its association with the Nazis and disappeared during the postwar years.) As an ardent eugenicist, Yerkes hoped to harness his scientific ingenuity to the project of designing a more perfect human race, and viewed chimpanzees as ideal subjects for experiments in selective breeding, heredity, sterilization, and whatever else might further his mission to eradicate human imperfection. Since the ability to breed chimps was critical to his research, Yerkes considered the arrival of Madame Abreu's infant to be a milestone.

Yerkes's enthusiasm for chimpanzees was not shared by Harvard. Ironically, as late as the 1920s, this bastion of higher learning was nervous that study of the apes in university-sponsored research might signal its support of Darwinism, still considered controversial in academic circles, and Yerkes was not allowed to bring even a single primate to Cambridge. This did not stop him.

As many psychologists after him would do, Yerkes turned his own home, in this case a small farm in Franklin, New Hampshire, into a research facility, known as the Franklin Field Station. In 1923, he purchased a male and female couple for $2,000, a small fortune at that time for research animals.

Ada Yerkes, his wife and chief assistant, made this project possible by acting as surrogate "mother" to this first pair of chimps. Defying the odds that doomed most chimps taken from Africa, Chim and Panzee survived their first few months, a triumph that motivated Yerkes to expand his population and establish a larger research colony. And very soon he had a place to put it.

Unlike Harvard, Yale saw the value in Yerkes and his chimps. In 1924, Yerkes was invited to move the Franklin Field Station to New Haven, Connecticut, where he set up the Yale Laboratories for Primate Biology, the first primate research laboratory in the country. At Yale, Yerkes pioneered a field called psychobiology, which involved comparative research on human and nonhuman primates, using his own animals for research. He appeared to have everything in New Haven under control but the weather, which was too cold for his chimps. In 1929, the Rockefeller Foundation (which had been one of the main financial supporters of the eugenics movement in universities) purchased two hundred acres in Orange Park, Florida, where Yerkes established the Anthropoid Experiment Station. Upon his death in 1956, the facility moved to Emory University in Atlanta, Georgia, where it remains today.

Yerkes's devotion to primates was based on his belief that they could be used as literal laboratories to test scientific theories that might ultimately benefit humans — perhaps even transform them. His work was the foundation for all the ape research that followed. Ultimately, it was Yerkes who set in motion a number of the forces that led to the birth of Nim Chimpsky in a research institution in 1973 and dictated the role Nim would play in one of the most famous experiments in the history of linguistics and primatology — the eponymous Project Nim.

Less than two weeks after Carolyn gave birth to Nim, he was sent to join a human family in New York City, as part of a study by Professor Herbert S. Terrace. Wanting to find out whether a chimp could learn to use American Sign Language (ASL), the Columbia University psychologist had designed an experiment that called for a chimp to be raised in the bosom of a family and taught human language just like any other child. The hope was that teaching communication skills to a "humanized" chimpanzee would shed light on how language is acquired by humans.

This was an extremely audacious, potentially paradigm-shattering study, for the dividing line between humans and animals has, for millennia, been drawn at language. And the fact that humans learn to speak while animals do not has implications that go far beyond the question of language. We have interpreted the "silence" of animals to mean that they are unable to think or to feel, and this in turn has been used to justify relegating them to a life of subservience and legally defining them as "property," available to anyone — for the right price — for any purpose. The belief that animals are removed from our moral sphere of protection goes back at least as far as Plato and Aristotle, who both agreed that the animal mind was empty. Descartes went Plato and Aristotle one better, announcing that animals, unlike humans, not only had no minds but had no souls, which reduced even further any moral claims they might make upon us.

Noam Chomsky, the brilliant Massachusetts Institute of Technology linguist known for his theories about a universal grammar that is inherent in the human brain and therefore exclusive to humans, is only the latest in a long series of thinkers to hew to this basic distinction between man and beast, which is deeply embedded in our culture and in our beliefs about ourselves. In naming his research animal Nim Chimpsky, Terrace was throwing down the gauntlet. His mentor at Harvard, the notable behaviorist B. F. Skinner, had been one of Chomsky's bloodiest targets. Skinner and Chomsky, both world-famous philosophers, had been at each other's throats for decades, long before Project Nim. Chomsky delivered a mortal blow to behaviorism as early as 1959, in a devastating review of Skinner's famous tome *Verbal Behavior,* published in the scholarly journal *Language.* By the 1970s, Chomsky had effectively annihilated behaviorism as a viable theory and severely undermined Skinner's notion that language could be learned. But Skinner's devoted students seemed not to know that behaviorism was dead. Terrace, while hardly a strict Skinnerian, conceived Project Nim as a direct challenge to Chomsky's primary thesis that language is inherent only in humans.

Terrace intended to teach his chimpanzee to use language just as humans do — and thus prove Chomsky dead wrong. The experiment's goal was to blur the language line between humans and nonhumans or even erase it. In the process, Project Nim threatened to put interspecies communication on a more scientific (i.e., credible) and meaningful basis.

Skinner gave Project Nim his full blessing. Hopes were high and the experiment looked promising, hence fundable.

This is Nim Chimpsky's story, from his birth in 1973 until his death in 2000. Nim was a genuine celebrity in his infancy and early adolescence, his life extensively documented so long as he participated in Project Nim. But what happened at the end of the experiment? Despite the adulation Nim received in the popular press, his narrative has not been an easy one to reconstruct. Animals, especially research animals, have hidden histories, most of them lost (and often deliberately kept secret) in the shuffle of their lives as they are moved from one facility to another. They die without much fanfare after years of service to the demands, often lethal, of science. Nim was a survivor. But his story has been swept under the rug, along with all the dust kicked up by the controversial study that bore his name.

To write his biography, I had to find the people who lived with Nim, diapered him, dressed him, brushed his teeth, kept him company at night when he was frightened, and even breast-fed him to comfort him and make him feel more like a member of the family. These are the folks, mostly students, who raised him while trying to teach him sign language during the almost four years he spent in New York, from 1973 to 1977. Then I had to track down those who encountered Nim in one of the several institutions where he found himself locked away during his later years. Some people, still feeling angry and/or guilty a quarter of a century afterward, did not want to talk about Nim, especially to a writer. But those who did had much to say. The time had come.

The people who knew Nim best still think of him more as a long-lost relative than an animal. At first, this seemed a little strange to me. Eventually, it made perfect sense. Nim's identity had been carefully constructed from birth to be more human than not. The people who originally took part in this experiment believed in it. They never thought of Nim as an ordinary chimpanzee — and still don't. Nim was raised to identify with humans; he wore human clothes, ate human food, and used a toilet (now and then), and it is likely that he thought of himself as human. Those who cared for him in his later years believe that, with a few exceptions, he liked people more than he liked members of his own species.

By any standards, Nim led an utterly unique life. By the time he was two weeks old, he had a first and last name, an address in an upscale New York neighborhood, and a human family, complete with a gaggle of siblings to call his own. Nim became a significant member of this household — for better and for worse — during his time there. Stephanie LaFarge, his surrogate mother, loved him tenderly, and he in turn loved her. But from early on, Nim had a job to do. Under Terrace's supervision, Nim's adopted family began teaching him ASL as soon as he was old enough to focus his attention, at about two months.

This was hard work, and Nim didn't always want to cooperate. But his ability to use sign language to converse with people, which began in the very earliest days of his life, would prove to be his lifeboat. For the next twenty-six years, he introduced himself to prominent psychologists, primatologists, animal advocates, and various members of his fan club. Many of them are still under the spell of his legendary charm, mischievous sense of humor, and keen understanding of human beings. Ultimately, Nim was able to handle them more skillfully than they could handle him. But he was a chimpanzee with one foot in the human world and one in the wild, which made it hard for him to be content in either place. Inevitably, Nim's divided nature presented a huge challenge to his caretakers. It also proved to be his salvation. Throughout his life, his sizable vocabulary, complex personality, and human-like desires attracted all kinds of people to his side and ensured their continuing loyalty.

Project Nim could only have launched in the early 1970s (in spirit still really the sixties), when minds, along with government and institutional funding for novel research, seemed to enjoy a brief opening. Scientific interest in chimpanzees, fanned by research dollars, was growing quickly. Until that time, those scientists interested in cognition in animals had cut into their brains in order to look around, maybe take out a piece or two, sew them back up, and then observe the results. Then came a new, more imaginative, less invasive kind of research. A few maverick psychologists, under the influence of a more humane behaviorism, began to explore the animal mind without surgical intervention. But the questions these psychologists were asking had not changed for centuries. Could chimpanzees learn to use a human language? How do chimpanzees differ from humans? What can these creatures tell us about ourselves? Although the questions had remained the same, the means to find the answers were changing. The burning interest in chimpanzees and whether or not they could be taught to communicate in a human language had given rise to the codification of a small field called ape language studies (also known as language acquisition). Public interest in it was initially fueled, at least in part, by its romantic, Dr. Dolittle appeal, but its conclusions were viewed with skepticism by most of the scientific establishment. Some serious scholars, however, Herbert Terrace among them, scrutinized the results of the early language experiments and saw in them reliable, scientifically documented indications that *something* was going on in the chimpanzee mind that quite possibly had been overlooked for centuries, or at the very least never pinned down with accurate data.

Three pioneer experiments investigating the chimp's capacity for language were particularly important in paving the way for Project Nim. The first one was set in motion in the 1920s, when a husband-and-wife team, Winthrop N. Kellogg, a psychologist at the University of Indiana, and Luella A. Kellogg, also a psychologist, became intrigued by the discovery of several feral children in Europe and India and the subsequent debate on the effects of nature versus nurture on childhood development. If Winthrop Kellogg could have adopted a feral child or placed a newborn in the wild, he probably would have. Instead, he and his wife decided to reverse the situation and adopt a chimpanzee, the next best thing to a feral child for the purposes of their research. It was only natural for them to turn to Robert Yerkes for help with this project, since he was an ardent believer in the similarities between humans and chimps. Moreover, Yerkes had a lab full of chimps. Yerkes invited the Kelloggs to Florida and agreed to loan them one of his chimps for the experiment.

On August 30, 1930, Luella Kellogg gave birth to their son Donald. On June 26, 1931, a healthy seven-month-old female chimp named Gua came to live with the Kelloggs on long-term loan from Yerkes. (Gua, originally born at Abreu's estate in Cuba, was one of many chimps she sent to Yerkes; he eventually took over her entire colony.) For nine months, boy and chimp were brought up virtually as twins. They were dressed alike and fed the same foods (except that Donald refused raw vegetables) in an effort to treat them equally, the better to make a strictly scientific comparison of the details of their physical development, their behavior, and, the Kelloggs hoped, their speech. Each day the "siblings" were drilled for hours on individual words. In addition, Gua's surrogate parents manipulated her lower jaw, hoping to encourage her to get it moving. Although there was much chimp chat ("oo-oo-oo") from Gua, neither Gua nor Donald uttered word one. Eventually, Donald began making the same sounds as his simian sibling. When the Kelloggs started to worry that the experiment might retard their son's development, Gua, sixteen months old, was returned to a cage in Yerkes's facility and the experiment was ended. The Kelloggs were convinced of Gua's intelligence but concluded that the question of whether or not chimps could talk remained unanswered.

Two decades later, a similar experiment began. Keith Hayes, a psychologist employed by Yerkes, and his wife, Catherine, wanted to adopt a newborn chimp from the facility and raise her like their child. Yerkes, enthusiastic once again, loaned a female to the Hayeses, who named her Vicki. The Hayeses believed that they would succeed where the Kelloggs had failed because Vicki would be their beloved only child, with no competition from any pesky siblings. The project led to numerous frustrations for the Hayeses and no doubt for Vicki, who eventually learned impeccable table manners and four words — *cup, mama, papa, up,* spoken in what was described as a "hoarse stage whisper" — before the Hayeses gave up the project and their surrogate baby. Each word had taken Vicki six agonizing months to master.

But the Hayes experiment was not a dead end, for all their hard work had been recorded on video, which yet a third husband-and-wife team of psychologists, R. Allen Gardner and Beatrix T. Gardner, of Reno, Nevada, would unearth a decade and a half later. Watching the tapes closely, the Gardners made a brilliant discovery about Vicki's aptitude for language, which the Hayeses had failed to see. Although their chimp had a terrible time learning to speak, there was ample evidence that she comprehended spoken words and could make herself understood by gesturing or inventing creative ways to express herself. For example, one time when Vicki wanted to go out, she ripped a photo of a car from a magazine and brought it over to her mother. The Gardners hypothesized that chimpanzees did not have the same vocal apparatus as humans, but that they might be able to learn another language, one not inimical to the limitations of their physiology: American Sign Language (ASL).

In a seminal 1966 experiment, the Gardners began successfully teaching a chimp they named Washoe to use sign language. Washoe, who had been purchased from a government research facility in New Mexico, was the first chimpanzee to learn ASL. The fact that chimpanzees could communicate through a learned visual language was indeed a breakthrough, and the Gardners' study was the bedrock of a small but growing movement in ape language research. The same year the Gardners began working with Washoe, David and Ann Premack, psychologists working at the Yerkes facility, designed a language based on small colorful plastic chips that had assigned meanings, which a chimpanzee named Sarah learned to use productively. In another equally fascinating project, psychologist Duane Rumbaugh (who would eventually marry Emily Sue Savage and work with her as a team) devised a symbolic language called Yerkish, based on a series of abstract modern symbols, which a chimpanzee named Lana learned to use.

The field was blossoming into a full garden, with sufficient variety and potential to expand. Yet there was absolutely no agreement on what constituted language, whether gestural or symbolic, when chimpanzees were involved. These chimps were learning, in effect, languages that had been invented for them. Even ASL (which conservative linguists might not in any case deem to be an authentic language) when used by chimps was hardly the same version that human signers learned. And beyond the question of how to define language, when the chimps learned these modes of communication, were they simply imitating their teachers, or did they actually understand the words? And if they understood the words, could they use them in the same way as humans? This was only the beginning of the avalanche of uncertainties in the ape language field.

Terrace planned to answer some of these questions. The Gardners' work with ASL had the most immediate relevance for Terrace. In 1967, he had gone to Nevada to see Washoe at work and to study the Gardners' training techniques, but he was dismissive of what they had achieved. The New York psychologist believed that Project Nim would leapfrog over the Gardners' work, leaving them far behind. Since Terrace felt at the time (though he has since reconsidered) that the Gardners had already proved that a chimp could master sign language, he felt no need to have his study demonstrate that point again. Instead, he focused the design of his experiment on a much more ambitious goal — to study how the chimp *used* ASL, in the hope that he could prove that Nim's signing bore the marks of human language. Not only would Nim have to demonstrate that he comprehended the meanings of individual signs, but he would have to string the signs together to express new thoughts and ideas.

Terrace was proposing to enter a brave new world, for proving that language should no longer be viewed as the dividing line between nonhuman primates and ourselves would be tantamount to a scientific revolution. This boundary, in effect a massive wall, protects our belief in the uniqueness and the superiority of the human species. Even many of those who have long since accepted Darwinism are heavily invested in maintaining the distinction, yet Terrace had the hubris to think that Project Nim could erase it. Before he could dream of taking down this wall, however, he would have to penetrate the thicket surrounding it, which was dense with all kinds of linguistic tenets that define human language and distinguish it from the verbal communications of nonhuman species. Noam Chomsky had planted this thicket, and to gain entrance, Terrace would have to play by Chomsky's rules.

Chomsky, now better known to the general public for his political views than his scholarship, has nonetheless dominated the field of linguistics at least since the 1960s with his notion of transformational generative grammar, which is a series of criteria for what he believes sets language apart as a uniquely human construct. To put it simply, according to Chomsky, human language is an orderly system of symbols that is governed by a set of rules, otherwise known as syntax, which is the essence of language. Without this underlying and innate structure of grammar and syntax, there can be many forms of communication, for example, animals grunting to each other in the wild about the presence of food or danger, but no communication that is more complex than that — no language. Chomsky further maintains that humans have the innate and exclusive ability to develop the capacity to use this structure, which he refers to as the "language organ." Linguist Steven Pinker calls it the "language instinct." Agreeing with Chomsky, Pinker asserts that the capacity for language comes from within, which is to say, it is not a result of cultural influences, and cannot be taught to any other species. "People know how to talk in more or less the sense that spiders know how to spin webs," writes Pinker. "Spiders spin spider webs because they have spider brains, which give them the urge to spin and the competence to succeed."

When Terrace named his experimental animal Nim Chimpsky, he was putting the world of science on notice that he intended to challenge the ironclad authority of the famous linguist and his acolytes. The goal of Project Nim was not only to teach Nim to sign proficiently but also to prove that he was using language in a way that was comparable to how humans used it. In more traditional animal behavior experiments, the pigeon either pecked the target or didn't, the rat either learned to eat or starved, the monkey either died of depression or did not, offering clear and quantifiable data. Videos of chimps signing or data collected from handlers on the spot were more ambiguous, more subject to interpretation and debate.

Naysayers would argue that Nim was using language like a chimp, merely imitating his trainers. Accurately measuring language skills in an animal would be far more difficult than Terrace had imagined. Could any legitimate scientist talk with an animal — and prove it? Thomas Bever, the skeptical but open-minded psycholinguist who signed on early to the Project Nim team, wondered what the chimp might say if he really did learn to talk. "We were only going to know we were successful if we walked in one morning and Nim demanded a quarter to call his lawyer to get him out of the joint," he said years later. As historian Erica Fudge noted, "If we could hear them speak, we might not want to hear what they say. That's the danger."

Academics were divided on the subject of ape language but mesmerized nonetheless. If Terrace could prove that chimps were talking, a revolution really was at hand; if they were merely mimicking their trainers, however, the charade needed to be exposed and funding withdrawn. Chomsky found the whole endeavor to be absurd: "It's about as likely that an ape will prove to have a language ability as there is an island somewhere with a species of flightless birds waiting for human beings to teach them to fly."

Most scientists agreed with Chomsky and concluded that the possibility of interspecies communication was science fiction, not a subject for serious research. Adversaries of the ape language projects sharpened their knives, even as Nim's signing vocabulary grew. Project Nim would generate a firestorm, threatening to burn down the house of ape language studies.

As the debate rages on into the twenty-first century, language research with animals has gone through multiple transformations. Most psychologists are no longer arrogant enough to presume to teach animals a rigidly defined human language in order to learn more about human (or animal) nature. Today, researchers study *animals'* language, culture, and cognitive abilities — even their laughter. One recent experiment demonstrated that mice — possibly the most disposable research animals of all — empathize with each other's suffering. Few scientists doubt that animals are sentient, self-aware beings. However, what this revelation will mean for nonhuman species remains to be seen. Meanwhile, there is abundant evidence that animals can communicate to each other — and to us. We in turn are becoming better listeners, observers, and trainers. The story of what happened to Nim Chimpsky offers us a unique perspective on how far we have come in our efforts to understand the human as well as the animal mind.

■ ■ ■ ■

PART ONE:
PROJECT NIM: NEW
YORK CITY

■ ■ ■ ■

Bill Lemmon with his children Peter and Sally, at home with Pan and Wendy

CHAPTER 1
EARLY DAYS ON THE CHIMP FARM

Nim's story begins at the research facility in Oklahoma that was founded by the notorious Dr. William Lemmon. Early in his academic career chimpanzees became the focus of Lemmon's lifelong research, and helped to make him — for a time — the most prominent psychologist in Oklahoma. Over several decades, he authored many of the state's mental health policies, helped to shape numerous public programs, and virtually founded the clinical psychology department at the University of Oklahoma (OU), where he remains a legendary figure thanks to his early chimpanzee experiments. From its inception until its demise, Lemmon ran the Institute for Primate Studies (IPS), the place where Nim Chimpsky was born. Lemmon bred and owned Nim. As a result, the psychologist was responsible, often behind the scenes, for every major event that shaped the chimp's life, both before and after Project Nim.

Virtually everyone who ever had anything to do with Lemmon (Bill, as he was called) or his chimpanzees came away with strong feelings about the psychologist, but what those feelings were varied considerably. Some loved Lemmon, some despised him, and some still won't speak about him at all because it's just too painful. Lemmon, who has been dead for more than two decades, remains a controversial figure in Norman and the wider primate world, where his unconventional methods of animal husbandry and research are often attacked. He ruled his chimpanzees with an electric cattle prod, as many unenlightened keepers still do, and tried every possible disciplinary technique, including shock collars, all kinds of guns, and a pair of Doberman pinschers trained to tree escapees. (This last was not an effective method; the chimps dominated the dogs and ripped one of them apart.) When asked by a friend, "How do you discipline a chimpanzee?" Lemmon responded, "Any way you can."

The chimps learned to respect their keeper. Lemmon's graduate students also understood their place. One claims that he locked her in a cage inhabited by a few adult chimps, just to see her reaction. She survived to tell the story, one of many about the sadistic pleasure Lemmon took in pushing people to the edge. Lemmon's protégés, employees, and patients all worshipped him — or fled.

Still, however much he was feared by both his experimental animals and his students, Lemmon was one of a very few researchers in the 1960s who had any expertise in raising and breeding chimpanzees in captivity, where they rarely survived or reproduced. Lemmon and his carefully selected graduate students studied chimpanzee mating habits, sexuality, and social development, and they even collected data on the personalities of individual chimps. Unfortunately for Lemmon, and for the field in general, little of this research, apart from a handful of articles, was ever published. Lemmon's vast knowledge of chimpanzees mostly benefited those who became members of his prestigious inner circle in Norman. Ultimately, the scientific community labeled his work "anecdotal," their way of deeming it worthless. For better or worse, he was an outsider who was destined to remain on the margins because he refused to maintain his academic status by regularly publishing his results or writing books. In the long run, this arrogance did not serve him or his animals well. But in the short run, it made IPS, known as the "chimp farm," a compelling place for students to cut their teeth on primatology.

Lemmon was born in Cleveland, Ohio, in 1916. A prodigy of sorts, from a working-class family, he earned his doctorate at Ohio State University, where he studied with Carl Rogers. The promising young psychologist had a background in biology and a passion for the theories of Sigmund Freud. By twenty-eight, Lemmon had married, fathered three children, and become the director of clinics in the psychology department at the University of Maryland. There he fell in love with one of his graduate students and moved on to the next chapter of his life.

Dorothy Lemmon — known as Dottie — met her husband-to-be in a classroom, where she found herself enthralled by his erudite lectures, liberally sprinkled with literary references and stories about his personal experiences. Dottie was said to have had a Mona Lisa smile and a dark, mysterious appeal. After Lemmon divorced his first wife he and Dottie promptly moved to Norman in 1945, where Bill had been offered a position in the department of psychology at OU, and where they had two children, Peter and Sally. Dottie, like her mentor and husband, became a clinical psychologist. But she opened an office at a local mental health center, maintaining as much distance as possible from Lemmon's university sphere. Throughout her life, Dottie's carefully nurtured independence from her powerful husband was critical to her emotional survival. She had her own practice, her own friends, and even her own plants — in a greenhouse where her husband was not welcome to dig around. He had a greenhouse too, separate from hers, where there was more than enough dirt.

However, the greenhouses, as well as the chimpanzees, came later in the marriage, some years after the Lemmons found an affordable farm, which they bought in 1957. Located on the outskirts of Norman, on East Lindsey Road, it was a private paradise just a short distance from the OU campus. The original wooden farmhouse, built in 1907, was far up on a hill, at the end of a long, winding driveway, surrounded by 140 acres of meadows, woods, and ponds. There were few amenities — the house had no bathroom or running water — but the land was spacious and ideal for farm animals, or any other kind of animals. At the time Lemmon bought the farm, animal behavior and comparative psychology had already become the focus of his research, and he envisioned turning the place into a research institute, which he would stock with multiple species. He promptly began to design one, which was constructed over a period of years, as funds became available.

Although Lemmon supplemented his university income with money from a highly successful private practice, as a professor in the 1960s he made a modest salary, so it took some time for his dream to become a reality. Meanwhile, he started to purchase exotic birds and small mammals the way other people buy baseball cards or stamps, grabbing one of each kind to round out their collections. By the early 1960s, the Institute for Primate Studies had come into existence on Lemmon's farm, and moving there enabled the psychologist to add more birds as well as border collies, spider monkeys, gibbons, sheep — and anything else he could get his hands on. Lemmon liked to purchase one or preferably two of each species, Noah's ark–style, so that they would breed and he could scrutinize their mating habits, gestation periods, and physical and psychological details of reproduction. He sold the resulting offspring to other researchers or gave them away to friends. On occasion, he did more elaborate, and less humane, behavioral experiments on his animals. The farm allowed him to be more ambitious. Hidden away from OU, Lemmon had a new sense of freedom.

Over the years, the old wooden farmhouse was transformed into a modern residence covered with a pinkish stucco surface, and other buildings were constructed to house Lemmon's growing menagerie. The animals appeared content and well cared for. The grounds were dotted with jerry-rigged pens and numerous gardens where flowers, fruit trees, and vegetables were plentiful. Both Lemmons were amateur horticulturists, in their separate greenhouses, and the farm, though not a lavish place, had a genuine elegance of sorts, a seedy rustic charm.

Lemmon's popularity as a professor and a psychotherapist grew as rapidly as his farm. Well known on campus for his idiosyncrasies, he was admired by his students for his refusal to conform to convention — in either the academy or his personal life — regardless of the consequences. Even Lemmon's attire challenged university standards. At a time when most OU professors wore jackets and ties to class, Lemmon, a proto-beatnik, with wild bushy eyebrows and a well-trimmed goatee, wore leather sandals

Bill Lemmon in his greenhouse

over bare feet and shaved his head. During cold spells, the professor donned a belted trench coat, the collar flipped up, as if he were a spy. Typical OU faculty members dressed up, not down; they also did not keep cobalt-blue hyacinth macaws, the largest species of parrot in the world, in their campus offices.

Not surprisingly, Lemmon was a target from the very beginning of his time in Norman, where everything he did was noticeably different from what other professors were doing. Already in 1946, the dean of the university was asking Lemmon (in a letter on official stationery) to wear socks and shave off his signature goatee, as people were beginning to "think he was eccentric." Lemmon continued to wear his sandals barefoot but immediately shaved off his goatee — and grew it right back.

But the problems between the charismatic Lemmon and the conservative university, which started early and escalated for years, went far deeper than surface appearances. The more consequential trouble had to do with Lemmon's academic views, the radical nature of his chimpanzee research, and the highly irregular relationships he fostered among his students, his colleagues in the clinical psychology department, and even the patients in his private practice. Lemmon, inhabiting some parallel chimp universe, had much in common with Alfred Kinsey. He shared Kinsey's intensity, his originality, his love of controversy — and his interest in sexuality. By the 1970s, Lemmon was doing research on clitoral orgasms in female chimpanzees. Operating on the cutting edge, he exerted a magnetic effect on many of those in his sphere of influence, who saw him as a visionary, a leader. Lemmon, however, would never make a significant contribution to his field. His ideas were often too far out to be fundable — even if they were in fact doable.

Eccentric as he was, no one could deny

Lemmon's popularity on campus, which irked other professors in the psychology department. Undergraduates lined up to get into his famous introductory courses, and graduate students clamored for acceptance into his program, known as the Psychological Clinic, to undergo Lemmon's intensive training program for therapists. Lemmon wanted only the brightest, most devoted acolytes, and in a grueling process of selection he handpicked each student for the program. Other professors competed for the same students and lost. For students, getting a green light from the master therapist was equivalent to a coveted membership in a club.

Lemmon turned the Psychological Clinic into his headquarters. The clinic operated out of a building on a separate area of campus known as South Base, which was a short distance from the main campus, and Lemmon ran it virtually as his own private enterprise. Home to his delightful macaw as well as other research animals he occasionally brought in for observation, it had an atmosphere the students found exotic and appealing. Lemmon's students functioned almost like a cult, supporting each other and worshipping their leader. They filled his workshops to capacity, and used him as an advisor for every decision large and small. An invitation to Lemmon's "home" — IPS — was a badge of honor.

Lemmon had a mystique, an aura. Students literally scrambled to get physically near him, and some even emulated his personal habits. If Lemmon smoked a certain brand of cigarette in class, his students switched to that brand. Once he conducted an experiment to see how far they would go to imitate him. He began smoking big stinky cigars — and observed that the smokers in his entourage did the same.

As a prerequisite for entrance into Lemmon's clinical program, his students had to undergo psychotherapy or some alternative therapy with a faculty member or with the master himself. Lemmon, of course, was the most revered and feared therapist of all. Students were often both therapist and patient, simultaneously in therapy with one of their professors while treating one of their peers. The interior of Lemmon's building on South Base looked more like a real clinic than an academic setting. There were small offices, each one with a couch, where Lemmon and his graduate students saw private, paying patients in between classes and training sessions, day and night. Other professors, along with associates, often moonlighted in the building to augment their modest academic salaries with fees from patients. Some of the professors who didn't moonlight charged those who did with unethical conduct in an academic building.

Lemmon never took his opposition, mostly experimental psychologists in the department, too seriously. But ignoring his critics did not make them go away. They scrutinized Lemmon's program ever more carefully in an effort to gather ammunition to destroy it and snatch his students. Lemmon's conservative colleagues wanted to see some rats and pigeons and some grants to support them, not to mention an end to the lucrative therapy sessions, which they viewed as a disgrace to the department. Lemmon had no intention of preaching the theories of B. F. Skinner, or what he called "rat science." He was a Freudian, which was unusual for a clinical psychologist. Even more unusual, he did Freudian-type research on his chimpanzees, hoping to explore their early development and how their personalities formed.

Lemmon was best known in Norman for his highly successful chimp breeding program and for his long-term cross-fostering experiments, which began in 1962 with the purchase of his first two chimpanzees, Pan (born in Ghana) and Wendy (born in Sierra Leone). The young chimps, a year old when they arrived, were raised in the Lemmons' home with their two human children, Peter and Sally, ages eleven and ten. (Three half siblings from their father's first marriage made periodic visits.) Peter Lemmon, who remembers Pan and Wendy fondly, describes them as "his first two hairy brothers and sisters." There would be many more.

Convinced that comparative studies between humans and chimpanzees would lead to new insights into the evolution of the human brain, something researchers still knew very little about, Lemmon wanted to find out everything he possibly could about chimpanzee behavior and early development. The key, he believed, was raising the chimps in human homes, where their "humanness" could be reinforced and made more distinct and observable. Lemmon planned to cultivate a colony of human-raised chimps that were kept isolated from members of their own species, and a parallel colony of chimps reared by their natural mothers and living in a large social group. When in a whimsical mood, he wondered, occasionally to the press, whether or not chimps could learn to talk, understand the

Peter Lemmon holding Pan and Wendy

value of a dollar, or drive cars. As of yet no one had proved otherwise. Chimp genetics, DNA forensics, the discovery of AIDS, the Endangered Species Act, and Project Nim were still years ahead.

Pan and Wendy were the beginning of all Lemmon's aspirations. For their first few years, the young chimps were attention magnets and about as big a novelty in Oklahoma as the first Model T. People had seen a few chimps in movies or on television but never up close and personal. Eager to show them off, Lemmon allowed those he trusted to hold them and interact with them, which was a rare treat. His chosen students lined up to help collect detailed data, sometimes hour by hour, on Pan and Wendy's development. They were magnificent ambassadors for their species, and simultaneously remarkably like human children, which made them infinitely endearing. Lemmon's associates had adopted all kinds of animals in his wake, mostly exotic birds and monkeys, and now they wanted their own chimps too. Lemmon, eager to collect more data for his research, set out to bring more chimps to Norman.

Getting hold of infant chimps during the 1960s was a difficult and expensive proposition. Pan and Wendy had been born in Africa and purchased through a commercial dealer, the usual way of obtaining research animals. But for his next round of studies, Lemmon wanted even younger babies. As a psychologist, he believed that the less time they spent with their natural mothers, the more quickly the infants would bond to their human mothers. With his customary resourcefulness, Lemmon turned to the world of roadside circus performers to open up new sources for chimpanzees. He spent months making contacts and building relationships with several breeders, including a colorful chimp trainer named Mae Noell, who lived in Tampa, Florida, with her husband, Bob, and a colony of performing animals, known as Noell's Ark. For generations, her chimps had been sold to entertainers all over the country. Noell had only disdain for researchers and wanted her infants to remain with their natural mothers for several months, even years if necessary, to make sure they were ready to leave home before they were sold. But Lemmon's powers of persuasion were enormous. He worked on her, writing letters in which he argued that behavioral research, unlike medical research, was benign; he explained that Noell's chimps would be living like kings and queens in human homes — the homes of OU psychology professors whom Lemmon had personally chosen for this singular honor — where they would get better treatment than they would just about anywhere else.

In 1965, Noell finally relented and informed Lemmon that two of her chimps were expecting babies. Lemmon wanted both. He had selected Vera Gatch, a popular OU professor, to become the first woman to adopt a baby chimp in Norman. Gatch had been a graduate student at the University of Maryland with Dottie and had followed the Lemmons to Norman in the 1940s. A loyal friend and colleague, Gatch made an ideal spokesperson for Lemmon's research. She also looked the part of a conservative, middle-class mom, with her fitted shirtwaist dresses and neatly styled hair. However prim, she shared her mentor's passion for primates. Gatch lived alone, and the newborn chimp would be her first and only child.

In December, Gatch flew to Tampa to pick up the infant, just four days old, and bring her home. She named the baby Maebell Twilla Gatch (called Mae after Noell), dressed her in fetching baby clothes, and took the infant all over town, as if she were human. Local headline writers went nuts — "Woman's 'Baby' a Chimpanzee," "College Apes Study Humanology" — as Gatch, with the utmost seriousness, described herself as a typical adoring mother.

Six weeks after Mae arrived, her half sister, Lucy, was born on schedule. Lucy moved in with Jane and Maurice Temerlin and their eleven-year-old son. Maurice Temerlin, whom everyone called Maury, was then chairman of the OU psychology department. Both he and his wife had been

Lemmon's students, patients, and protégés; Jane Temerlin became Lemmon's assistant at IPS, while her husband was next in line, like a son, to inherit Lemmon's mantle. The Temerlins lived close to IPS and were often there, socializing with the Lemmons and their chimps; their son, Steven, and the Lemmons' son, Peter, who were the same age, took care of the animals together after school.

Soon Lucy and Mae were well ensconced in their middle-class, seemingly ordinary homes. People who read the local papers in Norman, which reported on the chimps as though they were celebrities, bought into the fantasy. After a while, catching sight of a chimp in a Norman supermarket or on campus was a thrill but not a shock.

The experiment launched with promise; having two cross-foster families enabled Lemmon to do comparative studies. In his enthusiasm, Lemmon wanted to go further, acquire more infant chimps, collect more data, design more experiments for the infants, and expand the scope of his research. His aspirations grew more grandiose and more expensive. To further them, Lemmon began paying more attention to creating a breeding program of his own, which would be the answer to both his research and his financial problems. Breeding animals had always fascinated and challenged the psychologist. Now he set about it systematically, taking in any adult chimps who came his way and seemed like potential breeders, and placing their offspring in human homes as close to IPS as possible, hoping to enlist adoptive parents as volunteer researchers in his cross-fostering studies. Inevitably, as his bizarre adoption program expanded to homes around the country, it attracted the attention of the national media.

Before reality television, there were game shows. When Mae was not quite one year old, Gatch was invited on *To Tell the Truth,* where the chimp mom and psychologist stumped the whole panel of celebrity experts. Once Lemmon's adoption experiment hit prime-time television, the psychologist began receiving letters from families all over the country who wanted to adopt a chimp and participate in what had been described as a unique and worthwhile scientific experiment. Mothers pitched themselves to Lemmon, detailing their virtues and their inexplicable desire to raise a nonhuman baby. Prospective parents often came through Norman to visit Mae and Lucy in their homes, or at OU, where their "parents" were respected professors.

Lemmon had elaborate and changeable plans for experiments he wanted to do, most of which, unlike his cross-fostering project, remained fantasies. Scientifically viable or not, however, this project constituted the most radical behavioral experiment ever witnessed in Oklahoma. "In the 1960s, cross-fostering chimps was very avant-garde, especially in the heart of the Bible belt," says Kirby Gilliland, a psychology professor who joined the OU faculty the following decade. "We were just beginning to understand our relationship to chimpanzees and how close they were to us biologically. But many people still thought this was a crazy thing." Skepticism about chimp research went far beyond the Bible belt. When Jane Goodall walked into the jungle in 1960 to study her first troop of chimpanzees, people thought she was nuts too. It would be years before her colleagues took her observations seriously.

Lemmon had confidence in the ultimate significance of his work, and a primate institute to back it up. But the immediate reality looked more like a circus act than a scholarly experiment, pushing the envelope of acceptable research at OU. Although Lemmon's admirers considered him a pioneer, his detractors did not like pioneers. And while it may have been the sixties, his home base was Oklahoma, not California or New York. Resentment of Lemmon's campus popularity, distinctive clinical program, crowd-pleasing chimpanzees, and booming private practice grew rapidly, fueled by Lemmon's fame — or notoriety, as many viewed it.

In 1967, several members of the psychology department orchestrated a quiet meeting with the American Psychological Association (APA) to complain about their colleague. As a result, the APA threatened to withdraw its accreditation of the entire psychology department unless OU reined in the maverick professor. The complaints against Lemmon were all true. His faculty was incestuous, composed of his own students who were hired back into the department, and his academic program did not conform to the usual balance of theory and practice; Lemmon never published regularly or won any outside grants for the department. Ultimately, as a result of his various transgressions against the rites and rituals of conventional academia, Lemmon lost control of his department. First he had to agree to ask Maurice Temerlin to step aside as chairman. Temerlin, who was often seen in the company of his chimpanzee "daughter," was considered far too weird to be a department head, and OU administrators were highly skeptical of his "groundbreaking research" with Lucy. Temerlin was allowed to continue teaching, but Lemmon had to acquiesce in the hiring of Dr. Lauren G. Wispe, a social psychologist with a Harvard degree, as the new chairman of the department.

Wispe was generally disliked on campus. But he had been hired to clean house, and he did his job. Two years after Wispe's arrival, Lemmon was summoned to a meeting with OU president George L. Cross, who informed him that a decision had been made to put the entire clinical department "on hold" for one year, while the psychology department was reorganized. Lemmon's Psychological Clinic, the seat of his power, was to be terminated; therefore his position as director no longer existed. Lemmon's students would be moved into other divisions to finish up credits and graduate on schedule. Lemmon protested angrily, to no avail. Though he quickly organized his own political defense outside the university — state officials wrote letters to protest the decision, and the Oklahoma legislature, in a dramatic act of support, passed a resolution noting the widespread influence of psychologists who had been trained in Lemmon's clinic — it was all too late. The administration stood firm.

By 1969, Lemmon had lost his students, his faculty, his South Base building, and his status in the psychology department. He went from being a god on campus to being a pariah. His students were in shock. Two of his young faculty members, Bill Trousdale and Bill Mummery, desolate over their mentor's fall from grace and the termination of the program in which they had been teaching, committed suicide — a brutal epilogue to the bloodbath.

Ironically, the one thing Lemmon did not lose was tenure, which President Cross could not legally terminate. Lemmon continued to teach his popular introductory psychology course on campus; he also continued to attract students to his honors seminars, which he moved to the farm. Transferring his power base from South Base to IPS, Lemmon made the farm the new headquarters for all his activities, which were still many and diverse. His private therapy practice continued, but now the patients came to his home office, a room that featured his favorite chair, which was covered in a cow skin from his own herd,

IPS cages

and a reproduction of a Picasso sculpture of an ape. With fewer academic demands on his time, Lemmon was able to redirect his considerable energies to an expansion of his chimpanzee studies, which encompassed his breeding program, a variety of experiments, and a vast correspondence with primatologists, zookeepers, and primate researchers around the world — in short, anyone who wanted to purchase a chimp, get rid of one, or study chimpanzee behavior.

Among the researchers were Allen and Beatrix Gardner in Reno, Nevada. Lemmon had corresponded with the Gardners for many years about their sign language experiments and the care of their chimpanzees. In fact, it was he who had arranged for the Gardners to get Washoe from the Aeromedical Field Laboratory at Holloman Air Force Base in New Mexico. Like typical researchers, the Gardners traded in their chimps as soon as they became older, larger, and less tractable. Washoe had been with the Gardners for almost four years when she was deemed ready for retirement. The Gardners wanted to send Washoe, accompanied by one of their assistants, a graduate student named Roger Fouts, to Norman; Fouts had cared for Washoe for three years and been one of her ASL trainers. The timing was ideal. It was 1970, less than one year after the Psychological Clinic had been terminated, and Lemmon was especially receptive to projects that might open up new sources of revenue for IPS. Since Lemmon thought of ape language studies as the next big thing — the latest trend in chimp research and potentially a magnet for grants — he agreed to take Washoe and help Fouts get an assistant professorship at OU while Fouts finished up his doctorate. Washoe was moved into a cage at IPS, and her young keeper, the hottest new psychologist on campus, brought ape language studies to Norman.

The transition was traumatic for both

Fouts and Washoe. Although Washoe had spent her first months of life in a cage with other members of her species, she had been isolated from them for almost four years while living with the Gardners. At IPS, she had to learn to live with her own species again; as a dominant female, she made the adjustment relatively quickly. Not so Fouts. Although he had been catapulted into the best job thus far of his short career, the young psychologist had no idea what he was up against at IPS. The Gardners had failed to warn him that Lemmon thought of himself as a god and would expect Fouts to become one of his many minions. Fouts, insecure, sensitive, and convinced that he knew far more than the IPS director about ape language, had no interest in pleasing Lemmon.

Nevertheless, the handsome, charismatic researcher managed to inaugurate a sign language program in the psychology department, using several of Lemmon's younger, cross-fostered chimps, including Mae and Lucy (Washoe could not be safely handled by novices and was not removed from her cage unless Fouts was present). This unique program took off, attracting graduate students from around the country, which pleased OU administrators, and Lemmon too, who convinced the university to give IPS an annual budget of $50,000 to maintain the chimps.

Though Fouts had brought students, funding, and a newfound sense of prestige to IPS as well as to the psychology department, Lemmon refused to give his underling any authority over the chimps. In fact, Lemmon expected Fouts to follow his orders while continuing to take care of the chimps and generate more outside funding for them. In return, Lemmon was prepared to take the young psychologist under his wing and into his inner circle of believers. But Fouts was not looking for a father figure or a therapist. He just wanted to be around chimpanzees, get his Ph.D., support his wife and three children, and have a good time.

In the book he later published in 1997, titled *Next of Kin,* Fouts describes his confusion about his career and the sensation of having lost his way when he got to Norman. He had an intense dislike of Lemmon and found Lemmon's attitude toward his chimpanzees to be reprehensible. There was so much tension between him and Lemmon that Fouts could barely stand to be at IPS some days. But Lemmon, unlike Fouts, thrived on tension. He thought of the naive psychologist as nothing more than a new toy. He played with Fouts and watched him squirm.

Fouts stayed in Norman for a decade of drama and hard times, during which he saw the comings and goings of dozens of chimps. The most celebrated of them, and the one who would pose the biggest threat to the preeminence of Fouts's own chimp, Washoe, was Nim Chimpsky, who was born several years after Fouts's arrival at IPS.

Herbert Terrace, Stephanie LaFarge, and Nim © **Harry**
Benson

CHAPTER 2
LAUNCHING PROJECT
NIM

In 1968, the first chimpanzee was born at IPS. By 1985, the year IPS closed down, seventy-two infants had been born to twenty-two female chimpanzees. Carolyn, Nim Chimpsky's mother, was William Lemmon's most productive breeder. An exemplary and overworked mother, Carolyn eventually gave birth to fourteen infants, including five sets of twins, all of whom were taken from her within weeks of their birth, a fact of life in captivity that she never appeared to accept. Imported from Africa as an infant in 1955 and sold to the Chicago Zoological Society, Carolyn had arrived in Norman in 1966 at age eleven, after demonstrating an unacceptable level of antipathy toward the public: she spat and hurled her feces in the faces of gawking zoo-goers with uncanny precision. Dr. Gene Shreiber, chief curator at the Chicago zoo while Carolyn was there, described her as difficult and sullen, which was not atypical of wild-born females languishing in zoos. When Lemmon agreed to take her, along with two other troublesome adults, Shreiber was relieved he'd found a decent place to send them.

In Norman, where there were no irritating gawkers, Carolyn seemed more at ease right away. Although she continued to spit at visitors, as did many of her mates, she must have felt that she had found a more congenial home. For the first time, she was spending more time with chimps than humans and eating decent food. Lemmon fed his chimps a recipe called the Radcliffe Diet, a mix of whole grains, vegetables, beef (from his own cows), vitamins and other nutrients, and a dash of castor oil, all of which was shaped into individual loaves and baked in his own kitchen. Each chimp received a loaf for breakfast and another one for dinner. In between, they snacked on fresh fruits — apples, persimmons, mulberries, pears, and peaches — picked right from the orchards planted at IPS for this very purpose.

Although Roger Fouts described him as being close to a monster, to his credit Lemmon housed his chimpanzees in small social groups where they could mix, mingle, and select their mates. They could also kill each other — and on occasion tried to —

but more often they formed tightly knit bonds and hung out together, like a fraternity group. Early on, unlike many other primate researchers of the time, whose chimps regularly succumbed to depression and illness, Lemmon had realized that keeping chimps occupied was key to their ability to survive in research facilities. The majority of the adults lived in a series of large cages that could be linked together by opening several manually operated guillotine doors; outside runs on one side of the building, and eventually a roof playground, gave them more options for socializing and moving around, and allowed them to occasionally see the sky. They rotated through the building and the space, depending on the research under way. The younger chimps did even better. When the weather was warm, some of them were taken by boat to a man-made island behind Lemmon's house where there were no cages at all. Chimps are not monogamous and like to have sex with multiple partners. So, in addition to the healthful diet he fed them and as much fresh air as possible, Lemmon allowed his chimps to select their own sexual partners.

By today's standards, Lemmon's setup was a dreary, crowded, woefully inadequate cement prison. His chimps had no full-time access to trees, soft grass, or anything else resembling nature. But at the time, IPS was far better than other research facilities and zoos, where chimps were locked down in small cages and often prevented from touching each other. Thanks to the conditions he established at IPS, Lemmon's chimps reproduced with regularity, which amazed others in the field. They wrote him letters begging for advice with their chimps, who often would not eat, let alone mate.

Carolyn produced her first baby, Ahab, two years after her arrival in Oklahoma. Nim was Carolyn's seventh infant. (Two died at birth, but each had a surviving twin.) Pan, Nim's natural father, displayed great interest in Carolyn but, unlike her, none in their offspring. Male chimps typically have little to do with raising their infants, even in the wild. Pan and Wendy were the first two chimps Lemmon brought to Norman. Dale Peterson, in his superb book *Eating Apes,* pithily describes the usual way in which baby chimps were captured in Africa prior to the 1970s: "Shoot the mother, remove baby."

Pan freely mated with Carolyn and Wendy as well as several other females. He was a large, barrel-chested, dangerous male who was known to be Lemmon's personal favorite. As the oldest and strongest member of the colony that gradually developed on the farm, Pan became the alpha male. There are many stories about Lemmon's attempts to dominate Pan, even after he was older and huge. In one, Lemmon is said to have brought Pan into his kitchen, where they sat at the table, face-to-face, sharing a bowl of popcorn; Lemmon ate the popcorn with one hand and held a gun with the other. Chimps don't ordinarily share their food, but apparently they will when looking down the barrel of a gun.

The director collected guns and occasionally used them to shoot snakes in the pond behind his house. The chimps were frightened by the shots but more frightened by the snakes, which was Lemmon's excuse for using the reptiles as target practice. Not that Lemmon required an excuse for anything he wanted to do.

According to Roger Fouts, Lemmon used a two-by-four to beat Pan into submission. "The other chimps were absolutely terrified by Lemmon's dominance of Pan, the powerful male who dominated them," wrote Fouts in *Next of Kin.* "When Lemmon entered the chimps' building, many of them would approach their human master in a chimpanzee posture of submission, bending low to the ground while extending a wrist limply and pulling back their lips to show all their teeth in a grimace of fear. Lemmon would then place his hand against the cage and the chimps would kiss his large silver ring." Fouts claims that the ring displayed a coiled snake with glistening ruby eyes.

Whether or not such a scene ever took place — and I could find no one to verify it — Lemmon was certainly capable of cruelty. But it is difficult to know exactly what went on at IPS because there are so many different versions of every story. Peter Lemmon does not recall ever seeing his father wearing such a ring. Nor did he ever witness his father beat or abuse a chimpanzee, including Pan, he says. But there is no doubt that Lemmon fostered a kill-or-be-killed atmosphere both within the cages and outside them. If it could be said that Pan ruled over the chimpanzees, it could also be said that Lemmon ruled over Pan — and Fouts. Although Fouts viewed himself as being on the side of the animals, against Lemmon, the two sides were not that clearly defined. Fouts, like everyone else who worked at IPS, not only carried a cattle prod but also had occasion to use it (he referred to the rod as his "superego"), and it's not hard to see why. Newborn and infant chimps are so sweet and fetching that it is hard to believe they will grow up into menacing wild animals. But each and every one, including Nim, did. Fouts could handle them only because he convinced them he was in charge.

Newborns presented Lemmon with several options. Each one was either sold off for a fee or placed with participants in the director's cross-fostering project. Lemmon had a waiting list of people who wanted a chimp. The list included researchers, rodeo clowns, and couples who just wanted to have one of the adorable creatures to raise in their own homes, as they'd read about other people doing. Ironically, Lemmon preferred the entertainers to the scientists; circus and rodeo people lived with their chimps and taught them manners around humans, while researchers kept the chimps at a distance and returned them to Norman, often sooner than expected and not always in good shape. If the chimps recovered and were still young, as was frequently the case, Lemmon sent them out again, bouncing them around from project to project or home to home until they were too large to handle, in effect burned out and dangerous, at which point they were generally returned to IPS.

Herbert Terrace, the behavioral psychologist at Columbia University, was one of the people on Lemmon's waiting list. The two psychologists had started corresponding in the 1960s, when Terrace was in the initial stages of planning what he hoped would be a trailblazing ape language project. Terrace insisted on getting a male infant. Thus far, other notable language researchers, such as the Gardners, Rumbaugh, and Premack, had used females (Washoe, Sarah, Lana), possibly because they are smaller and, at least in theory, not as destructive as males. Terrace felt that using a male would be one more way to distinguish his experiment from the work of his predecessors. He did not appear concerned about the danger factor, perhaps because he had little prior experience with chimps.

During the research phase of his project, as he carefully laid the groundwork for his ape language study, Terrace visited chimp facilities at the Yerkes laboratory at Emory University in Atlanta, Georgia; at Holloman Air Force Base in Alamogordo, New Mexico; and at Lemmon's IPS, in Norman. Afterward, eager to obtain a chimp, Terrace wrote to Lemmon and told him that the Institute was "orders of magnitude more sophisticated and humane" than all the other facilities. The two psychologists occasionally bumped into each other at conferences, and they stayed in touch over the years, with Terrace expressing an interest in the results of Lemmon's cross-fostering data. By 1968, Lemmon had five newborn chimps living in human families. The Norman psychologist claimed to have demonstrated that chimps raised by humans develop more quickly than those raised by their natural mothers: the cross-fostered chimps moved around earlier, were more responsive to people, and were generally more alert and independent than the chimps in Lemmon's control group. The significance of this study was unclear, yet it was a revelation to Terrace, who had no idea what raising a chimp would be like.

Terrace, known as Herb, is a short, stocky man with a doughy face, a trademark moustache, and a no-nonsense style. He has a reputation for being unfriendly, arrogant about his own work, and little interested in anything else. Even during the sixties, he personified the science geek, the reverse of cool. Born in 1936, the son of Polish immigrants, he and a sister, Dorothy, grew up in Brooklyn. Dorothy, ten years older than her younger brother, was rarely around, and Herb recalls spending much of his childhood alone. Their father supported the family as a house painter, and their mother took care of the children, both of whom were pushed hard to concentrate on their schoolwork. (Dorothy became a medical doctor, and died unexpectedly of a brain tumor.) Terrace attended Stuyvesant High School, a highly competitive public school for bright New York City students with a scientific bent; won a full scholarship to Cornell University; and ended up in a doctoral program at Harvard, where he studied with B. F. Skinner. He had the good fortune to assist Skinner in a series of precedent-setting studies that proved pigeons could learn through trial and error. The results received considerable academic acclaim. Terrace left Harvard wrapped in the Skinnerian mantle to pursue research into animal cognition, which in those days was relatively virgin territory. At the tender age of twenty-five, he became one of the youngest and most promising faculty members in the psychology department at Columbia University.

Dr. Thomas Bever, currently a psycholinguist on the faculty at the University of Arizona, was a colleague of Terrace's in the psychology department at Columbia during the 1970s. Bever was immediately captivated by Terrace's plan to raise a chimp in New York and teach him ASL, for Bever, like Terrace, was interested in language. As Terrace continued to conceptualize his experiment, Bever made an ideal sounding board for detailed discussions on the mechanics of language acquisition. He had been trained by Skinner's nemesis, Noam Chomsky, whose office was just down the street from Harvard at MIT. Project Nim, as it would soon be officially named, grew out of a desire to settle an old score between Skinner and Chomsky. As noted earlier, while Chomsky believed that the ability to develop language is not learned but inherent in humans and only humans, Skinner disagreed, arguing that language skills are acquired through training and could in principle be learned not just by humans but by other animals too. "Herb was not an enthusiastic Skinnerian," says Bever, who enjoyed sparring with Terrace. "But he was trained to think that Chomsky was wrong." Skinner's young disciple wanted to name the chimp he intended to study either Noam Chimpsky or Neam Chimpsky. Bever suggested Nim Chimpsky. Terrace went along with the name change because, as he explained in his own book, *Nim,* published in 1979, "If Chomsky was changed to

Chimpsky, then Noam should be Nim."

Terrace invited Bever to become co-director of Project Nim. Philosophical differences between them had never interfered with their friendship. Both were bachelors and ambitious intellectuals, men who wanted to make their marks. Terrace needed a psycholinguist, and Bever wanted to be part of what was potentially the splashiest, most prominent experiment at Columbia — though he had no desire to be responsible for a live chimpanzee and understood that Project Nim belonged to Terrace. They decided to begin their collaboration by designing some preliminary research projects that might inform the shape of Project Nim. According to Bever, these early experiments focused on "structural learning" in pigeons and helped to sharpen their ideas about how language is actually learned. (Terrace had a lab filled with pigeons at Columbia.) "We both agreed that language is highly structured," explains Bever. "So, how could any animal, human or chimp, possibly learn such a complex thing? We started with the idea that maybe if we could teach pigeons structured learning, we could begin to see if they had any hierarchical organization, sort of analogous to phrase organization." But their studies didn't go anywhere, because, as Bever puts it, pigeons are "really stupid" and "teaching them even one sequence is not an easy thing to do." The two men were eager to climb up the research food chain from pigeons to chimpanzees, widely considered to be the brightest animals in the jungle — and in research labs.

Two years before Bever joined Project Nim, Terrace had had his first hands-on experience with a chimpanzee. In 1968, Lemmon informed Terrace that an infant male chimp had suddenly become available. Lemmon assumed that, like most of the researchers on his list, Terrace was waiting eagerly for a chimp. He wrote to Terrace describing the baby chimp, who had been fathered by Pan and born to a female named Maude on February 12. Abe was only the second chimpanzee to be born at IPS — a mere eight days after the very first. The infant had been separated from Maude on his third day and given to a graduate student, who brought him home to her apartment, where she was bottle-feeding and mothering him. Lemmon and his faithful assistants had kept careful notes on all aspects of Abe's development, a few of which he mentioned in the letter: "Abe prefers to be held by women and has a miraculous effect on them. Their bust increases by six inches and they simply must hold him." Lemmon suggested that Terrace bring Abe to New York and begin his experiment. "A set of diapers, baby shirts, terrycloth towels, a crib, nursing materials and a drugstore is all you need," he reassured Terrace, still a bachelor. "I know. I have five children and two grandchildren."

The Columbia professor was taken aback by the sudden offer. At that moment, the campus around him was seething with political unrest and myriad demonstrations. There were times when Terrace had to elbow his way through hordes of milling antiwar protesters just to get to his office in Schermerhorn Hall, Columbia's labyrinthine science building. He was not political, except when it came to his own projects. Bever later described his colleague as a closet liberal who kept his distance from the social upheaval around him primarily because it had the potential to interfere with his research, which included trying to launch his ape language experiment.

Terrace had been moving slowly and strategically into the language field, and he didn't yet feel ready to launch Project Nim. He had no funding, completed proposals, adequate staff, or infrastructure set up for the project. He thought it would be hard to convince his potential funders (not to mention himself) that he could manage a chimp in New York City, where no one had ever, to his knowledge, raised a cage-free chimp before. Still, Lemmon's offer was tempting. He specified only three conditions regarding Abe, who, even in New York, would remain part of Lemmon's cross-foster study: the chimp had to be reared in a home environment, kept away from other chimps, and returned to Norman when he became difficult to handle, a few years hence. Ultimately, Lemmon wanted to breed him.

Terrace, eager for some firsthand experience with a chimp, agreed to take Abe. But he was not going to launch his big experiment until he felt more prepared. He viewed Abe as a practice chimp, a warm-up experiment in preparation for the *real* one in the future. His first challenge was to figure out where to put Abe. He could hardly bring him home. There was no Dr. Spock for raising chimps, and Terrace's own apartment was more of a bachelor pad than a nursery. Terrace, who had probably never changed a diaper in his life, called Stephanie Lee, a former student of his and an experienced mother, to ask for help. Unlike Terrace, she thrived on spontaneity and loved having animals around her. She immediately agreed to take the chimp into her own home.

For Stephanie, this story really begins in 1961, when she took her first psychology class at Columbia University as an undergraduate. It was a large, impersonal lecture taught by Terrace, to whom she was immediately attracted. The rising star on the psychology faculty, he impressed her with his vast knowledge, Harvard credentials, and piercing blue eyes. Terrace noticed her as well. "She was the smartest student in the class," he says. At twenty-four, she was a little older than the other students, confident, self-possessed, and strikingly beautiful, with long dark hair and a slim figure. Terrace felt flattered by her attentions. The sixties had passed him by, but he could see that Stephanie Lee (later LaFarge) had the intellectual chops, as well as the desire, to be more than a wife and mother. Married at the time to Ralph Lee, a New York artist and performer who later became well known for his innovative theater work with massive, imaginatively grotesque puppets, Stephanie lived in a bohemian environment, worlds apart from the sterile labs of Columbia. At nineteen, she had found herself married and nursing her first child. Two more followed like clockwork. Stephanie took care of the children while Ralph focused on his theatrical career. But by her mid-twenties, she had finally started to turn her energy toward her own goals.

Since childhood, Stephanie had dreamed of becoming a psychologist. Terrace took his unusually sophisticated student under his wing and into his confidence. He was just beginning to formulate his ape language experiment, which he discussed for hours with her, immodestly comparing himself to Darwin and Galileo. Stephanie bought every word. If Terrace was arrogant and egotistical, she saw only his brilliance and authority. Listening to him talk about his chimp study made her feel as if she too might play a part in making scientific history. She was not particularly interested in language per se, but the idea of interspecies communication enthralled her.

Terrace became Stephanie's mentor and, briefly, her lover. In the sixties, as the second wave of women's liberation rolled through universities, professors and their students had sex more frequently than administrators or anyone else cared to admit. According to Stephanie, their affair ended in 1963, when the Lees suddenly moved to Seattle, Washington, where Ralph had a job; Stephanie enrolled at the University of Washington to complete her degree. As it turned out, juggling a family, school, and a move to a city where Stephanie had few contacts was not as easy as she had expected. So when the family returned from Seattle a year later, Stephanie had not been able to complete the coursework for her degree. Two years after that, in 1967, her academic career still on hold, she took a job as a teacher in a Montessori nursery school on the Upper West Side of Manhattan.

In 1968, after Abe had been offered to him, Terrace, who had been out of touch with Stephanie, tracked her down and discovered that she was teaching, taking care of three children, and contemplating a return to school. When Terrace explained the situation with Abe, Stephanie found that her enthusiasm for his ambitious project had not diminished. She still believed that Terrace was going to change the world, and she wanted to participate in any way she could. If he needed a mother for Abe, there was surely no one more qualified for the job. Stephanie was already knee-deep in diapers, pediatricians, and mashed bananas. She figured one more mouth to feed, even a chimp's, wouldn't make much difference. From her perspective, the opportunity to play a role in Terrace's experiment was a great honor.

Soon afterward, Terrace flew to Norman to pick up Abe, who was by then six weeks old. The healthy, happy foster baby was handed over to the nervous psychologist. Back in New York, Stephanie, Ralph, and their children — Heather, age nine; Jenny, age eight; and Josh, age five — plus a Danish au pair, Dorrit Lyngsie, hired by Terrace to help with the chimp, prepared for their new charge. Terrace came directly from the airport to the Lees' apartment, where they immediately renamed the chimp Bruno, conferring membership in the family, and took in the baby with tremendous if naive enthusiasm.

According to Terrace, the goals for Project Bruno were minimal. The Columbia professor only required evidence that a human household could cope with a chimp and in turn that a chimp could survive the climate in New York City. (Bruno did contract pneumonia while he was in New York, but he recovered.) Of all the children, Josh was the one who grew closest to Bruno. He was five, considerably older than the chimp, but displayed a similar level of energy and was able to roughhouse and tumble with Bruno for hours. Lyngsie and Bruno, however, were inseparable. Jenny Lee recalls that when Bruno bit Lyngsie, she would bite him back on the ear, which shocked him as well as the children, who were not used to nannies or disciplinarians. But by the time Bruno was six months, Lyngsie was the only person who could control him.

Stephanie describes Bruno as a very sweet chimp who generally got along well with children. Like the dominant male that he was, he treated the Lees' home like his castle, which others entered at their own peril. There were inherent risks in just having him there, but there were also rewards. The children were mesmerized. "Some kids watched television," says Josh. "We had a chimpanzee."

But two months after Bruno arrived, with the antiwar movement reaching a fever pitch, the Lees made the decision to go to Europe with Joe Chaikin, the founder of the Open Theater (OT), the hippest, most political theater collective in New York. Ralph had gotten a job as a member of the company. Of course, he would have preferred to go alone, leaving his wife and children (and chimp) behind, but Stephanie, tired of playing the dutiful mother, refused to stay home. She understood that Europe, alive with antiwar ferment, was the place to be, and that traveling with the Open

Josh Lee and Bruno

Theater would be the experience of a lifetime. The whole family boarded a cruise ship bound for England (the Open Theater had been hired to provide the entertainment), with plans to travel in a van around Italy and France for six months.

Only Lyngsie remained after the Lees vanished from Bruno's life in early May. Terrace put four female students in the Lees' apartment with them. Despite a flock of unfamiliar babysitters, Terrace claimed there were no problems with Bruno. "I am still amazed at the ease with which Abe seems to adjust to the wide variety of people who care for him," he wrote to Lemmon in a progress report. "Abe is thriving." (Lemmon apparently did not yet know that Abe had become Bruno.)

Inspired by Chaikin and the Open Theater, the Lees never looked back. Although Stephanie felt a bit guilty for abandoning Bruno, she now considered political activism to be the primary focus of her life. Stephanie and Chaikin fell into a brief sexual relationship on the way over to Europe. But once there, she was still Ralph's wife. Nonetheless, she and the children had to sleep outside in their Volkswagen bus while Chaikin and all the actors and performers, including Ralph, slept in small hotels as they moved from one town to the next; the OT budget didn't provide for family members. Stephanie made the best of it. Chaikin was a god, and she felt lucky to be part of his entourage at all.

When Stephanie and Ralph returned in the fall, Bruno remained with his babysitters and was not invited to join them in their next home, a loft in Westbeth, the first artists-only residence in New York's Greenwich Village, where Chaikin also lived. (Says Jenny, "It's a shame we never had Bruno or Nim in Westbeth, the one place where a chimp would have fit in.") It was a tumultuous time for the Lees. Their marriage, by mutual agreement, was over, although they still lived together. Ralph took a job at Bennington College and commuted back and forth between New York and Vermont. Stephanie returned to Columbia to finish her undergraduate degree in preparation for supporting the children as a single mother.

During Stephanie's absence, Terrace had begun some preliminary (and unsuccessful) experiments with Bruno, attempting to teach him the rudiments of ASL. But when the Columbia demonstrations swept up his graduate students and several of Bruno's trainers took to the streets, leaving Terrace without adequate assistance, he made the decision to put the whole project on hold. He had a sabbatical coming up and wanted to go to London. In June of 1969, Bruno was sent back to Oklahoma. No tears were shed for the departing chimp, for no one in New York had any more use for him.

When Bruno returned to IPS, he was fourteen months old and had never met another chimpanzee since being taken from his mother. In letters between Lemmon and Terrace arranging for the chimp's return, Lemmon offered to keep Bruno in a "human environment" to allow Terrace to pick up his research with the chimp upon his return from England. But Terrace had never done any serious research with Bruno, nor did he want the chimp back. Terrace required a fresh, newborn animal with a clean psychological slate. But it would be years before he got one.

Finally, in November 1973, Lemmon notified Terrace about Carolyn's unexpected male infant and offered to send him to New York. The IPS director again assumed that Terrace would be enthusiastic and grateful. Once again he was wrong. Terrace panicked, even debated turning the chimp down. Still a bachelor, he needed a full-time mother for the chimp in order to accept Lemmon's offer. And in another replaying of history, he thought of calling Stephanie. True, Stephanie had run out on Bruno, but Bruno had been merely a rehearsal chimp, no more than a lab animal returned at the end of the experiment without remorse or reflection. Terrace enjoyed working with Stephanie and wanted to do so again. By 1973, Stephanie had graduated from Columbia, divorced Ralph, and become the head teacher of a Montessori school. A few years earlier, she had met W. E. R. LaFarge, a poet and playwright from a wealthy family, who was a board member of the school and one of its founders. They had fallen in love, married, and moved into a brownstone that was big enough for their combined family, which comprised seven children — Stephanie's three and her husband's four. When the call came from Terrace, whom she had not heard from for years, Stephanie was about to apply to graduate school.

Now thirty-six, Stephanie might have changed names and husbands since last she had seen Terrace, but she had lost none of her enthusiasm for her mentor's research. Moreover, the timing was ideal, for she would need to do a Ph.D. thesis for her graduate degree, and she knew that raising a chimp under these circumstances would virtually guarantee her a doctorate. This was a strong motivation, but not the only one. The concepts underlying Project Nim appealed to her too, and she also felt that the children would benefit from being steeped in a major scientific experiment.

Stephanie flew to Norman on November 25, 1973, to pick up the newborn chimp and bring him home. Terrace, too busy to accompany her, sent her off on her own, confident that she could handle the return trip. Stephanie felt honored to have been selected as the designated mother for this chimpanzee. In all the excitement, she never considered the long-term consequences of Project Nim. She focused on her immediate task — to nurture the chimp as if he were her own flesh and blood and teach him ASL. With Bruno, she had been babysitting; this felt more like adoption.

Stephanie spent her first day in Norman closely observing Carolyn and Nim through the bars of the cage. She had never been in a research laboratory or in close proximity to adult chimps, which is, especially on day one, an overwhelming and frightening experience. LaFarge stayed close to Lemmon as she watched Carolyn and her baby. She was awed by the IPS director and never questioned anything he said or did around his animals. "He was somewhere between Albert Schweitzer and Emperor Jones," she says. "Here an environment that resembled a zoo, with animals in concrete cages, with lots of guns and cattle prods around to control them, but at the same time, Lemmon and his wife were *feeling* for these animals as if they were people."

On Stephanie's second evening in Norman, she returned to Carolyn's cage, again accompanied by Lemmon, this time with a dart gun in his hand. Lemmon's MO when removing infants from their mothers was to sedate the mothers with Sernalyn, a drug that produces a groggy, hallucinatory state of mind accompanied by immobility. Without the tranquilizer, the mother chimp would have been quite capable of killing any human or animal trying to take away, or even approach, her new baby. Carolyn clung tightly to Nim, breast-feeding him, as Lemmon and Stephanie drew near. Stephanie recalls locking eyes with Carolyn — mother to mother — when she first approached the cage. She saw rage in Carolyn's eyes. "She knows," Lemmon whispered into Stephanie's ear, confirming her hunch. Stephanie had no qualms about taking this baby from his mother, however. She viewed herself first and foremost as a scientist doing research that had the potential to benefit humankind. The cruelty implicit in what was about to happen was an acceptable part of the research. It would be years before she would make a connection between the anger she had glimpsed in Carolyn's eyes and the events that eventually shaped Nim's life — and years before she would feel a sense of responsibility for her own role in setting those events in motion.

The chimps in the adjacent cages began to hoot in protest, as if they too knew what was about to happen. Then Lemmon shot a dart into Carolyn's thigh. After several minutes, still breast-feeding her baby, Carolyn fell to the ground, her eyes open. The trick was to grab the baby immediately after the mother was immobilized and before she accidentally rolled over and crushed him. Paralyzed, Carolyn watched as Lemmon rushed into her cage to peel the infant off her body. Hours later, Carolyn, still in a stupor, was staggering around her cage, searching for her baby, while Nim, diapered and swaddled in Stephanie's arms, was getting to know his new mother, preparatory to embarking on his strange journey.

Stephanie spent the next two nights in the Lemmons' pink house on the hill, pacing back and forth with a crying baby in her arms. On the third day, both she and the chimp began to relax. It was just in time. That afternoon, Stephanie was booked on a flight back to New York. When she boarded the plane, she was carrying Nim, hidden in a blanket, sleeping peacefully. Buckled into her seat for takeoff, Stephanie felt a surge of contentment at being alone with Nim for the first time. He was so much like a human baby that she knew instinctively what to do with him. Halfway through the flight, she could no longer resist unveiling her baby to show him off to the flight attendants. Their mouths dropped open and they squealed with delight when they discovered the tiny chimp. Lining up to see Nim, the attendants took turns holding him in their arms. One of them whisked him off to the cockpit to meet the pilots like a VIP. As Stephanie was already discovering, Nim's mere presence could turn any ordinary situation into theater. Flying home to New York, she knew she had been given a front-row seat on what was destined to be a tremendous show, way more spectacular than anything she had previously seen.

As every mother knows, traveling with a baby for the first time can be a litmus test. Nim's flight from Norman was blissfully uneventful. Stephanie's confidence soared as she hugged the chimp to her body. Her task was to make Nim feel like one of her own, just as she was trying to do with her new husband's four children, and she felt sure she could succeed. As she came down the jetway into the terminal with Nim in her arms, she was very much the picture of a beaming new mother. For his part, wide-eyed with pleasure, the infant chimp clung to her the same way he had to Carolyn in Norman. Project Nim had begun.

Stephanie LaFarge, WER LaFarge, and Nim

CHAPTER 3
"BRADY BUNCH —
PLUS CHIMP"

Nim Chimpsky was about to enter what Herbert Terrace believed was an ordinary family, where the chimp, and the psychologist himself when needed, could be successfully integrated into the mundane, everyday life of a busy, affluent household. Stephanie assured Terrace that Nim could be slipped into her domestic scene without any glitches. She wholeheartedly bought into the fantasy that she would be raising Nim as her new baby. Conveniently enough, since Terrace had not yet managed to win any grants for the study, her husband, W. E. R. LaFarge (known as WER, which rhymes with *beer*), offered to pay Nim's bills. Nonetheless, WER was not as eager as Stephanie to bring this new creature into their already complicated lives.

WER LaFarge had been born into an old, distinguished Boston family, the latest in a long line of powerful men who had become legends in their own time. John LaFarge, WER's great-grandfather, was a celebrated nineteenth-century watercolorist; C. Grant LaFarge, WER's grandfather, was an eminent architect who helped to design, among other notable churches, the Cathedral of St. John the Divine in New York City; Oliver LaFarge, WER's uncle, won a Pulitzer Prize for his first novel, *The Laughing Boy,* read in high schools to this day. WER's father, Christopher LaFarge, was also a writer and an accomplished architect. He had married Louisa Hoar, a member of a Massachusetts family prominent in politics, which made its fortune in manufacturing electrical wire. The Hoars boasted of an ancestor's signature on the Declaration of Independence, two U.S. senators, and a Harvard University president. The marriage of a LaFarge to a Hoar created a nexus of power, wealth, cultural accomplishment, and expectations that entered the very DNA of their offspring. It also left many of them, like WER, feeling the heavy burden of having to live up to the family legacy. WER was the fourth generation of LaFarges to attend Groton, then Harvard.

While at Harvard, WER fell in love with a Radcliffe girl, Ann Burkett, an intelligent, unpretentious woman from a small town in

Maine. After graduating, the couple married in 1955 and returned to New York to begin their own family. They produced four attractive blond children in quick succession — Louisa, Annik, Albert, and Matilda. WER had ambitions to be a writer, like his father and other LaFarges before him, and he also strove to reproduce the patrician lifestyle of the LaFarges, raising his children in an elegant brownstone on the Upper East Side of Manhattan. WER's mother, not known for her warmth, had died of cancer when he was twelve years old, and his father, whom he tried hard to emulate, succumbed to a cerebral hemorrhage at the age of fifty-five, two weeks after WER and Ann were married. Ann had always found her father-in-law's authority over her husband problematic. But his death upset WER to the core, and she felt that he never truly succeeded in overcoming his grief. Until then Ann had never noticed any cracks in WER's well-polished façade, but suddenly she saw that he was unsure of himself and of what he wanted to do with his life.

Ann did not come from generations of wealth and power, but she understood the weight of WER's family history. She believed that despite whatever WER went through after his father's death, their marriage would survive, and she did what she could to hold the family together. Ann ran a well-regulated household, one that was formal and refined enough to please her husband, who thrived on the rituals that had been touchstones of his rarefied childhood. He ordered his suits from a tailor in London, and he kept his shoes shined and his hair cut short. Formal dinners with polished silver and ironed tablecloths were de rigueur. He and Ann had tea in the afternoon, cocktails each evening, and dinner at seven o'clock. The children went to bed when they were supposed to. Says Ann, "I thought our life was perfect."

Albert LaFarge, WER and Ann's son, describes his father as "a member of the establishment with a capital *E*." The children had a European au pair and wore uniforms at their top private schools. On weekends, they dressed in penny loafers and pullover sweaters. During the summer, they went to their country estate, a spectacular four-hundred-acre farm on the Narrow River in Rhode Island that had been in the LaFarge family since the nineteenth century; WER worked in the same cabin that his father had used as an office. The farm was a natural wonderland untouched by development, and the single place on earth where WER felt truly at home.

As the fifties turned into the sixties and a whole generation began to seethe with rebellion, WER began to feel like a hollow man, constricted by the very lifestyle he had worked so hard to perfect. The sixties hit WER like a tab of bad acid that he could not get out of his system. He tormented himself with philosophical questions he could not answer, and in the process tore himself apart. WER had become a stranger to his own children, and they could not understand the unhappiness that had taken their father from them. They wondered if he was having a nervous breakdown. Ann remembers going into WER's office one afternoon and seeing a folder on his desk labeled "New Life." In his systematic way, he was collecting information on the counterculture as he struggled to break away from centuries of LaFarge tradition and figure out his own beliefs.

WER observed the revolution going on around him, and he came to believe that he was part of the problem, part of the bourgeoisie that maintained and supported the war in Vietnam. He had never had to earn a dime, but he suddenly understood that poverty and wealth were charged ideological issues. For the first time, he felt some responsibility for all the trouble and suffering in the world. To make amends, he began selling off family stock in corporations that were supporting the war, and giving away large chunks of his money.

Seized by self-doubt and a new passion for advocacy, WER took off for California to turn his life around. Ann remained behind with the children, hoping to preserve the routine that structured their lives. "It was as if he needed to shed his whole life like a skin," says Albert, who watched his father's transformation through an eight-year-old's eyes. When WER returned, he looked completely different. He was wearing casual clothes, had a long ponytail, and was carrying a shoulder bag that the children described as "a purse." Albert thought he was virtually in costume: "He looked like he was poor, even though he had millions of dollars in the bank." Ann did her best to stand by her husband and help him get through his *crise de conscience.*

In his zeal to be more active in his community, WER took a seat on the small board of the Montessori school that his children had attended and that he and Ann had helped to found. There he met and became involved with Stephanie Lee, who was then a teacher at the school and the liaison to the board. Stephanie's parents were not millionaires, but they weren't poor either. She had grown up in New York City with a Park Avenue address. Her father, Victor Ratner, was an executive at CBS, and her mother, Letitia Ide, was the first female dancer to partner with José Limón on stage. Stephanie had grown up in an artistic milieu, enjoying all kinds of freedoms, yet she seemed to speak WER's language and understand the struggle he had been through to get away from a life that he no longer wanted. *Repression* was not a word in Stephanie's vocabulary. Powerful, independent, and seductive, she led WER downtown to a part of Manhattan he had never seen.

WER had written a satirical play about his family, which had been successfully produced in California while he was living there. (The uptight protagonist wears a Brooks Brothers suit in the first act; by the final scene, he is wearing a dashiki.) But WER had few artistic connections in New York. Through her involvement with Joe Chaikin, Stephanie, of course, was at the vortex of avant-garde theater in the city. She had the network that WER had only dreamed about entering. He longed to meet Chaikin and get a play produced by the Open Theater. Chaikin was looking for a

117

biographer and agreed to talk to WER. But the two men had nothing in common and there was no creative spark when they came together. Chaikin wanted WER to write *about* the Open Theater, not *for* the Open Theater. He had no desire to produce WER's plays. In the end, none of this really mattered to WER. He was changing his life, entering the art world, and thinking about the relationship between art and advocacy. As he became more involved in the downtown scene, his depression began to lift.

The Lees and LaFarges had several dinners together, as if the two couples were going to become best friends. Stephanie and Ralph, still sharing the same apartment in Westbeth for the sake of their children, had a conspicuously open marriage; Ralph was teaching at Bennington College, where he was seeing one of his students, and commuting back and forth to New York. (Casey Compton, the student, would become his second wife.) Stephanie tried to shield her children from the evidence of her new affair — she appeared alone for breakfast each morning before they all went off to school — but certainly Ralph had no illusions about the presence of a new man in Stephanie's life. Nor did he object. Ann, however, was not "liberated" and she took her marriage vows seriously. She was horrified by her husband's most indiscreet affair.

But WER was too carried away with his passion for Stephanie to bother hiding his feelings. He could no longer be depended upon to come home at night for dinner, and when he did show up, he spent the whole evening talking on the phone with Stephanie, as if they were in high school. Assuming that their infatuation would end, Ann did everything she could to save her marriage. She even went downtown in her efforts to bring WER back uptown. At Stephanie's suggestion, she joined a women's consciousness-raising group that met weekly in Westbeth. Ann believed this would allow her to monitor Stephanie's behavior and also to get some support from the other members, who included, among other writers and artists, Grace Paley. The women sat on the floor in a circle and took turns telling their stories. When it was Ann's turn to speak, she explained that Stephanie, sitting right there, was sleeping with her husband and that she felt irate and miserable about it. But she had not anticipated the response from the other women. In their view, monogamy was a straitjacket, not an optimal way of life. They were feminists, searching for ways to liberate themselves from men.

No one was going to pin a scarlet letter on Stephanie's chest. Everybody there was thinking about or actually doing some version of the same thing.

WER finally moved out of his house and into a small apartment on the West Side. He told Ann that he wanted both her and Stephanie in his life, and he had a plan: he wanted to marry Stephanie and make Ann his mistress. For Ann, this was the last straw. She filed for divorce. Stephanie and Ralph, who by this time had also divorced, shared joint custody of their three children. At Stephanie's suggestion, WER hired the same lawyer that she had used to dispose of her husband.

WER loved his children and felt tremendous guilt about leaving them behind with his wife. All he wanted from the settlement was joint custody and a chance to integrate the children into his new life. Everything else, including money and property (with the exception of the farm in Rhode Island), was meaningless. But Ann was hardly in the mood to give WER anything, especially her children. "WER had hired a young woman lawyer who didn't know what she was doing," she recalls. "My lawyer mopped the floor with them."

In the 1970s, judges were not inclined to

give custody to fathers who had committed adultery and abandoned their wives. WER was completely devastated by the decision to award full custody to Ann. He and Stephanie decided to get married, which they felt would normalize their relationship, both to the children and to the outside world. The couple found a Jungian minister, an acquaintance from the Village scene, to perform a church service, but no one, not even the children, was invited to witness the ceremony. In Stephanie and WER's view, marriage was a technicality, not an event.

Their father's dramatic change of heart and wives was disturbing to the LaFarge children. The second Mrs. LaFarge could not have been more different from the first one. The two women had different styles, politics, and talents. Ann made the children simple hamburgers and frozen vegetables for dinner; Stephanie spent hours in the kitchen and pulled perfect soufflés from her oven. Ann lived on the East Side; WER and Stephanie made their new home on the West Side. The one constant was a town house.

The home WER purchased for himself and his new wife represented a serious investment in his relationship with Stephanie. Located on West 78th Street, it was a three-story sandstone building, built in the

1920s, with intricate hand-carved architectural details. A stone stoop led to a solid oak door that was painted black. Inside, the house had a formal entrance featuring a huge mirror and pocket doors that disappeared into the walls. The living room walls were covered from floor to ceiling with elegant rosewood bookshelves — perfect for displaying WER's collection of treasured books, including many first editions. The house boasted five bedrooms and a renovated gourmet kitchen that opened up into a separate dining room, where Stephanie served feasts for her husband and their small army of children. Outside the kitchen door, a patio caught just enough sun for a potted herb garden. A circular metal stairway spiraled down to a backyard one story below, which was mostly used by the dog, a German shepherd named Trudge, who would become Nim's best buddy. In the basement, a separate apartment was rented out to an obscure soap opera actress named Betty Buckley, who occasionally banged on the front door to complain bitterly about the constant noise upstairs. Little did she know a chimp was about to move in and add a few points to the decibel level.

WER's four children lived primarily with their mother in her brownstone, also coincidentally on 78th Street, but across town, on the East Side. Louisa, Annik, Albert, and Matilda (Tildy) referred to WER and Stephanie's house as "West" and Ann's house as "East." The East Siders were familiar with every bump and stop on the 79th Street crosstown bus, which they rode frequently, traveling between their parents' homes. Stephanie's three children, Heather, Jenny, and Josh, lived more or less full time with her and WER, traveling downtown to visit their father in Greenwich Village on weekends. The children's comings and goings followed a regular schedule that was posted each week in the kitchen.

Stephanie, WER, and the "LeeFarges," as some of the children called themselves, moved into the brownstone almost a year before Nim arrived. Marika Moosbrugger, a colleague of Stephanie's from the Montessori school, was invited to take a room on the third floor, which pleased the children. She had taught the LaFarge siblings, and she acted as a buffer and friend to all the children as they faced a difficult transition.

The new arrangements were especially tough on the four LaFarges. For them, traveling to the West Side was like going to another country. "I'd sit on the crosstown bus looking at all the other fathers," Tildy remembers. "They had short hair and were carrying briefcases. My dad had a ponytail and carried a pocketbook." Their father's new life made them feel like outsiders. WER wanted them to switch to more progressive schools and let their hair down too. He hoped that Stephanie would rub off on them and help them open up. But across town, Ann deeply resented the bohemian atmosphere that WER and Stephanie were creating. She discouraged her children from becoming too ensconced on the West Side and wanted them home as much as possible.

Louisa, the eldest LaFarge daughter, was the most receptive to her father's transformation. She dropped out of the conservative Brearley School on the East Side and switched to Calhoun, an experimental high school on the West Side, which Stephanie's daughter Jenny also attended. Louisa was as comfortable with Stephanie as she was with the laid-back atmosphere of the house. Albert and Tildy made the best of their father's new life, while Annik kept her distance from the whole scene, surfacing only occasionally at dinnertime.

Stephanie reached out to the LaFarge children, trying to find ways to bring them into the fold. "WER and my mom genuinely had some dream about these two groups of kids coming together to celebrate this wonderful family," says Jenny. "But none of us were particularly interested." At one point, WER purchased an old yellow school bus and removed some of the seats so the seven children could comfortably spread out. On their first family excursion in the bus, to Washington, D.C., the kids complained of stomachaches for most of the drive. No one was happy.

Despite bumps in the road, these seven very different children had one important thing in common: the experience of divorce. They were each trying to manage an intricate web of familial relations while going to schools all over the city, not to mention extracurricular dance classes, piano lessons, and volleyball games. Just figuring out what clothes to leave out for school, which textbooks to pack in the morning, or what address to write down on a school form required a brain-splitting amount of attention. Nothing was easy or obvious. But Stephanie and WER wanted the children to feel loved. "Stephanie was in heaven because she had so many opportunities to be the shrink," says Moosbrugger. "There was always one issue or another erupting between the kids, and we had meeting after meeting to discuss it."

At the time Nim suddenly became available, Stephanie and WER were actually thinking about having another baby. It was a new marriage, and Stephanie liked having babies; she thought one more might bring the two disparate groups of children together. But the idea of adopting a chimp instead seemed to her like the ideal solution. She encouraged Terrace, ready or not, to accept Nim and begin the experiment. The high drama of the situation — the urgent need for a surrogate mother — appealed to her.

WER was considerably more circumspect. He felt deeply ambivalent about the whole enterprise. Had he been able to turn Nim down and still keep Stephanie happy, he almost certainly would have done so. He worried about the effect Nim would have on his marriage and his already frayed relations with his children. And he was not, as it turned out, an animal lover. Stephanie gave him little choice, however, framing the adoption of Nim as part of her career path. As she explains, "It would have been hard for him to have said no to Nim because he wasn't a pet; this was an intellectual project."

After years of taking a backseat to Ralph,

Stephanie wanted to focus on her own career, and she convinced WER to take in the chimp. "Stephanie always got what she wanted," Moosbrugger comments. "WER would have done anything she asked. If Stephanie decided to get a Ph.D., she would get it. If Stephanie decided to get a monkey, she would get that too." Moosbrugger shared WER's fears. "I was totally mixed up about it," she recalls. "Until I held Nim in my arms."

The plan, sketchy at best, called for Nim to remain in his human home as long as possible, even into adulthood, up to age ten or eleven, in order for him to become one of them — Nim Chimpsky LaFarge — and have enough time to fully develop his language skills. Once acculturated to family life, Nim would presumably be motivated by the same mysterious factors that move human children to learn how to communicate. From Terrace's point of view — which is to say, that of a Skinnerian — the chimp's mind was pliable and impressionable, like putty. Of course, this was a highly speculative assumption. Washoe had demonstrated to the Gardners that a chimp could learn words, but whether a chimp could use language structurally and systematically to communicate his thoughts was the most critical question for Project Nim.

In reality, Terrace knew little about chimpanzees or their culture. (He may not have believed that they even had a culture.) Nor did the LaFarges. They were parents, not primatologists. The question of whether or not they would succeed in constructing Nim's identity as a human and be able to collect viable data on how his mind actually operated generated a mix of intellectual excitement and suspense around the project. Terrace was confident that Nim would pick up language naturally, like human children. But his confidence was not based on any experience with chimpanzees. Abe/Bruno had come and gone without any fanfare, and there had been little systematic attempt to teach him much of anything.

On December 1, a bitterly cold day, Jenny, age twelve, accompanied WER on a drive out to Kennedy Airport to pick up Stephanie and Nim. Jenny was the one child who totally supported her mother's decision to take in the chimpanzee. She had not focused much on Bruno, but five years later her maternal instincts were beginning to blossom. Right from the start, Jenny insisted on being part of Nim's life. A feisty, independent preteen, she shunned Barbie dolls, preferring animals to people. Jenny had even convinced her school to give her a leave of absence so she could fully participate in Nim's care at home and attend regular meetings concerning the experiment at Columbia. She proudly became the youngest member of the Project Nim team.

Jenny remembers standing in the airport, watching intently for her mother, until Stephanie emerged from the arrivals gate carrying what appeared to be a small bundle of baby blankets in her arms. When she reached the nervous dad and her bubbling daughter, she unwrapped the package to reveal a scrawny, black, hairy creature with long arms and a pacifier in his mouth. He was whimpering happily as Stephanie put him in Jenny's arms. For Jenny, the bond was instant. But when Stephanie gave Nim to WER, the chimp began to cry and didn't stop until she took him back. It was one of those moments that both she and Terrace noted as possibly prophetic. Several years later, Terrace speculated that WER simply had the misfortune of being the first male to come between Nim and his new mother: "Nim's reaction to WER seemed downright Oedipal," he wrote. On the drive home, Nim went back to sleep and Jenny asked the obvious question: was this a new baby or was it a new pet? The response was silence. No one could think of a simple answer to this complex question, which would haunt Project Nim for its duration. But for the moment, Jenny had a new brother.

What immediately surprised the whole family was that Nim was so easy to be with, to comfort and hold. He looked, acted, and felt like a real baby. He sucked eagerly on his bottle, burped contentedly after a few pats on the back, slept most of the time, and cried when he was put down, preferring to be held. Tickling and kissing made him ecstatic. "All he wanted to do was cuddle with his new family," says Moosbrugger. If WER harbored fears that the chimp might be something out of a David Cronenberg film, they appeared to be groundless. The baby was adorable.

Although Nim bore a close resemblance to a human infant, the LaFarges could not help but notice the differences. Human babies are soft blobs of flesh that have to be carefully held and supported. Nim was far from helpless. It was not possible to drop him. He clung tightly to whoever was holding him, and if he did slip, he simply grabbed something on his way down and hung on. Diapering him was an unforgettable experience. Chimps can grasp with their hands and their feet, so getting a diaper on him before he grabbed it with his prehensile fingers or toes was never easy, especially since Nim hated wearing anything on his body. Nevertheless, Project Nim required him to play and look the part of a human baby. Besides, he needed some clothes for warmth. Moosbrugger knitted him colorful striped sweaters and quickly became his number two caretaker. She couldn't get enough of him.

Stephanie tried everything she could think of to make Nim feel part of the family. She had always loved the intimacy between mother and child, and she found something even more exhilarating about her closeness to Nim. After all, he was so much less helpless and so much more responsive and interactive than a human child of that age. "I felt freer with him than I did with my own children," she says. "He was less vulnerable to being screwed up by me." Nim was trying to breast-feed on her, which initially made her uncomfortable. But she decided to go along with it, mostly because it was hard to stop him from doing anything he wanted to do. Stephanie also enjoyed the process and believed that nursing Nim would comfort him and make him feel more connected to her. Of course she had no milk for Nim, and the feedings soon gave her mastitis and had to stop.

Most nights, Nim slept in between Stephanie and WER, which, after the first few months, began to bother the new father. They could have sex only if the chimpanzee was in a deep slumber. If Nim was awake, WER couldn't get near Stephanie. Insisting that newborn chimps required physical intimacy with their mothers, she had no intention of peeling him off her at night until he was a little older and more confident. WER had long since given up making demands on Stephanie, apart from a sit-down dinner each evening, but allowing Nim to take over his bedroom made him feel as if he had been supplanted in his own home. WER expected more from his new wife. He was used to a certain amount of control and respect.

Nim's pediatrician, Dr. Steve Lerman, made house calls, which always turned into a spectacle. Dr. Lerman happened to have a son who had been born right at the same time as Nim. During his first few visits, he brought the baby with him, to compare their rates of physical development. At about one month, the two babies were roughly equivalent, both lying on their backs together. Two weeks later, the doctor's baby was still lying there, but Nim was beginning to roll over. A few weeks after that, the doctor's baby was still immobile, while Nim was scooting all over the house. At two months, Nim could scale any wall that had a molding he could grip with his fingers and toes. He became stronger and more agile with each week.

Despite the tension in the bedroom, Nim's first months passed relatively smoothly. Stephanie integrated him into her routines, whether doing errands, cooking dinner, or going to her weekly psychotherapy session, where Nim slept quietly on her chest as she lay on the couch and talked. Moosbrugger and Jenny were also confident with Nim, taking him from Stephanie when she needed a rest. Then there was Maggie Jakobson (now actress Maggie Wheeler of *Friends* fame), only fifteen, but bold enough to knock on the LaFarges' front door, introduce herself, and ask to see the chimpanzee, whom she had heard about at Calhoun, where she went to school with Louisa and Jenny. Maggie was not friends with either one of the girls, but she was obsessed with primates and more than anything else wanted to meet and hold one. Stephanie, open to virtually anyone and anything, invited Maggie in. Maggie quickly made herself indispensable, becoming Nim's number one outside babysitter.

The project attracted bright students from universities all over the East Coast who were thrilled to meet the chimp and get a behind-the-scenes glimpse of a noteworthy experiment. Volunteer helpers lined up, hoping for a chance to babysit the chimp. A few of them got themselves fired right away. Stephanie terminated one the day she came home and found him in a deep slumber, during which Nim had gone up to a room on the third floor of the brownstone, opened a window, and climbed out on the ledge. When Stephanie found him there, he was happily sitting outdoors, watching the people and cars go by. Trudge, their loyal dog, was sitting in the room with his eyes on the chimp. After that experience, a sign was made for the street door that read "Danger: Live Chimpanzee Experiment" and a greater effort was made to Nim-proof the house, which was gradually transformed into a safe playground. Everything that was valuable or breakable was packed away or otherwise put out of the reach of Nim's dexterous fingers and toes. The LaFarges were learning chimp care on the job. The only formal training they received was in ASL.

Like any healthy male chimp, Nim had no trouble establishing his authority. He soon ran the household, supplanting WER as the top male. The chimp could not be contained. Every inch of the brownstone became his turf. The living room, Nim's headquarters, where everybody hung out, looked like a Haight-Ashbury crash pad. It was devoid of furniture save for a king-size water bed and the floor-to-ceiling shelves that held WER's treasured books and expensive stereo equipment. The floor was covered with a thick white shag rug strewn with oversize cushions on which Nim bounced around when he wasn't sliding up and down the banister or hanging from light fixtures. Says Tildy, "The living room was all about sitting on the floor, which at the time I thought was really weird. Most of our friends had couches in their living rooms." But Stephanie and WER liked to sprawl out on the rug, light up a joint, and listen to music with whoever happened to drop by. Nim would take a puff on the joint too — and inhale with pleasure. (A few years later, he would ask for a joint in sign language by combining three signs: "stone," "smoke," "now.")

After a cover story in *New York* magazine described Project Nim as a "scientific revolution with religious consequences that occurs once every few hundred years," Nim became a local celebrity, greeting his fans on the street. He thrived on being the center of attention and made it nearly impossible for anyone else to get any. WER became more unhappy week by week. A few months into the project, he took to locking himself in his office on the third floor of the house. Stephanie had to walk upstairs and fetch WER for meals. She often begged him to come downstairs and spend some time with his children.

WER began to insist on a few changes. He felt that Nim was old enough to move out of his mother's bed and give his "parents" some privacy. Stephanie had to agree. A tent-like construction that Ralph Lee had once built for Bruno was taken out of the closet and reconstructed in a corner of the dining room. There were platforms at various heights to climb on, as well as a hammock for Nim to swing in; the contraption zipped up the front and, in theory, could not be opened from the inside. Everyone hoped the novelty of this cozy little space would keep Nim amused long enough for him to fall asleep.

During the first night Nim spent zipped inside his new bed, he screamed louder and longer than ever before. His cries were so disturbing that a neighbor thought a child was being abused and called the police. When they arrived at the front door, Stephanie explained that they were not child batterers but scientists, and all the noise was part of an important experiment. No arrests were made. Like everyone else, the officers were charmed as soon as they met the young chimp. But separating Nim from Stephanie was not going to work — neither for her nor for him. She could not stand to hear him wail or deny him comfort. What she regarded as WER's refusal to acknowledge the chimp's needs infuriated her. Stephanie began to wonder if WER had any paternal feelings for the chimp at all, at the same time that WER's children were wondering if he had any paternal feelings for them. From WER's perspective, Nim and Stephanie were ruining his life.

The children, as children will, exploited the tension between WER and Nim. Whenever anything was missing or turned up broken, Nim was blamed. Stephanie saw what was happening, but there was little she could do about it. The children were teenagers; they thrived on undermining their parents' authority, which happened to be Nim's expertise as well.

At some point during any given evening, Nim would do something to torment WER. The children enjoyed watching their father squirm. They secretly looked forward to the moment when the fun would begin, and they were rarely disappointed. WER was an obsessive-compulsive who needed every-thing in its proper place. Somehow, Nim knew that the hottest button he could push was connected to WER's most sacred pos-session: his collection of books in the floor-to-ceiling rosewood shelves, carefully ar-ranged by subject and size. When WER settled down in the living room after din-ner, surrounded by his books, Nim waited for his opening. At what he deemed, for reasons of his own, to be the perfect mo-ment, he raced to the wall and ran his hands over the bottom shelf of books, knocking every single one onto the floor. Then he reversed course and ran back the other way, knocking every book off the next shelf, and the next and the next, until every book within reach of his long arms lay on the floor in a heap. As he got bigger, he could go higher and higher. Predictably, WER leapt to his feet screaming: "Stop! No! Bad!" But there was no stopping Nim.

When he was done, Stephanie picked up all the books off the floor and put them back on the shelves. They could have moved the books out of the room, but WER wanted them around him, where he could see them, and besides, packing them all up would have been a victory for Nim.

"Nim must have sensed WER's negative feelings, for more and more he resisted being held by him," Terrace wrote. But according to Jenny, Nim didn't particularly like Terrace either. The chimp would begin acting out the minute the Columbia professor walked through the door. Jenny and Stephanie were convinced that Nim liked only women; but as he grew older, this turned out not to be the case. He simply appeared not to like Terrace or WER.

"Nim was like throwing a grenade into the family," says Albert. "We were already a very fragile household, and there was a lot of animosity between the stepsiblings. So there was a great deal of angst mixed in with the excitement around Nim. We didn't really understand the science. But we knew intuitively that it was important. In the beginning we could see that Stephanie and Dad had this passion to discover something vital about what makes us human, which was amazing. But it was also painful and quirky."

Albert remembers rolling around with Nim on the water bed before dinner. "We'd all be there with Nim watching *The Brady Bunch* on television," he continues. "We were this postmodern Brady Bunch — plus chimp."

Occasionally, the blended family — plus chimp — experienced "normal" times that were thoroughly enjoyable. They liked to cook together, crowding into the kitchen, sometimes for hours, to prepare elaborate dinners that ended with fabulous home-made desserts. Stephanie created a kitchen culture where all the children, including Nim, were welcome to help. Lingering visitors — friends, colleagues, and graduate students — were invited to stay and eat. Stephanie and Jenny often made big pots of spaghetti or sloppy Joes for twenty. When the family dined alone, Stephanie made her signature soufflés.

Stephanie put Nim's high chair at the dining room table. The goal was to keep him in it for as long as possible. Until he learned to use silverware himself, Jenny sat next to him and fed him. Nim ate everything he could get into his mouth. He loved bananas, as well as ice cream and Jell-O, which Stephanie made from scratch with real juice, gelatin, and fresh fruit. One night they

Jenny Lee and Nim at home on West 78th Street
© Harry Benson

were having Jell-O for dessert. When the bowl was put out on the table, Nim became overly excited and wanted to devour it immediately. Jenny forced him to wait until he was served. Nim started hooting, louder and louder, until he was so revved up that he couldn't wait any longer; he sprang up onto the table and dove face-first into the bowl. The whole family burst into hysterical laughter as Nim vacuumed up the dessert. At moments like these, the antics of an infant chimp trying his best to behave like a little boy brought them together and helped them feel like members of one family.

In every respect, Project Nim was Terrace's baby. But he was surprised to find how little effect he was able to have over how the chimp was being raised. A frequent visitor throughout the first few weeks, Terrace came by the brownstone to give Nim at least one bottle a day. But the LaFarges did not observe a schedule, so Terrace never knew whether or not they would even be home when he called or arrived. Jenny intentionally disappeared when she saw him coming, and as Nim grew older, he did too. According to Stephanie, none of the children liked Terrace. They felt the professor failed to relate to them or acknowledge their contribution to Nim's well-being. Jenny, especially, was miffed. More than the others, she was involved in all aspects of Nim's daily life; she loved the chimp like a brother. The children experienced Terrace as an intruder, someone who interrupted the natural flow of life at the brownstone.

Not insensitive to his unfriendly reception, Terrace eventually stopped coming by unless he was invited or was meeting a guest there. Stephanie didn't miss him. She felt that Nim's aversion to Terrace and WER was a natural stage in the chimp's emotional development. Had they all been in the jungle, Nim might not even have given his biological father the time of day; mothers raise their infant chimps. Adult males are not part of their daily lives.

As Nim became bigger and more disruptive, the LaFarge home devolved into chaos. Terrace longed to get Project Nim on track. In his view, Nim was becoming more difficult to control because Stephanie had failed to train him, indulging her own laissez-faire attitude toward discipline. Terrace's criticisms, all thoroughly discussed at meetings, annoyed the whole family. From their point of view, Nim was thriving; Terrace simply had no idea what living with a chimp was like.

Terrace felt that his lack of authority in the LaFarge home might stall the progress of Project Nim. Theoretically, the brownstone was Terrace's research laboratory, which he should have been able to run as he saw fit. But after only a few months, Terrace understood the error in his thinking: "It is one thing to explain to a graduate student why it is important to switch bird number 36 from condition A to condition B for two weeks and another thing to tell a member of someone else's family never to allow Nim to touch a bookshelf." After several more heated discussions with Stephanie, Terrace realized that she was not about to change her views or cede her authority over rearing Nim. Terrace had lost control of his chimp.

But he remained in charge of Project Nim and decided to begin collecting hard data from Nim. Hoping to take the experiment to a new stage and reassert his influence over it, he argued that Nim was ready to participate in structured language sessions. Only two months old, Nim was already a proficient imitator of human behavior. Terrace noted that when he stuck out his tongue at the chimp, Nim happily mirrored the gesture. Surely this capacity for imitation would serve him well in learning to sign. Nim's infancy was over — it was time to begin his education.

Stephanie, Moosbrugger, Jenny, and several of Terrace's graduate students had been taking a class in ASL at the New York Society for the Deaf, and Terrace had also hired a tutor to go to the LaFarge house and meet with as many family members as happened to be around. No one involved was fluent in ASL, but everyone knew a few words, which they had used around Nim (along with English) since his arrival.

After much discussion, Terrace and Stephanie agreed to begin his formal training with the sign for "drink" (the thumb is extended from the fist and moved to the mouth in a smooth gesture). The teacher, in this case Stephanie or Jenny, would take Nim's hands and mold them, as if they were clay, into the precise shape of the sign. The Gardners had used this technique successfully on Washoe. Molding is simple, although it requires some trust between teacher and student, who are in physical contact. At first, Nim resisted the entire process and wanted none of it. But his teachers persisted until Nim relaxed and began to participate, even enjoying the sessions. Two weeks after his instruction began, Nim signed *drink* to Stephanie without any prompting or molding. It was a landmark moment, the first of many. Terrace, to be sure that Stephanie had accurately observed the sign, developed criteria for adding words to Nim's vocabulary list. Each use of the word had to be observed by three different people over at least five successive days. Most important, Nim had to use the word spontaneously, without any prompting from the humans around him. Nim's teachers regularly molded his hands into other signs and within two months, he mastered "drink" as well as "give," "up," "sweet," and "more."

The LeeFarges hung a blackboard on the dining room wall to keep track of Nim's stats. At dinner, Stephanie announced the next word that Nim was to be taught, and reported on his daily progress to the family. In his effort to bring order and structure to Project Nim, Terrace began weekly meetings at Columbia for his team — which now consisted of selected graduate students and volunteers as well as Stephanie and Jenny — to discuss the chimp's behavior, teaching strategies, and language theory in more detail. (Nim was not present.) Various experts were invited to attend the meetings, comment on the reports, or offer advice. Nim's vocabulary was growing week by week, along with his confidence and physical strength, and Terrace believed the chimp was making good progress.

"Nim's early mastery of signs was very encouraging," wrote Terrace. "But even though Nim learned his first sign before most children speak their first words, I did not regard Nim as a prodigy." Terrace pointed to evidence that both deaf children and chimpanzees learned to sign before human children learn to speak, which meant only that Nim was on schedule. That is, he was on the same schedule a human deaf child might be on. But as far as chimps were concerned, he was learning faster than Washoe, and at a younger age. In a very real sense, Nim was competing with Washoe for potential grant dollars. Terrace hoped that the proposal he and Bever were about to submit to the National Science Foundation and the National Institutes of Mental Health (NIMH) would finally get the project funded so that it would no longer be dependent on the generosity of WER La-Farge, who was currently its only financial backer, and who was growing unhappier by the moment at having to share his wife and his home with a chimpanzee who didn't even seem to like him.

Nim's progress dazzled the family. They watched in amazement as he began using sign language to make requests and get attention. Stephanie, proud of Nim's success, felt that whatever she was doing in raising Nim was working. Terrace was not so sure. As a scientist, he felt pressure both to document Nim's process of signing more carefully and to maximize his production of signs. He wanted more statistics as evidence that Project Nim had launched with success. To get it, he demanded a tougher, more structured program for the chimp. According to Jenny, who regularly attended weekly meetings at Columbia, discussions about the lack of discipline in Nim's home life became more and more heated. Stephanie refused to push the chimp harder. Like parents with clashing philosophies of child rearing, arguing over whether or not their child was ready for kindergarten, Stephanie wanted to give Nim a longer infancy, while Terrace, the overachiever, wanted the chimp to get to work.

As the chimp's mother, Stephanie believed that she alone had his best interests at heart. She had been trained as a Montessori teacher and had clear ideas about the way that children learned. Stephanie wanted the experiment to consider the social aspects of Nim's language development. She believed that if she confined her role to setting up a nurturing environment for Nim, the learning would take care of itself. She argued that too much interference could actually slow Nim down. "As the critter's mother, she had a lot of authority," says Jenny, who witnessed countless arguments between Terrace and Stephanie. "But there wasn't much she and Herb agreed about."

The original premise of Project Nim had called for the chimp to be treated like a human child and allowed to learn language naturally. But from Terrace's perspective, the original premise was not working.

Stephanie's emotional attachment to Nim had become an impediment. The rift between Terrace and Stephanie, the two most critical individuals in Project Nim, grew wider, impeding dialogue and making it difficult to reach decisions on how to proceed.

Terrace was not about to rip Nim from his mother's arms — there was nowhere else for the chimp to go. But Stephanie found herself in an impossible position. Her influence over Terrace and the direction of Project Nim was eroding, which made her feel even more protective of Nim. She liked taking care of him and having him in her family, but she did not want to participate in the language training if it meant sitting the chimp down for three hours a day and drilling him on words. In designing the project, Terrace had combined the jobs of mother and teacher, which Stephanie found untenable. She made the decision to resign as Nim's teacher. Separating teaching Nim from mothering him made perfect sense. She could still attend meetings and influence the direction of the project, but she would have more time for her husband, who needed her attention.

Terrace was not averse to this solution; he began a search for another teacher. But sending new people into the LaFarge house to work with Nim was not so easy. Neither the chimp nor his family members welcomed outsiders, but the chimp was a particular challenge. The LaFarge house was Nim's turf. He had a talent for getting out of any situation that did not please him, often by using his teeth; before he was one, he noticed that sinking his teeth into human flesh could be quite effective. Stephanie tried out all kinds of techniques to alter this behavior. Biting him back, a technique that had worked with Bruno, had no effect on Nim; he was so muscular that Stephanie was afraid she would break one of her teeth on him. Moreover, Nim loved to be bitten back. For him, physical discipline was just a game, more attention. "His physical prowess just escalated," says Stephanie, describing the problem. "If he wanted to defy you, he had the upper hand in every way. We tried to spank him, hold him down — just stop him. But frankly, you could not punish him." In despair, she gave up on coercion and tried to manipulate him psychologically. When he behaved badly, she turned her back to him and began walking out of the room. The threat of abandonment made him panic. He stopped whatever he was doing and ran after Stephanie for a hug and reassurance. Nim learned to sign "sorry," and did so often. Stephanie, Marika, Jenny, and Maggie all successfully used this technique to handle him, but others still had a hard time.

"I was holding him in my arms once and he just suddenly bit my breast," recalls Tildy. "This was the first moment that I realized he was not really like a human baby even though he was wearing diapers." The biting was unpredictable, which made the children wary. "We had to be careful when we opened the front door and first walked into the house," says Josh. It was Nim's territory. Nevertheless, Josh and Albert tumbled noisily with Nim all over the house. They liked to play really rough together and throw Nim up into the air, onto the water bed — anywhere. Nim loved bodily contact. But Albert recalls one incident when he and Josh pushed the chimp too far. "We were all playing and Nim suddenly bit me on the back," he says. "It made me realize that we had our boundaries, which we had been taught, but he did not. I got the message."

Holding the chimp's attention for longer than even a few minutes was a talent, and one that most of Nim's trainers needed to develop. Once he was no longer a baby, Nim's phenomenal mobility made him ever more astonishing to play with. By the time he was six months old, he could bounce off walls, crawl up or down any surface, and move so quickly that he required close supervision twenty-four hours a day. His babysitters took a deep breath when the chimp went to sleep — and tried to catch a wink themselves. Taking care of a young chimp requires endless reserves of nonstop energy; next to chimps, human infants move like sloths.

As Lemmon had discovered, human-reared chimps were more precocious and willful than those raised together in captivity or in the jungle. Both have prodigious strength, but the chimps who don OshKosh and learn to eat spaghetti with a fork also excel at handling people. There was no cage for Nim at the end of the day while he was with the LaFarges. Nim picked his companions and refused to spend time with people he didn't like. He tested people, checking out their strengths and weaknesses before he decided whether to pounce or not. *Mano a mano* with Nim every minute of the day, the LaFarges had good reason to contemplate his personality, and they wondered how much of it had been shaped by them, though they were not asked to keep any records of Nim's behavior or their time with him, apart from the language research. Terrace had little interest in the chimp's personality. If this little "person" had an inner life, evidence of it was considered anecdotal and of no value to Project Nim unless it negatively affected his concentration or created a disciplinary problem.

Nim's "terrible twos" came early, before his first birthday. The little person's animalness surfaced, making him harder to control and often unpredictable. When he wouldn't listen, brush his teeth, or sit still to work on a new sign, Terrace blamed his unbridled and unacceptable behavior on his permissive mother, who had turned her home into a chimp house instead of turning the chimp into a well-behaved child.

But in the spring of 1974, Terrace had more immediate, practical problems on his mind. In his view, Nim's life had become a house of cards: the graduate students who had been helping to care for him were about to go off for their summer vacations, and the LaFarges were stretched to the breaking point. It was Terrace's responsibility to come up with a plan for the summer and find Nim a new teacher to take over his language training. This time, Terrace wanted someone who would respect him, be able to discipline the chimp, and move the study forward at a more rapid pace. Terrace had been an A student his whole life. He expected nothing less from Nim.

Terrace put together a patchwork plan for the summer. The first part fell into place when Maggie Jakobson, Nim's teenage babysitter of choice, offered to take Nim to her parents' house in the Hamptons — a one-hundred-year-old clapboard palace decorated with contemporary art, surrounded by perfectly manicured lawns with a swimming pool in the back — for the month of June. Although she never thought he would agree to it, Terrace accepted her offer. He himself planned to take Nim for the following month, bringing him to the summer house he had rented in the Hamptons, which was near the Jakobsons' and big enough for Stephanie and whoever among the children had not escaped to camp. In August, the LeeFarges would take Nim to WER's farm in Rhode Island. Meanwhile, Terrace looked for money and staff to hold the project together. Nim would learn one new sign that summer: "eat." It was the only sign Terrace himself ever taught the chimp.

Stephanie LaFarge and Nim

CHAPTER 4
TROUBLE IN THE FAMILY

Terrace (or more likely Nim) had a knack for attracting wealthy, adoring females who could keep the chimp in fashionable clothes, ripe bananas, and well-furnished homes. Maggie Jakobson, age fifteen, who wore a WIN (Whip Inflation Now) button upside down on her sweater so that it read NIM, was one of the first. From Terrace's perspective, the LaFarge family appeared as impenetrable as a brick wall, but Maggie had leapt over that wall and landed in the center of Nim's life, exactly where she wanted to be. She was a born operator, and no one loved the chimp more than she did. So, the charming, willful teenager made the decision to dedicate her life, or at least a month of it, to Nim.

At fifteen years of age, even Maggie was stunned when Terrace and LaFarge agreed to give her full responsibility for Nim. Of course, Maggie had led them to believe that her parents had approved the idea. This, however, was a slight exaggeration. Mr. and Mrs. Jakobson had been left entirely in the dark about the whole plan until the last moment. At the end of May, Maggie casually informed them that Nim would be a guest in their summer home for a month. Appalled by the idea, they tried to nix it. The Jakobsons had met Mr. Chimpsky only once, when Maggie smuggled him into their Upper East Side brownstone for a sleepover date; she revealed Nim to her parents only when they entered her bedroom to kiss their daughter goodnight. Loving the drama, Maggie threw off her covers and revealed a sleepy chimpanzee snuggling with her. Neither parent found his presence in their daughter's bed very amusing. But it was late, so they all went to sleep.

Maggie explained to her unhappy parents that it was impossible to change the summer plan; Professor Terrace and the La-Farges were all counting on the house. Unable to rein in their daughter's passion for Nim, the Jakobsons put their valuables in storage and hired a Wesleyan student with a driver's license, who apparently liked chimps, to watch over Maggie while Maggie watched over Nim. Then they fled to Europe, preferring to be in another country while Nim rearranged their furniture and climbed their walls.

Perfect for humans during the summer, the Hamptons is even better suited to chimps. The weather in June, hot and sunny during the day and cool in the evening, is ideal. Maggie and Nim, just seven months old, seemed made for each other. Unlike many of the adults in Nim's life, Maggie had few rules, ample energy, and a love of pizza and ice cream as intense as his own. Maggie was with Nim all day, and at night he slept by her side, tucked right into her bed.

Maggie was so tight with Nim that it seemed as if she could read his mind, which enabled her to head off trouble when she saw it coming. She would whisk the chimp away before he could break anything, hurt anyone, or be hurt himself. Maggie was adventurous with Nim, but when she made a mistake, she made sure not to repeat it; she struck drive-in movies off Nim's activity list after she discovered that the other patrons did not appreciate a chimp who hooted louder than the soundtrack.

Maggie gave Nim the month off from any language work. She wanted him to climb trees, chase birds, and learn how to build drippy sandcastles. Nim had been to the park but had never spent time in the country. Maggie, accompanied by her own baby-sitter, filled Nim's schedule with swimming lessons in the pool (he finally managed to put a toe in the water), trips to the ice cream parlor (peach was his favorite flavor, and he was partial to cones), excursions to the beach, and hikes around the area. Nim befriended a little black pug next door with whom he played happily for hours. Maggie thought they looked alike and wondered whether Nim believed the dog was another chimp.

By this time, many of the people who had been regularly integrated into the chimp's routine had, like Maggie, developed a strong attachment to him. Extremely affectionate, especially to women, Nim could readily communicate his desires, which made him a highly interactive, mesmerizing creature. Stephanie described him as trilingual, claiming that Nim understood spoken English, had a developing vocabulary of signs, and, of course, frequently sounded off in his natural tongue, despite being isolated from his species. Nim appeared to understand people and wanted to be around them every minute of the day. No one who has spent time around chimpanzees can deny that they have easily identifiable emotions, much the same as ours. According to LaFarge, whenever she cried in Nim's presence he brought her a tissue. His intense, human-like eyes, large and wide, had a gravitas and a depth that were haunting. Nim did not forget people, and people never forgot him. As Terrace once told a reporter meeting Nim for the first time, "Once you get a look at Nim, it is difficult to take your eyes off him."

In June, while Nim was living at the beach with Maggie, Jenny Lee suddenly collapsed onto the floor in the middle of a dance class and could not move her left leg. Her instructor, insisting that the show must go on, ordered the child to stand up and dance. Insisting that she was in terrible pain, Jenny refused, and an emergency call brought Stephanie to her side. She too was more than a little skeptical about her daughter's collapse. Nevertheless, she took Jenny home and put her to bed, where she remained for three days, while her siblings, none of whom gave her any sympathy, speculated about why she was feigning illness.

On the fourth day, Jenny's doctor ordered a bone scan in the hospital and discovered that several bones in her leg had shattered, despite the fact that there had been no prior fall or accident. The mystery was solved during surgery when the doctor discovered the remains of a cyst that had grown inside the bone and burst, causing the pain and damage.

Entombed in an enormous cast, Jenny remained in the hospital for six weeks learning to walk again, her guilt-ridden mother by her side, and both of them separated from Nim for the duration. The good news was that the tumor was benign. Jenny would fully recover. But before the diagnosis was made Stephanie had been terrified that cancer would take her daughter's life, and she was overwhelmed with guilt at the thought that she had neglected her own child while she focused on Nim. She felt she was being given another chance to be a better, more attentive parent, and she was determined to put her own children ahead of Nim, who for the first time since his arrival was no longer the most significant other in her life.

At the end of June, Terrace took Nim to his rented house at the beach, where Stephanie and her daughters had been scheduled to join them. But Jenny was still recuperating, and consequently, her mother rarely visited Nim. Her absence, however short-lived, caused hardship for Terrace. He spent more time than he ever had before with Nim, but he had no desire to become Nim's primary caretaker, twenty-four hours a day. Once again, he was forced to recognize that the project would not survive without a reliable, full-time staff. In September Terrace's teaching schedule would resume and he would have to return to a lab full of neglected pigeons to continue the learning experiments he had been conducting on his birds for twelve years. He had yet to raise a penny for Project Nim and was haunted by the prospect of having to end the experiment altogether.

Marika Moosbrugger picked up Nim at the end of July and drove him out to WER's farm in Rhode Island, where all the Lee and LaFarge children were gathered under one roof. It was an extraordinary reunion. Nim was ecstatic when he saw Stephanie. He grinned, hooted, and hugged her; he even groomed WER's hair, a sign of affection. One afternoon Stephanie brought home a baby goat to amuse them all. They took long walks along the Narrows River, which ran through the LaFarge property, with Nim, Trudge, and the young goat trotting after them. Jenny's health improved. The month went by quickly, and all of them were sorry when it was time to return to the city and their busy lives.

In September, with everyone back in New York, an increasingly desperate Terrace arranged for a loan from his university to keep the project going. Columbia bailed its professor out of a jam, fully confident that Project Nim would be recognized as the vanguard of ape language studies and that the grants would eventually roll in. Although several similar projects were going on in other parts of the country, none of Nim's peers had been raised from birth in a human family and immersed in language in quite the same way. Terrace had recently signed on two consultants, Dr. Lois Bloom and Dr. Ursula Bellugi, both prominent psychologists in the field of childhood development, whose names added heft to his grant proposals and emphasized the link between apes and humans. The loan allowed him to hire a full-time, experienced ASL teacher. Equally important, the university provided a suite of small rooms in Schermerhorn, the science building where Terrace had an office, which would serve as a chimp-proof classroom. There, Nim could work one-on-one with a teacher while others observed him through a two-way mirror. For the first time, Terrace would have his own laboratory space for Nim, and the chimp would have regular hours outside the LaFarge brownstone.

Data collection continued to be Terrace's most pressing problem. He was used to a sterile laboratory where the animals, mostly pigeons, were caged and docile. Contrary to his original optimistic assumption, collecting solid data amidst the chaos of family life on West 78th Street had turned out to be virtually impossible. Nim often signed spontaneously, which made the sign difficult to capture. When Terrace came to work with Nim in the LaFarge home, the chimp was often uncooperative and refused to work. Records on Nim's progress were so unsystematic that Terrace feared peer reviewers might challenge their accuracy. In his new space at Columbia, he planned to set up a video camera to record every session. The instructors would also write daily reports, so there would be both print and video records of every moment they spent with Nim.

Even Stephanie, Terrace's harshest critic, agreed that the new setup might work for Nim, and for her as well. Having made it clear that she wanted nothing to do with the language acquisition aspect of Project Nim, she agreed to keep the chimp in her family so long as he was out of the house for a fixed number of hours every day. She thought of it as sending him off to school. She had, after all, done the same thing with her own children. Now ten months old, still in diapers, and with a vocabulary of six signs — "drink," "up," "sweet," "give," "more," "eat" — the young chimpanzee was about to turn a big corner in his life.

Terrace was in dire need of an experienced ASL teacher. He turned to the New York University Deafness Research Center for candidates. There he found Carol Stewart, age forty, who had been teaching at the Southbury Training School, a state mental hospital in Connecticut founded in 1940. Southbury had a reputation for being underfunded and overcrowded; the majority of residents were profoundly retarded, and most lived out their lives on this prison-like campus for decades. Stewart had been teaching ASL to residents with some success in what she believed was a breakthrough program. She described her pupils as "perpetual rockers, the ones who knock their heads against the wall, the eaters of their own excrement." Some of them, she claimed, were able to communicate with their parents for the first time after learning ASL.

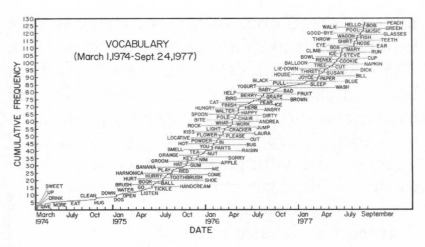

Vocabulary chart

But Stewart was critical of the quality of life offered at Southbury and wanted to leave the place behind her. After eight grueling years in the facility, she was thrilled by the prospect of working with a single chimpanzee on a unique and scientifically significant experiment. Terrace was in turn drawn to her tremendous enthusiasm for the job. Bill Tynan, Stewart's bearded thirty-two-year-old boyfriend, had worked with Stewart at Southbury. He happily moved to New York with her and enrolled in school at Columbia on the GI Bill. His résumé listed an assortment of jobs, including one at *High Fidelity* magazine, where he had learned to set up complex video equipment. Terrace offered Stewart the position of head teacher and took on Tynan as a part-time member

166

of the team, responsible for the technical aspects of the experiment. As a student, Tynan would get course credit instead of a salary, which was fine with him. Tynan was totally captivated by Nim. He declared himself a psychology major and threw himself into the project. A few months after they began working for Terrace, Tynan and Stewart were married.

Terrace found Stewart's approach — rooted in behavior modification — worth trying. In fact, he appeared ready to try anything on Nim, within reason, if he thought it might get the chimp to work harder. At the other end of the spectrum from Stephanie, Stewart was rigorous and demanding, intent on setting up a tightly structured environment for Nim. She developed a strict curriculum for his teachers, family members, and babysitters to follow. Her first goal was to get everyone who had any involvement with the chimp on the same page. She stressed the importance of consistency, particularly with regard to punishment, both in the classroom at Columbia and at home. Reward and punishment were second nature to a Skinnerian such as Terrace, so he was eager to try out Stewart's methods. (He had once used a cattle prod on Nim; this appalled the La-

Laura-Ann Petitto and Nim at Columbia
© Harry Benson

Farges, who vetoed it at a meeting.)

Nim started his new regime slowly by going to school three days a week from 10:30 in the morning until 1:00 in the afternoon. Laura-Ann Petitto, an ambitious undergraduate from Ramapo College in New Jersey, often transported Nim from the La-Farges' home to Columbia for his classes. Later, Nim had to stay for a second session in the afternoon, which ended at five o'clock. In between lessons that lasted for two hours (or however long his attention held out) he played in a small room set up with a swing and toys. Maggie and Jenny frequently went up to the campus to care for him during these breaks. For Nim, used to the permissive environment of the La-Farges' Upper West Side brownstone, it was as if he had suddenly found himself at a military academy. Upon entering the classroom, he was required to hang his coat on a hook, sit down at his little desk, and pay attention — no screeching, bouncing, biting, or joking around. If he misbehaved, as chimps are wont to do, Stewart stuffed him into a specially constructed four-foot-square box that sat in the corner of the room for what Terrace described as a "time-out" period. The box, made out of plywood, had no windows and hence no light.

The first time Nim was forced into the box, Terrace heard him crying hysterically from the next room but didn't intervene. The second time Stewart put Nim in the box, Stephanie and Jenny were there and watched the drama unfold from behind the two-way mirror. Nim cried out uncontrollably again, banging on the wood, desperate to get out. "It was unimaginably cruel," Jenny recalls. "Here we were raising the chimp as a human and locking him in a box when he was bad." Though she was not allowed to intervene, at the next formal staff meeting Stephanie, backed up by Jenny and a handful of Nim's minders, demanded that Stewart desist from using the box. However effective Stewart's methods at Southbury might have been, Stephanie argued that they were not appropriate for working with Nim. From infancy, Nim had hated being alone anywhere, for any amount of time. Besides, he was not retarded. Quite the opposite — he was a highly intelligent chimpanzee. Stephanie feared such treatment would have long-term deleterious effects on him. Jenny, outraged by what she describes as "torture," was too young for her opinions to be taken seriously, but that didn't stop her from making them known to Terrace. In a rage, she accused him of animal abuse. Terrace, irritated that the LaFarges had become advocates for Nim rather than Project Nim, supported Stewart. If Nim's vocabulary grew, the box would stay.

At weekly meetings, Stephanie continued to rail against Stewart and her box, taking the position that it was not only cruel but would impede Nim's progress in learning language. The two women argued over Nim's sensitivity to people and whether or not he identified with humans. When Nim was given a group of photographs to sort —

170

images of chimpanzees, including one of himself, mixed up with those of humans — he would put his own picture in the pile with the humans. "I don't think Nim had any concept that he was a chimpanzee," says Bob Johnson, a burly Vietnam vet who was getting his undergraduate degree in psychology at Columbia when he first started babysitting for Nim. "It is possible that he looked at us and expected that one day he too would grow up and lose all his body hair."

Johnson, like Tynan and some of the La-Farges, frequently discussed what might be going on in Nim's mind, though these kinds of speculations, riddled with unscientific assumptions, were tabled at the weekly meetings. Johnson, who had begun working for Project Nim at about the time Stewart arrived, never liked her techniques or her claustrophobic classroom, which he boycotted. But he did take care of Nim after class, earning a small salary through Columbia's work-study program. Nim was always elated when he saw Johnson on campus. Within months, Johnson became one of the chimp's most reliable handlers, and he joined the chorus against Stewart — and her terrifying box. Although Stewart had no academic training and only her experience at Southbury to rely on (her methods had apparently worked in Connecticut, and had never been questioned), she didn't hesitate to take on her opponents, including Stephanie, arguing that using the box was the only way that she could dominate Nim, a prerequisite for teaching him ASL or anything else.

Apart from the box, what seemed to disturb Nim most about the new classroom setup was the squeals of rats wafting through the wall from a psychology lab next door. Whenever Nim heard them, he leapt into the arms of the closest human being. According to Stephanie, one afternoon when she arrived to pick him up, Nim escaped from his classroom, found the lab, and opened the cage doors, setting the rats free. Somehow Stephanie managed to make a game out of catching the rats and putting them all back into their cages. Stephanie was pleased that she had not had to resort to any disciplinary measures but was able to cajole Nim into rectifying the chaos he had created. She considered this evidence in support of her approach to educating Nim.

Initially frightened by this new environment, Nim learned the rules quickly. As months passed, he began to do some work for Stewart, but he was becoming more jumpy and impatient, eager to leave the classroom hours before the end of his day. Stewart had promised Terrace that her methods would accelerate Nim's acquisition of words, but they didn't. The chimp picked up no more than one new sign a month, and even that was a struggle. Terrace still believed that Stephanie had been too permissive, but he was forced to admit, as he wrote in his account of the experiment, that "the LaFarge home provided a greater opportunity than the classroom, and Nim often used signs at home in more interesting ways." Eager for more progress, Terrace sent Stewart to West 78th Street to train the chimp. She brought the box with her, hoping it might encourage Nim to settle down and work. But her authority, with or without the box, evaporated when she faced Nim on his own turf.

Terrace realized he had a problem. The structure that he had tried to put in place for Nim was a complete failure. His weekly meetings at Columbia where the methodologies were reviewed had become a battlefield on which Stewart and LaFarge fought for Nim's soul — or at least his brain.

LaFarge, always passionate, became more so, insisting that Stewart try to use psychological manipulation rather than brute force to control Nim. Ahead of her time, as the concept of a human-animal bond would not be acceptable in psychological circles for at least another decade, LaFarge stressed her personal relationship with Nim and factors such as emotional bonding and empathy. She had intuited that it was impossible to work productively with Nim — or any other chimp — without first developing a certain amount of trust. Like two mothers arguing over whether or not to use corporal punishment on their children, both Stewart and LaFarge held their ground. The weekly meetings went from bad to worse as they turned into angry philosophical debates, where Terrace felt he could barely get a word in edgewise. At one point, he assigned everybody in the room articles to read, thinking he could turn their disputes into a more constructive seminar that he could lead, but it was hopeless. The power struggle between Stewart and LaFarge superseded any theoretical discussions. Their opposing views on discipline were, however, only part of the broader problem. "There was an incredible level of basic stupidity about the nature of chimpanzees," Johnson comments. "Do chimps really learn sitting at a desk? Why did Nim have to hang his jacket up on a hook? What did any of this have to do with language?"

Terrace argued that raising Nim as a human, which included structure and discipline, had everything to do with his ability to acquire language. But the psychologist had little interest in what Nim was communicating — in any language — or how the people raising the chimp felt about him. For him, the only measures of Nim's progress were the number of signs that he acquired and his ability to use them.

The public never saw any of the internal squabbles or heard anything about the box, but they heard plenty about Nim, who was a magnet for publicity. Who could resist a talking chimp? Reporters wanted to speak with Nim. Terrace both welcomed and tried to control the press, using it to attract attention to the experiment and maintain his own authority over Project Nim. The first stories, mostly puff pieces, rolled off the pages of mainstream papers like freshly baked buns — sweet, warm, and easy to digest. Few reporters asked tough questions, wondered about who was paying the bills, or considered the ethical implications of Project Nim. They assumed, as Terrace suggested, that Project Nim would go on for years to come, while the myriad anecdotal revelations gradually morphed into scientific fact. As Nim entered the public imagination, the anthropomorphization of his personality became more surreal. Television raised Nim's profile even further, especially in his home city. David Susskind, the combative late-night local talk show host once aptly described as an "endearing narcissist," invited the talking chimp onto his show, a staple for New York City insomniacs, for a live chat. Terrace, who never missed an opportunity to broaden the audience for Project Nim, accepted; LaFarge, who was more realistic about the potential danger, understood that there was a risk, but she liked risks. So together they took the chimp to the studio, hoping that Nim would rise to the occasion, feel flattered, and have fun without causing an undue amount of damage. As the threesome walked out onto the set and the cameras rolled, Terrace and La-Farge held their breath. On his debut visit, Nim signed to Susskind and crawled all over his lap. The audience laughed noisily each time Susskind winced or made a weak attempt to keep Nim at bay — an impossible task. Nim was a huge hit.

But the scene could easily have gone another way. At any moment, Nim could have sunk his teeth into the host's neck or ripped the shirt off his back. Nim could not be trusted to do the right thing, especially in a new situation. But that was precisely what made him a hit on the Susskind show: he introduced a palpable element of danger. When he grabbed at Susskind's clothes and rumpled his hair, Susskind was visibly frightened, and the audience gasped with pleasure as the stiff interviewer became unraveled. But Nim behaved. Terrace could never have safely handled the chimp alone; throughout the evening, LaFarge made sure Nim felt appreciated, rather than challenged, and kept him calm by offering a constant stream of treats and praise. Susskind was charmed and repeatedly invited them back. Nim had made a new friend.

Nim's television appearances led to a photo spread in the *New York Post* showing him hard at work in his classroom. The photos looked staged, and to some extent they were, but Nim really did do his work at a desk where he was forced to sit, like human children. Thanks to the *Post,* his fame spread. The press frequently called Columbia and the LaFarge house, requesting photo ops and interviews with his family. ABC contacted the LaFarges to discuss a sitcom based on their lives with a chimpanzee. Nim Chimpsky had become a household name in New York, following in the footsteps of another chimp, J. Fred

Muggs, who began his television career in diapers, appearing on the *Today* show with news commentator Dave Garroway from 1953 to 1957. But like Nim, Muggs became more unpredictable as he grew bigger. He was eventually fired after biting Martha Raye in the arm, and ended up working at Busch Gardens in Tampa, Florida.

All the showbiz hoopla around Nim could not resolve the internal struggles over discipline, staffing, and training techniques. With Terrace's team split into two opposing camps, new volunteers felt compelled to choose one or the other. As morale reached new lows, Terrace continued to stand by Stewart so long as her methods could not be proven wrong. Eventually, however, Stewart's results were her undoing; Nim's progress in her classroom was slowing down. After almost nine months, in May 1975, Terrace fired her, just as everybody was taking off for the summer. "My main objection to Carol's approach was that it was too simplistic," he concluded in his account of the whole debacle. "Nim would bite or scream for various reasons. To follow automatically each instance of biting or anti-social behavior with the same punishment could make matters worse." According to Johnson, Terrace had absorbed the arguments made by his own graduate students — and claimed them as his own. Says Johnson, "That was the only way we could effect any changes."

Firing Stewart was a popular move among Nim's caretakers. Only Bill Tynan, Stewart's husband, considered leaving. But in the process of working with Nim, he had developed a personal attachment to the chimp, and he felt committed to the project. Nim respected Tynan, and they often spent whole days together. Moreover, Terrace had grown dependent upon him to solve all kinds of technical problems in the classroom to keep the data flowing. Tynan stayed on after his wife left.

In June, as classes ended and students scattered, Nim's schedule fell apart. Terrace hadn't yet replaced Stewart, which compounded the problem of keeping the project going. But there would soon be other problems. Nim, about to turn one and a half, had worn out his welcome in the La-Farge home. Stephanie and WER's marriage was in trouble, and the chimp's human siblings were investigating boarding schools. WER began spending more time in Rhode Island at his farm. When he came to New York to visit his children, he was despondent, closing himself off in a small room on the third floor of the house. In a poem called "dear Gleaming Family," WER wrote: "I think this man / is leaching into madness / I don't like him / but I think the water / is low in his tub / his wife may be / already a widow / knowing it, knowing it, his children victims . . ."

By summertime, Stephanie was on the verge of a decision that would haunt her for years to come. Once again, she had come to the realization that she couldn't take adequate care of her family and Nim at the same time. Equally important, she had begun to feel that her relationship with Nim would be compromised by the demands of the experiment. She refused to be the kind of mother Terrace wanted for Nim. She felt Terrace was treating her like a glorified babysitter and that he was no longer even listening to her. Still anxious for more progress, Terrace kept insisting on more structure and discipline. But he would never get it from LaFarge.

Perhaps Terrace had not understood that both LaFarge and the culture had changed during the 1970s. Terrace may have missed out on the women's movement, but LaFarge had not. She had left her first husband, taken responsibility for her children, gotten a job, enrolled in graduate school, and remarried, all on her own terms. If Terrace had assumed that Stephanie would not question his authority due to their brief affair or his comparatively lofty academic status, he was seriously mistaken. LaFarge's romantic illusions about many aspects of her life — Project Nim, Terrace, and WER — were fading.

LaFarge finally told Terrace that he needed to find another home for Nim. It was over. Terrace did not beg her to allow Nim to stay. But Jenny did. She took the news hard. Outraged by her mother's decision, she implored her to stand by Nim, her "brother," to protect him from whatever Terrace had planned. WER alone was pleased that Stephanie had decided to give up Nim, but the decision did not bring the family back together. If WER thought that without Nim, Stephanie's attention would return to him, he was mistaken. WER needed to find a more traditional wife who, at the very least, would make him the center of attention in his home. He took off for Rhode Island and didn't come back. "He just left town," says Albert LaFarge. "We got a postcard from him with a change of address. We didn't even know there was a divorce going on." Says Stephanie, "Neither did I."

In the summer of 1975, after Stephanie had made her decision to let go of Nim, Terrace again rented a beach house and invited the whole LaFarge family to join him for a vacation. It was a peace offering and a way to keep Nim and everybody else under one roof while the panicky psychologist figured out what to do next. He was still struggling to hold the reins on his experiment, generate grant proposals, snag new volunteers, and solve his most perplexing problem: how to capture accurate and convincing data from a chimpanzee. Nothing was settled, including Nim's next address.

Everyone began to relax at the beach. Terrace thought Stephanie might even relent and agree to keep Nim for as long as she was needed. Their first days, which passed in a bliss of vacation highs, were idyllic. Trudge and Nim chased each other around the house until the dog flopped down, exhausted. They all cooked together, watched horror movies late into the night, and willingly shared responsibility for Nim. The chimp appeared content, not taciturn or difficult. But by the end of the first week, the same old issues began to emerge — the arguments over how to control Nim. Terrace and Stephanie were unable to agree on much or come to an understanding on how they might work together in the future. Stephanie demanded more control over Nim. By turning her into a babysitter and stripping her of any impact on the project, Terrace had effectively demoted her, and she was no longer willing to accept her lowly status.

Living together under one roof had made their differences crystal clear. No one was better with Nim or closer to him than Stephanie, but Terrace finally understood that she would never submit to the dictates of Project Nim. That was true. And she, in turn, understood that Terrace had staked his whole reputation on this bold experiment, only to have to face the fact that he had never had any real control over the chimpanzee. From the start, Nim's heart had belonged to Stephanie. When she was around, Terrace could barely get Nim's attention. The two of them agreed that Terrace had to find another home for Nim.

Now Terrace intended to give the chimp a different kind of mother, someone who would put his research project first. Stephanie's concern about Nim was more maternal than scientific, and he wanted that imbalance to be corrected. To him, Nim was a research animal, albeit a socialized one. The next phase of Project Nim would be controlled by Terrace. Or at least that was the plan.

Delafield

CHAPTER 5
THE MASTER OF DELAFIELD

Screened by majestic trees, protected by iron gates, and barely visible from the street, the Delafield estate was a hidden haven in Riverdale, New York, just a stone's throw north of Manhattan across the Spuyten Duyvil Creek. Only a handful of people at Columbia even knew it existed. In 1964, Edward Coleman Delafield, president of the Bank of America and an avid botanist, had donated the property to the university. Used briefly by Grayson Kirk as a residence during his tenure as president of Columbia, the elegant nineteenth-century Georgian-style mansion was a jewel set on seventeen acres of manicured lawns and exotic gardens. The property also included a large greenhouse and a small cottage. Like a back-lot reconstruction of an antebellum plantation sitting in a corner of the Bronx, the estate was a complete anomaly.

Delafield had given the property to Columbia imagining passionate young environ-mentalists contemplating the flora and fauna in his backyard, using the place as an agricultural field station. When they were tired of smelling the flowers, they could walk down a hill and sit by a large pond, or continue all the way to the Hudson River. For many years a devoted gardener had maintained the grounds as if Delafield himself were still in residence. But by the mid-1970s, Columbia students were into molecular biology, not botany, and Delafield, which had been empty for ten years, had fallen into disrepair, a disheveled pile, less a home for the likes of Scarlett O'Hara than for Miss Havisham.

In the course of investigating properties owned by Columbia, hoping the university might donate one to Project Nim, Terrace eventually stumbled across Delafield. In a moment of whimsy, he imagined Nim living in luxury, catapulting down its garden paths and climbing the trees, each one labeled with its Latin name on a tasteful plaque. He could literally have his own rose garden only seven and a half miles from the main cam-pus, which, incidentally, would make life incredibly convenient for the professor, who was due for a sabbatical in the coming year, 1976. But it was by no means certain that the university would turn Delafield over to Terrace. He was frantic. If he didn't get some funding and a place for Nim to live, he would spend his sabbatical trying to explain to his colleagues how he had muffed the chance of a lifetime. With the LaFarges finally out of the picture, Terrace had an opportunity to seize control of Project Nim and start anew — that is, if he could fund it.

Ironically, when Stephanie left, the only reliable revenue stream Terrace had went with her. For the past nineteen months, even while his relationship with Stephanie was disintegrating, WER had paid all Nim's bills and never asked Terrace for a penny of reimbursement. In 1974, the National Science Foundation had flatly turned Project Nim down and, worse, discouraged Terrace from reapplying. The National Institutes of Mental Health had also turned him down but at least had left the door open for him to reapply. Both government agencies regarded the investigation of language acquisition as controversial, unpredictable, and expensive. Terrace's preliminary results, presented in the sunniest possible light, reported that Nim could sign and had acquired a modest vocabulary, but even so, the data had not been impressive enough to garner major support. As Terrace feared, foundations were concerned — and justifiably so — about his ability to collect accurate data. Patching together a major experiment with a crazy quilt of teenage volunteers and students, all coming and going, sometimes week by week, was amateurish at best. And now, the most famous chimp in the world, or at least in New York City, was about to become homeless.

What Terrace needed was a full-time, paid staff to live with Nim, part-time ASL teachers to run the classroom at Columbia, and data crunchers to make sense out of the daily accumulation of notes, photos, videos, and other materials. What Nim needed was human continuity. He formed strong attachments to people and became upset when they disappeared from his life. Even handing him off from one person to another as the keepers changed shifts was becoming more difficult. Nim could not be left alone, not only because he was a valuable experimental animal but because he became frightened and prone to tantrums. To get through the next year, Terrace needed a budget in the neighborhood of $200,000.

Once again, Terrace turned to Columbia University for help. He submitted a request for the small cottage at Delafield, fully expecting to be turned down. But he had underestimated the degree to which Nim had seized the imagination of the Columbia community. Still tainted by bloody images of cops clubbing students on the 116th Street campus seven years earlier, the university needed some good press, which Nim could easily provide. Much to his surprise, Terrace was presented with the keys to the entire Delafield kingdom. Nim was not going to move into the cottage, but into the twenty-one-room mansion.

Delafield raised Project Nim to another level. Suddenly, Terrace's ragtag army of volunteers morphed into a privileged team of research assistants who deserved nothing less than the best Columbia had to offer. Replacing the LaFarges' brownstone on West 78th Street with a historic landmark was like a shot of adrenaline. The possibility of working in such a magnificent setting attracted new staff and another round of media attention to the experiment. Volunteers who had remained loyal when Project Nim floundered were rewarded with a classy new workplace. At the end of the summer, the regular weekly meetings at Columbia resumed with fresh energy as Terrace formulated plans for the next phase of Project Nim. The focus of the weekly meetings shifted from heated disagreements over language development and discipline to Terrace's priority: how to collect accurate data while maximizing Nim's language skills. The psychologist purchased pocket-size tape recorders for trainers to use to make audio notes on the spot whenever Nim signed or did anything else that might indicate his growing facility with ASL. Terrace needed the data to be not only accurate but also convincing enough to keep foundations involved over the long haul, some ten years or so at least.

The first priority for moving the chimp to Delafield was to Nim-proof the mansion. A construction crew, consisting mostly of students, made a home for the chimp in one half of the mansion, installed a heating system (it had been a summer palace), and devised ways to protect the original fixtures, including hand-painted murals of old New York, still in mint condition. (One mural featured a painted sun that, at a certain hour of the day, was bathed in the rays of the actual sun as they poured through the window.) Equally important, Nim himself had to be prepared for the move, which was his first major transition since being taken from his mother shortly after birth. None of the LaFarges would be moving to Delafield with him. (In fact, as it turned out, they would rarely even visit.) Terrace had to put together a whole new "family" to live at Delafield with Nim. In his determination to restructure the whole project in the hopes of putting it on a more efficient and scientific basis, Terrace returned to his original notion, which LaFarge had rejected — namely, that Nim's mother and teacher should be one and the same. This time around, there was no resistance from his staff.

But who would get the job? During the excitement over the imminent move to Delafield, Laura-Ann Petitto began emerging as one of the most capable and committed of the pack of volunteers who had spent time with Nim on West 78th Street. Petitto, affectionately called "Potato," was not the least bit starchy. She was small, attractive, and eager to dedicate herself to both Terrace and Nim. Petitto felt a passion for animals. She expected to work with them for the rest of her life, maybe go off to Africa and do research. She had taken a class in ASL and worked hard at earning Nim's affection. She was good with him, sensitive to his moods, and able to handle him by herself. Terrace admired her energy and intellect. Like many of his students, Petitto looked up to Terrace and felt awed by the scope of Project Nim. She wrote a strong undergraduate thesis on language acquisition based on her time with Nim. Petitto believed in Terrace and in Nim's potential to "talk" in signs.

Terrace, known for being cold, if not indifferent, to most students, found more than enough time for Petitto. When it came to women, the inscrutable psychologist wore his heart on his sleeve. "There was lots of gossip about her and Herb right away," says Stephanie LaFarge, who perhaps saw something of her younger self in Terrace's eager new protégée. His attraction to Petitto was so overt that other graduate students were miffed by the amount of attention and authority she received. Terrace offered her a full-time job as project director, with a salary, and, to sweeten the deal, he threw in the master suite at Delafield. To a working-class kid from Brooklyn, this must have felt like winning the lottery. Petitto put off graduate school and gratefully agreed to be both mother and teacher to Nim. Terrace, of course, hoped that she would be a scientist first and a mother second. At the very least, he expected she would challenge neither her boss's authority nor his goals, even if they might conflict now and then with the well-being of the chimpanzee.

In addition to Petitto, Terrace hired Amy Schachter and Walter Benesch, a couple who had occasionally worked with Nim over the past year and a half. Terrace invited them to move into Delafield, where they would share a bedroom. Schachter, age nineteen, had been working at the Bronx Zoo taking care of animals; Benesch, age twenty-four, had a degree in social work. Petitto, Schachter, and Benesch, who would be Nim's first full-time housemates since the LaFarges, were supplemented with a large pool of part-timers, including Joyce Butler, Susan Quinby, Bill Tynan, and Bob Johnson, who were to take regular shifts with Nim in the Schermerhorn classroom or at Delafield. At twenty-two months, Nim was about to have a new mother and a new extended family.

During the time the Delafield property was under construction, Petitto, Schachter, and Benesch took over full-time care of Nim in the LaFarge brownstone. The goal was to minimize the time he spent with the family and therefore his dependence upon them, so that he would be emotionally available to his new family. Believing it was in Nim's best interest under the circumstances, La-Farge intentionally distanced herself from him as she watched others take her place in the chimp's life. She also removed herself from the weekly meetings at Columbia, where all the plans for Delafield were thoroughly discussed. Bereft and guilty, she gave up any attempt to have even a minor impact on the next stage of Project Nim. For LaFarge, it was all or nothing. With little or no authority over the chimp, she could not see herself filling a part-time slot in Nim's day.

Unlike Stephanie, who understood and accepted that she was being replaced, Maggie Jakobson and Jenny Lee, furious with Stephanie for giving Nim up, continued to attend the Columbia meetings and assist with Nim during breaks from his classroom work. But the girls too would soon drop out of Nim's life altogether. "It was suddenly all about language acquisition and the rate it was taking place," recalls Maggie. "There was a new edge to the whole thing that made us feel uncomfortable. We were kids, not scientists." Without Stephanie, they had no real place in Project Nim.

During the transition, Nim continued to attend regular sessions at Columbia, where he appeared less interested in the acquisition of language than in the fine art of escape. The chimp became proficient at slipping through Terrace's restraints and amused himself by terrorizing secretaries in the building, who screamed in fear every time they saw him running loose through the halls. At the end of the chase, cornered and defeated, Nim would try to bite the hand that was clipping his tether back in place. Finally, by early August, to the relief of everyone at the university, construction at Delafield was completed and Nim's new home was ready.

One summer afternoon after Nim's regular session at Columbia, instead of taking him back to West 78th Street, Petitto drove him to Riverdale. Parking the car outside the gate, she gestured to the large house visible between the bars, explaining, in sign language, that it was where Nim was going to be living now. Whether or not he grasped that concept, the chimp certainly understood that something was up. Leaping into Petitto's lap, he clutched her tightly. His hair stood on end, indicating that he was scared to death. Petitto tried to calm him down while carrying him into the house for a tour, room by room. Nim refused to leave her arms. Many hours later, well after the sun had set, he finally fell asleep on the floor of his new bedroom, tucked in between

Petitto and Amy Schachter like a pea in a pod.

Delafield had been transformed into a "laboratory" that looked like a home for a hyperactive child who needed to be raised in isolation from his parents for their protection. A "Great Wall" divided Nim's living quarters — a bedroom, playroom, and bathroom — from the staff quarters, an area that was off-limits for Nim. Nim's bedroom featured an indestructible built-in loft bed. The pipes and wiring were buried deep inside the walls, where, everyone hoped, they would stay. At night, Nim would be locked in from the outside. Downstairs, during the day, he had access to the kitchen and other rooms. There were no cages at Delafield, only locks — on windows, shelves, and doors — which Nim quickly learned to open.

By any standards, Delafield was luxurious. It wasn't a tropical rain forest, which Nim presumably would have preferred, but it was a spacious, indoor-outdoor residence that could offer Nim far more room to move around than any apartment. Delafield came with a private park, acres of grass to run on, trees to climb, flowers to smell (and eat), and even a small pond where Nim would learn to catch fish with his hands or a net.

197

But he could not take advantage of everything that Delafield had to offer until he became adjusted to his new home.

For his first few weeks in Riverdale, Nim refused to be alone for even a minute, never letting the person with him out of his sight or, better, his reach. He seemed to understand that he had been sent to live in a new place, and he must have felt abandoned by his family. Chimpanzees have long memories and are known to hold grudges forever. In the wild, chimp mothers remain devoted to their offspring for at least four years. Humans, Nim was learning, were different, at least so far as he was concerned. The people he loved most would continue to abandon him, but this was his first experience of such a major loss.

Nim's days at Delafield were tightly structured and organized around language lessons. Terrace hoped that giving Nim a regular schedule would help the chimp learn how to be more self-reliant and to accept the demands that were made of him. He was growing up, but he still behaved in many respects like a baby. He still wore diapers, preferred to be carried rather than walk or scoot, and didn't like to sleep alone. Not unlike a human child, Nim insisted that someone remain in his room, if not his bed,

Nim fishing at the pond with Joyce Butler

until he fell asleep, whereupon the person would have to slip out from under Nim's body and sneak out the door. If the ritual was not executed with sufficient care, Nim would wake up and cry in piercing shrieks. "At times his cries subsided in a short time," wrote Terrace. "At other times, he woke up hours later and cried as if having a nightmare. Even though it was painful to hear his screams, I thought it was wise to ignore them lest Nim learn that screaming was a way of making his caretaker return.

But sometimes Nim's cries were so loud and persistent that we feared he might choke or pass out. On these occasions, I suggested that someone look into Nim's room to see that he was breathing normally." (Terrace himself rarely spent the night at Delafield.)

Bob Johnson, one of Nim's most consistent and competent babysitters, often put Nim to bed with a cup of hot tea laced with honey. (Nim liked to suck on the tea bags.) Once he was tucked under his favorite blanket and surrounded by his collection of stuffed animals, Johnson would tell Nim his birth story — not in signs but in a soothing, melodious voice. "It began with how he was born in Oklahoma with lots of chimpanzees and when he was a very little baby we brought him to New York," Johnson recalls. Nim's eyes would get glassy soon after the story moved to the city, and eventually he would fall asleep for about twelve hours. If he slept through the night, he woke up filled with energy and a bubbly, contagious enthusiasm. On duty every Saturday morning, Johnson would open Nim's door at 10:00 a.m., get him to brush his teeth and put on pants and a shirt, and go down with him for breakfast in the kitchen, where they would often make pancakes together, filling them with fresh fruit. Nim had a sweet tooth, and Joyce Butler, a part-timer who was writing her undergraduate thesis on Project Nim, invented a jelly omelet for Nim, which he devoured in his own particular way, picking up one end of the omelet and sucking out the jelly before eating the outside. Johnson always kept gum in his pocket as a treat, if not a bribe, and became known as "Uncle Gum" at Delafield. Three months after he began working on the project, Johnson was invited to live at Delafield and become the chief data analyst for Project Nim. He accepted the offer.

In September, after Nim had been at Delafield for one month, Terrace finally received his first grant, $10,000 from the William T. Grant Foundation. It wasn't a vast sum, but it was a vote of confidence that Terrace hoped would encourage other foundations to kick in. Visitors, television cameras, and new volunteers were lining up to "chat" with Nim, either at Columbia, where he could easily be observed through the two-way mirror, or at Delafield, where it was possible to stroll with him through the verdant gardens, which Nim loved to "help" weed. (Mostly he rolled around in big piles of leaves and tore branches from trees to build nests.) One afternoon, Tynan, now one of Nim's most competent handlers and favorite companions, was pruning the roses when he noticed Nim slyly eating the flowers behind his back. Tynan caught Nim's eye and shouted: "If you eat those flowers, I'm going to bite your ear!" Nim promptly removed a few petals from his mouth and put them "back" on the roses.

Terrace, hand in hand with Nim's keepers, designed a three-step protocol to screen out the less qualified among the volunteers lining up to work with Nim. Serious contenders had to take a basic class in ASL at New York University. Those who stuck it out were introduced to Nim in the presence of a third person, one of Nim's regular handlers. Sometimes this process occurred at Columbia while Terrace or Petitto watched through the two-way mirror; other times, however, volunteers were sent right to Delafield, which often ended in disaster. If they survived their first meeting with Nim, which could be difficult, especially if Nim felt he could get away with a bite, newcomers faced the final hurdle: time alone with Nim. If the relationship was going to work, it would be immediately apparent. Nim took every opportunity to test strangers, acting out and challenging their authority. On a few occasions, the minute

Nim was left alone with a new person he suddenly transformed himself into a "wild" animal, ripping off all his clothes (something he knew not to do around his regular handlers) and defecating and/or peeing all over the room. The stranger most often was at a loss to stop him and retreated, cowering, to a corner. The process seemed to amuse Nim, just the way he had seemed to enjoy trashing WER's books in the brownstone on West 78th Street. Novice handlers, especially those who were physically small, were putty in Nim's nimble hands. If the chimp sensed that he could get away with murder, the prospective volunteer was probably hopeless. In a sense, Nim selected his own keepers.

Even Nim's experienced handlers and housemates, such as Walter Benesch, had to work hard to keep ahead of the chimp. Over the course of his short life, Nim had absorbed an astounding amount of information about how ordinary objects in his home worked. He was particularly obsessed with locks and was able to open virtually every one that he could get his hands (or feet) on. Once successful, he would slip quietly through a door or window before anybody noticed that he was missing. The ensuing chase, complete with hysterical shrieks from startled bystanders, was icing on the cake as far as Nim was concerned. And it was all in good fun — except when it wasn't. Sometimes Nim broke through glass with his fists, cutting his hands as if it were nothing. Each time he mastered another lock on a window, cabinet, or refrigerator, Benesch would dutifully replace it with a new and more complex system. It was a game they played, like chess, each trying to outmaneuver the other. Getting in and out the side door, off the kitchen, required negotiating a series of locks on a thick Dutch door. Nim's human helpers had trouble remembering how to coordinate the locks in order to open the top and bottom panels at the same time. Nim taught himself to open the door in several minutes. Once he had done this successfully a few times, Benesch clocked him at ten seconds.

The kitchen door became a favorite means of escape. Nim would take advantage of any momentary distraction to let himself out the door, walk around to a window where he could see Benesch, and with a big grin on his face tap on the glass, signing "play" or "play me." He didn't really want to run away, at least most of the time. What he wanted was attention. Benesch lost him only once, when the gate was left open for a minute and Nim saw a young girl walk by on the street. He was attracted to children and ran after her to play, with Benesch dashing after him. Realizing the chase was on, Nim ran faster and slipped through a neighbor's front door, which happened to be open. (The neighbors, informed about Project Nim, had been asked not to call the police if they saw him, for fear that a trigger-happy cop might shoot him.) Benesch followed Nim into the house and grabbed him before he could do any damage. But when Terrace heard about it, the incident alarmed him so much that he created a new rule. From that day on, no one was allowed to take the chimp outside, even on the grounds of Delafield, unless he was on a tether.

Petitto, with Terrace's approval, developed a new pedagogical schedule for Nim in an effort to build his vocabulary more efficiently and improve his syntax. She selected new signs, instructed all the staff to use them the same way, and made a coordinated effort to reinforce Nim's vocabulary. Petitto threw herself into Project Nim, often working day and night. Both Thomas Bever and Terrace credit her with transforming Project Nim from a dysfunctional experiment to a more rigorously scientific one. Petitto organized the intake of data and record keeping, as well as the motley group of part-time staffers. "The new Master of Delafield blossomed into a proficient signer," wrote Terrace. "Of all of Nim's teachers, there is little question in my mind that Laura was the most effective and influential in establishing methods of teaching Nim to use sign language and for documenting his usage of language."

Though Terrace gave Petitto all the credit for Nim's progress, LaFarge, who never liked Petitto, argues that Nim was increasing his vocabulary at a more rapid rate simply because he was now older. Petitto's peers also resented her status, regarding her more as teacher's pet than as someone who was more capable than anyone else. "Laura was Herb's favorite," Tynan says. "She could do no wrong. But her abilities were no better or worse than anybody else's." From Tynan's point of view, the staff operated as a team, sharing information in late-night conversations, and the progress that was made was a result of their teamwork. Still, there's no denying that Petitto was smart, hardworking, and, unlike Terrace, skilled at attracting competent people to the project to keep Delafield well staffed. She was good at interviewing prospective volunteers, a necessity with students coming and going with the seasons, and keeping them content enough to stick around. Terrace felt dependent upon Petitto, just as he had felt dependent upon LaFarge, to keep the experiment going.

Each day students tabulated data by punching holes in cards every time Nim used a sign, learned a new word, or combined words; the cards were threaded on poles and eventually used to graph Nim's progress. They pored over hours of videotape, using a code to distinguish ASL gestures from ordinary movements. It was hairsplitting work. There were no sophisticated computers to crunch the data in the tiny office at Columbia where the cards were punched, tapes were transcribed, and Nim's linguistic abilities were translated into graphs and numbers.

The students also kept journals in which they recorded, in minute detail, Nim's daily activities: every sign, bowel movement (including frequent accidents all over the walls and floors), and act of aggression (also frequent). Every morsel of food that went into his mouth, down to the exact number of grapes, was counted and duly noted. In handwritten scrawls, sometimes at great length, each person recorded how his or her time had been spent with Nim. In these reports, Nim's handlers often included descriptions of their own feelings about the day — confessions, misgivings, and so on — in addition to purely descriptive material. Terrace, less interested in this material, never used the information in the diaries. Although quite revealing, the pages could not be turned into statistics.

After sessions at Columbia, Nim wanted to be outdoors as long as possible, walking down to the river to watch the trains go by, or exploring the edge of the pond near the mansion. When he was indoors, he washed dishes, sometimes over and over, inevitably breaking a few; did laundry (he was not good at sorting whites from the colored clothes); and cooked in the kitchen. He got irritated if dinner preparations began before he was available to help, as if he were the head chef. Petitto insisted on establishing a routine in the kitchen, a far cry from Nim's first years in the 78th Street brownstone. But the chimp thrived in the kitchen with Petitto, just as he had done with his first surrogate mother. He often pulled pranks on Petitto, catching her off guard. When she was busy cooking, he would steal her favorite spoon and hide it; after she spent a few minutes frantically searching for the spoon, it would magically reappear in its rightful place, as if it had been there all along. When Petitto found it, she and Nim would have a good laugh together.

Although LaFarge and Petitto both appreciated Nim's sense of humor, they did not agree on methods of chimp rearing. Petitto, unlike LaFarge, tried to maintain an emotional distance from Nim. "It wasn't until a year after the project began that I began to feel that I even liked him and I never thought of myself as his mother," she wrote in her journal. She viewed Nim as an animal, not a child, a perspective that must have pleased Terrace, who found her objectivity more useful than LaFarge's empathy. The psychologist believed that as Nim grew older, he needed less love and more discipline. Petitto's methodology seemed to be paying off. Nim was learning two new signs a week. Terrace's staff counted his signs one by one, as if they were pennies in a language bank.

By the end of Nim's first year in Riverdale, Terrace had a large grant pending from NIMH, which was his best hope for serious financial support. On August 3, a team from NIMH arrived at Columbia for an all-important site visit and took their seats behind the two-way mirror. Terrace had prepared for this event as if he were cram-

Nim washing dishes at Delafield

ming for the bar exam, and even Nim had rehearsed his performance. Whether Nim understood the stakes or not, he did well, impressing the observers, one of whom, Dr. Harry Boernstein, was fluent in ASL and able to read Nim's gestures and interpret them for the group. Terrace was awarded $140,000, a decent budget for 1977. If Nim continued to progress, there was every reason to believe that the project would be funded again the following year. For the first time, Project Nim was solvent.

But bad news was soon to follow. Petitto had postponed graduate school for one year, and she felt reluctant to give Terrace a second. Under constant pressure to write the grants, coordinate the staff, monitor the intake of data, and keep Terrace happy, Petitto was burning out. Tynan had watched her begin to crack. One night she wept in his room, agonizing over whether or not to leave the project. She felt like she was suffocating. There was not much more she could get from Terrace. He had given her a title, a salary, and authority over the chimp and the staff, and he had offered to add her name as co-author on any published articles generated by Project Nim. (It was an offer that he frequently made to students, in lieu of salary.) Terrace apparently hoped that his attentions would motivate his young protégée to stay. But they had the opposite effect: she decided to leave Project Nim and get on with her own academic career. In Bever's opinion, "She left to get away from Herb." Unfortunately, Benesch and Schachter quit the project at the same moment: Schachter had been offered a full-time job at the Bronx Zoo, where she would get a real salary, and Benesch, like Petitto, wanted to go to graduate school.

Once again, Nim needed a new mother figure, and Delafield needed a new manager. As he had before, when he lost key employees, Terrace contemplated terminating the project. But ending a landmark experiment just when the grants had begun to flow would have looked — and been — foolish. Despite his inability to keep employees, Terrace remained confident that Nim would break through the language barrier and make history. He believed — rightly — that Nim's rearing, even if chaotic, was virtually unique. Few psychologists working in the ape language field had considered putting their primates in language-rich environments where they would have constant exposure to ASL rather than intermittent lessons. At IPS, in Oklahoma, where Roger Fouts was embarking on a similar path, a few chimps were living in human families, but a greater number, including Washoe, were caged, removed for language instruction several times a week, and then locked up again. Nim lived with humans, slept on a mattress wrapped in his favorite blanket, and chatted in ASL each morning over breakfast.

Still, the long-term effects of living with humans — on chimpanzees, and on chimp language studies — remained unknown. At this point, Nim, the Gardners' chimps in Nevada, several in Oklahoma at IPS, and several more at the Yerkes Primate Research Center were learning at about the same speed. Like racehorses breathlessly running around the track, the chimps and the psychologists who were training them were headed toward an elusive finish line, where Skinner and Chomsky — each with an entourage of followers — stood, waiting to judge the race.

Whatever other uncertainties Project Nim faced, Delafield itself remained secure, and it was big enough to house one or two more chimpanzees, an expansion plan that Terrace had written into his latest foundation proposal. He felt that Nim needed not only a new mother but also the company of other chimpanzees, and he thought it would be interesting to teach a second chimpanzee to sign, perhaps with Nim's help, and compare their progress. Adding more chimps to the project would give him a wealth of new data. Terrace could not yet cry eureka, but he fully expected to someday. As he told a reporter, he even expected Nim to eventually "talk about an inner world — his emo-

213

tions and dreams." There was no end to the
fantasy.

Nim signing "cat" with Bill Tynan and Joyce Butler

CHAPTER 6
"PULL TICKLE"

Joyce Butler and Nim Chimpsky might as well have been cousins. The bond between them was so close that Butler took him home on holidays to see her parents. Their closeness had little to do with DNA and a lot to do with a more elusive chemistry. Young male chimps, not unlike some human males, require an alpha female to organize their lives. Butler ruled Nim. "When he was around, I was the dominant person in the room, and he knew it," she says. She matched wits with Nim, took him on excursions, and made him his favorite snacks and foods. She sweetened his chicken noodle soup with a cup of apple juice and put big chunks of fresh pineapple in his morning cereal. Butler trafficked in the small details that make all the difference in any youngster's life, human or primate. Other staffers watched her engage Nim for hours, never running out of ideas. If a part-time teacher or babysitter failed to show up for work, Butler filled the slot, sometimes spending twenty-four hours a day with Nim. After one such long session, she wrote in the journal of record: "I don't know who enjoyed it more, Nim or myself."

Butler was nineteen when Terrace met her and gave her a part-time job on Project Nim. One year later, he offered her $70 a week, plus room and board, to replace Petitto and move into Delafield. There was nothing that Butler wanted more.

Of all Nim's mothers, Butler felt the most enduring sense of responsibility for his welfare. Had Terrace anticipated the intensity of their bond, he might have been discouraged from hiring her. But there was no denying that Butler and Nim had a synergy that benefited the experiment. Butler brought out the best in Nim. Unabashedly reciprocating her affection, he became calmer in her presence and more willing to work. Sitting out on the great front lawn, Nim signed "pull tickle" to Butler, hoping that she might even satisfy his sexual urges. Butler laughed about his advances, unconcerned. At least he was signing, and even putting two signs together — a step on the way to language in the Chomskian sense, Terrace believed.

"Nim was so in love with Joyce," recalls Renee Falitz, a twenty-two-year-old professional interpreter for the deaf who moved into Delafield soon after Butler. Falitz became the first person to live with Nim who was fluent in ASL. A hearing person, she had first learned to sign as a means of becoming involved in the theater. Falitz grew up in Bayside, Queens (next door to Sid Caesar), watching her mother struggle to make a living as a professional singer. During her childhood, she hung around the theater, longing to be on the stage. But since, by her own account, she couldn't really sing, she discovered that she could gain access to the stage as a performing arts interpreter for the deaf. Over the years she shared the stage with such talents as Placido Domingo and Luciano Pavarotti. Project Nim appealed to Falitz's sense of drama, and Nim immediately swept her off her feet. She was not an academic, nor was she planning on becoming one. "I had to beg Herb to take me on and give me a room at Delafield," she continues. Only five foot four, Falitz could not physically dominate the chimp the way the others could, but her knowledge of ASL made her invaluable to the group.

Surprised that Terrace had no other fluent

signers on board, Falitz became the ASL expert in residence. She had little interest in language acquisition, but she signed more fluidly and naturally with Nim than the others did. Falitz noticed that several of Nim's teachers were sloppy about their signs, which made them more difficult for Nim to read. She tutored the teachers, explaining that signing was like handwriting, and the more legible it was to Nim, the faster he would learn to use it. Skeptical and not particularly interested in the nuances of ASL, Terrace hired her not so much because of her signing expertise but because he needed people who were willing to live at Delafield. There was no salary for Falitz. Instead, she got room and board. Although Terrace installed her in "the cook's room," a tiny bedroom in the attic on the fourth floor of the mansion, Falitz had never lived apart from her parents, and she was grateful to have a place of her own. She and her cat promptly moved into Delafield, where, like the others, she took orders from Butler as the new team pulled together.

Butler slipped into Petitto's role without any trouble. She was a natural leader — organized, efficient, and willing to take on responsibility. All these changes in personnel were hard on Nim, and Terrace wanted someone who might stick around for a while. Butler was not going to walk away from the chimp or the project. She had a grasp of the big picture and understood the science, while no detail concerning Nim's life escaped her attention. She tracked his vocabulary, made sure each person on duty cleaned his bathroom properly, and required them to report on his moods, pranks, fits, and diet. She suggested new ways to maintain control over him, told the staff which words to work on each week, and issued long lists of house rules, all of which were typed up and distributed in regular weekly handouts: "You put the toothpaste on the brush, which Nim takes. This does not mean eating the tube of Crest. He sits on countertop during this. There is no bouncing around with toothbrush in hand." She reminded the staff that Nim could not open "the refrigerator and get something to eat without first signing," nor was he allowed to bite into the Tupperware.

Butler made sure the staff — and Nim — understood the rules. The chimp had free run of a small gym but not of the laundry room or kitchen. Nim sat down to eat balanced meals three times a day, which had to include vegetables, yogurt, eggs, and pancakes. (He was not allowed to eat more than two yogurts a day.) Like Martha Stewart, Butler encouraged the staff to "cook up something that is nutritious, filling, and satisfying" in her weekly memos, which chided them for feeding Nim spaghetti night after night. On many evenings, she prepared his favorite dish herself, a multi-layered vegetarian lasagna baked in a loaf pan. Nim also craved pizza. If he heard Butler ordering one on the phone, he'd sit by the door waiting for it to be delivered. If anyone offered him a swig of beer, he accepted greedily, and often tried to nab the whole bottle. Like a rebellious teen, Nim picked up his teachers' vices along with their vocabulary. He demanded drags on cigarettes (Johnson tried to teach him not to "lip them," getting them all soggy), slurps from mugs of coffee, all the ice cream he could get, and anything else that his roommates regularly imbibed. "I never gave him coffee," insists Butler, who did not approve of offering Nim anything that might be addictive or unhealthy. But others were eager to barter with the chimp, cutting him some slack in return for a sign or two or a moment of peace.

Nim's favorite activities were off campus, beyond the Delafield grounds, in the opposite direction from Columbia. Weather permitting, Butler took him to a private estate in Katonah (owned by a wealthy Delafield neighbor who was impressed by the project), just an hour away, where they hopped into a canoe and paddled out to a small island. Butler couldn't wait to take off Nim's harness and set him free to run, climb trees, and just be a chimp. They ate a picnic lunch by the water and groomed each other. Desmond Morris once described primate grooming as something like human chitchat, a form of relaxed, intimate communication. Butler pulled ticks off Nim's back and rubbed Vaseline into his dry, cracked skin to soothe it. At the end of the day, Nim jumped right into the boat without any problem. He still lived in fear of being abandoned.

Bill Tynan, not yet living at Delafield, accompanied Butler on these day trips. (Terrace required that two people accompany Nim at all times when he was taken off Delafield property.) Tall, with thick hair and a full beard, Tynan had a strong relationship with Nim — and with Butler as well. The three of them began to function like a small family. In fact, Nim watched his two keepers fall in love.

Butler and Tynan relied on each other's help with Nim. A disaster of some sort often waited just around the corner. One summer evening, in the middle of a record-breaking heat wave, Nim woke up in the middle of the night and decided to visit Butler. Locked into his room from the outside, as always, he broke the glass panes of his window, scampered across the roof like a squirrel, and climbed into Butler's room through her window. Lying naked on top of the sheets, she had just managed to fall asleep, despite the heat. Nim gently placed one hand on her back, like a lover about to get into her bed. Butler froze. "It definitely did not feel like a human hand," she recalls. Instantly coming to her senses, she realized that she was only going to have one chance to grab the chimp before the situation escalated and he slipped back out the window and ran off; she did not want to spend the next several hours chasing a black furry shadow around the streets of Riverdale. Butler responded calmly, taking Nim into her arms and hugging him tightly while she shouted for Tynan, downstairs having a beer with other staffers, to come and help.

Eventually, Tynan moved into Butler's room — the master suite — which they shared with Speedo, a little mutt adopted from a shelter, and two cats. (Tynan and Carol Stewart subsequently divorced; he and Butler are currently married to other people.) Nim, allowed brief and well-monitored visits with these animals, loved them but probably would have killed them all, given the chance. He did not understand his own strength and had no qualms about using it when he felt the least bit threatened.

For their own protection, outsiders were not invited to Delafield to either meet the chimp or socialize with the staff in the evenings. At eight o'clock, after Nim went to bed, full-timers and part-timers often gathered in one of the many rooms to drink beer, smoke pot, or do crossword puzzles if it was Sunday. The atmosphere was relaxed, but there were no big parties. The last thing anyone wanted was a circus-like atmosphere, in which the chimp, dressed in his costume of human clothes, became the entertainment. But word was out, and curiosity seekers parked their cars in front of the gates, hoping to get a glimpse of Nim. Pedestrians walked by, shouting "Make him talk!" or "Hi, Koko!" confusing the chimp with Penny Patterson's popular gorilla.

Nim's roommates and teachers were careful to keep Nim out of the public eye most of the time, but they were not above using the chimp to pull off practical jokes. One Saturday afternoon, Falitz noticed a wedding going on in a synagogue down the street from Delafield; after the ceremony, the guests spilled out onto the grounds for the reception. For a lark, Falitz walked over with Nim. "We hid behind a tree, but the groom saw us, and he grabbed his wife in the wedding dress and shouted, 'Look over there!' pointing at us." When she turned around to look, Falitz and Nim disappeared behind the tree. When the groom turned around again, they popped back out and waved. This went on several times until the bride became furious with her groom's insistence that a chimpanzee had joined the wedding party. "She was ready to divorce him," says Falitz, still amused by the memory. Finally she and Nim came out of hiding to give them all a good laugh.

Tynan, Butler, Falitz, and Johnson anchored the Delafield team, while volunteers filled in the gaps. According to Butler and Tynan, Terrace brought in a string of inexperienced students on their way to graduate school or better-paying, less dangerous jobs. None of them lasted very long. Nim's temper tantrums, which were becoming more violent and destructive, scared novices away. If the tantrums weren't snuffed out quickly, they picked up momentum and lasted for hours. Butler was determined not to let Nim get away with these tantrums. In a memo to the staff, she wrote, "Don't let Nim fool you into thinking he is allowed to be a maniac just because he is a chimpanzee."

Toilet training was another problem that some were loath to contend with. "We decided to just take him out of diapers," says Johnson. "It was ridiculous. What did diapers have to do with language?" But getting him to use the bathroom was a daily battle. Any day that Nim was able to wear the same pair of pants from morning until evening was special, and designated as such in the reports. More often, according to the journal of record, Nim messed all over the house, sometimes in anger, sometimes accidentally; it was impossible to know for sure, although theorizing about why he did most things was an occupational hazard. As psychology students, the caretakers tried their own experiments. At one point, the staff decided to take Nim to the toilet every fifteen minutes, like it or not. This strategy worked better than diapers but was totally impractical.

It was difficult for those living with Nim to gauge his progress with much objectivity. As psychology students, they had studied the legendary and ever-fascinating case of

Clever Hans, a highly intelligent Arabian horse owned by Wilhelm von Osten, a German math teacher and horse trainer who had taught Hans to do addition, subtraction, and fractions and even tell time. Von Osten took the horse on the road, much to the pleasure of eager audiences, who asked the horse simple questions and watched him tap out the correct answers with his hoof. By 1904, the horse was causing such a huge sensation that a commission made up of thirteen prominent scientists was convened to determine whether or not the show was a hoax. The commission unequivocally pronounced Hans to be an authentically intelligent being. Three years later, Oskar Pfungst, a German psychologist who became curious about the horse, did more thorough research and determined that Hans got the answers correct only when he could *see* his questioner, who was inadvertently providing the necessary cues with his body language. (Von Osten claimed he had no idea this was going on.) The "Clever Hans effect" entered the psychological vernacular as a warning to researchers about the risk of compromising their results by their mere presence.

Butler made a conscious effort to distinguish instances when Nim mimicked her from times when he was actually signing. She felt sure she could tell the difference, but it was subtle. She considered the chimp's facial expressions, his eyes, and the speed of his gestures. His mood greatly affected his concentration and performance. But as Terrace knew, even on a good day, when Nim was engaged by the work, his signs remained open to interpretation. Terrace continued to consider new, more accurate methods to collect and verify data. At weekly meetings, the staff raised questions for Terrace about the handling and coding of data, or, say, Nim's confusion over particular signs (he juxtaposed "want" and "give"), and discussed how they could solve them.

Prior to Project Nim, none of the staff, with the exception of Falitz, had ever studied ASL or learned to use it in conversation, so once a week they attended an ASL seminar to improve their skills. Terrace took private lessons, refusing to learn with the group. Three years into Project Nim, fluent signers began showing up looking for work. Mary Wambach, a deaf woman who joined the experiment for nine months, signed fluently to Nim but saw irregularities in his responses. Wambach, who taught ASL in a deaf community, was not a native signer but had begun to sign at age nineteen when she was diagnosed as profoundly deaf. Although her first language had been English, she signed accurately in ASL and recognized that Nim's signs were something else. She informed Terrace and the others that Nim was learning a pidgin version of the language — not proper ASL, which has a structure and a set of rules. This, of course, made sense; apart from Falitz, none of Nim's teachers knew much sign language. They learned signs individually, word by word, the same way Nim learned them. The teachers were not far ahead of the chimp.

According to Falitz, the staff freely redesigned signs, loosely based on ASL, to make them easier for Nim to master. Part of the motivation for changing the signs was that speed was critical to Terrace. So if certain signs were difficult for Nim, such as signs that involved gestures in space, which were often done in front of the body, the staff might alter them so that they involved touch. As Falitz explains, "He was so egocentric and self-centered that if touching himself somewhere was part of the sign, he learned it twice as fast." Colors, for instance, usually signed in the air, were reshaped to touch down on Nim's stomach. Falitz began running seminars for the group, but she never understood why Terrace was hiring people who did not know ASL for an ASL project. Wambach's criticism went further. She thought that Nim should have been raised in a deaf family from infancy. Giving him to the LaFarges was like putting a child in an Italian family to learn German.

When native deaf signers came to visit Nim, they claimed to understand him more proficiently than his regular handlers. Johnson found this hard to believe. "Deaf people would come to Delafield and read Nim's signs in great detail," he recalls. "They'd say, 'Nim just told me he was hungry and would like to go inside and have a banana.' It was amazing. I'd be right there and all I saw was Nim sign a two-word combination — 'banana,' 'eat.' "

Wambach's concerns raised questions about the impact that deaf signers could have on Project Nim, and perhaps inadvertently about how Terrace's study might compare with the work done by the Gardners in Nevada, who had expressly designed their experiments to include deaf signers. Simply having Falitz sign at the weekly meetings and interpret for Wambach in the discussions brought a new dimension to their work. Wambach was not particularly critical of Terrace, who was older and far more established than she, but she wanted the staff to have a better understanding of the world of deaf speakers — those who used ASL because they needed a language.

Thanks to Wambach, the chimp project began attracting deaf volunteers (including one who is remembered for having *love* and *hate* tattooed on his knuckles), who formed a small subculture within Terrace's staff. In an attempt to bridge these two worlds, one night the deaf volunteers arranged to plug up the ears of the hearing staff and take them out to a restaurant for dinner. They were instructed to communicate exclusively in ASL from the moment the plugs were placed in their ears on the way to the restaurant, during the meal, and all the way back to Delafield. The hearing group found the experience to be a terrible struggle. But what made an indelible impression on Johnson was the way that everybody in the restaurant spoke really slowly and loudly to them, treating them as if they were all mentally incapacitated.

Meanwhile, Butler and Tynan had more mundane concerns. They worried not just about their fluency in ASL but about whether there was enough food in the house, a driver available to take Nim to Columbia for his language sessions, and a sufficiently secure environment to contain him given the constant escapes, which required daily repairs on locks, windows, doors, furniture, and objects that had once been considered unbreakable. Richard Sanders, a psychology student at Columbia who lived briefly at Delafield, turned around in the kitchen one evening and found Nim pulling a large wooden cabinet full of dishes off the wall. Sanders grabbed him, but Nim refused to let go and the whole cabinet came down on top of them. Though Nim was fine, Sanders emerged from the wreckage with a sore head.

Nim began by going to his Columbia classroom five days a week for three to five hours, but the schedule was cut back, largely because the chimp put up such stiff resistance. Even getting him to school three days a week was so much of a challenge that the Delafield group wanted his teachers to come uptown to Riverdale, where he was far happier and more willing to work. This made sense. The charts indicated that Nim was learning more language at Delafield than he was in his classroom, where the recalcitrant chimp often refused to cooperate. Butler, who sometimes drove him to Columbia and then spent a few hours in class with him, described him in the daily log as "a real shit" in school, and was very upset by his behavior. She wanted him to perform well and please Terrace, who watched through the two-way mirror as, over and over, Nim grabbed her hand and walked to the door, repeatedly making the sign for "open." If that didn't work, he'd sign "dirty," his word for needing to use the bathroom. Most of the time, he did not have to relieve himself, but just used "dirty" as a ruse to leave the room. (Nim cried wolf so many times that when he really did have to go, often he was denied permission and would mess in his pants.)

As the months passed, Butler felt increasingly protective of Nim and more unwilling to coerce him into going to Columbia, where he was overtly miserable. Getting him into the car, driving him to the campus, and tucking him safely into the classroom became an ordeal that she felt was productive neither for Nim nor for the project. But Terrace wanted the chimp at Schermerhorn. After Petitto's departure, the psychologist rarely went uptown to Delafield. He preferred that the chimp come to him, and he wanted handlers who could get Nim there. Butler argued with Terrace at meetings but never won. Reluctantly, Nim's housemates followed orders. Falitz puts it this way: "We

233

all loved Nim, so we tolerated Herb."

In his struggle to make the experiment financially solvent, Terrace ignored most of the demands from Riverdale, insisting that Nim keep regular school hours at Columbia, where he invited spectators to watch Nim sign through the two-way mirror and taped the sessions, giving the illusion that he had some control over the experiment. (According to Wambach, although Nim could not see people on the other side of the mirror, he could smell them and always knew they were there.) In fact, Terrace was once again losing control and he knew it.

Tynan had begun an independent study project with Nim, which involved art. He wanted to compare the chimp's colorful drawings with those executed by human children. As it turned out, Nim's ability to use line and color proved to be similar to that of human children in his age group. The drawings were done in Terrace's Columbia classroom, but Tynan used another professor as an advisor on the project. Chimp art, if there is such a genre, has a short and provocative history. Pablo Picasso hung a work by Congo, the most famous chimp artist in the 1950s, on his wall. Like humans, some chimps had more finesse in their works on paper than others, and their preference for particular colors and lines became distinct over time, like a signature. Nim used Magic Markers and would insist on a certain color one week and then switch to another the next. His careful scrambles of lines and color, though not artistically remarkable, turned out to have considerable monetary value, especially after Tynan's study received some scholarly attention. Terrace demanded custody of the drawings. Tynan refused to give them up, arguing that the drawings belonged to him, not Project Nim. The dispute eventually turned into a lawsuit, which was settled out of court. Tynan won and kept the original paintings, valued at $20,000 in 1977. Terrace was given a set of reproductions.

Tynan had no problem asserting his independence from Terrace, who had become dependent on him to handle Nim as well as all technical matters relating to the project. Tynan and Butler were Delafield's First Family, responsible not only for Nim's welfare but also for managing the staff and running the house. Replacing them would be tough. The Columbia classroom, like Stewart's wooden box, turned into the focus of a major battle between Terrace and those who were most intimately involved in Nim's care. Butler and the others were able to get

Nim into the classroom, but they could not force him to work there. Once more, discipline became a hotly contested issue. Terrace ordered the staff to withhold Nim's food on school mornings, hoping that Nim might work for his breakfast at Columbia. But interfering with Nim's morning routine did not help his frame of mind and made it more difficult to get him to school; he was jumpy and anxious to leave as soon as he got there. During this period, Butler described his behavior as "schizzy" in the journal. When Nim wasn't hyper, he might go into a deep funk, becoming too lethargic to work. Richard Sanders referred to this state as "stuperous." Nim's wide grin, a face he made when he was happy, with his rogue tongue dancing behind his teeth, appeared only when it was time to go back uptown to Riverdale.

Terrace, who occasionally drove Nim back and forth to Columbia, understood that the drive itself was becoming dangerous. Two people were required in the car, one to drive and the other to deal with Nim. If the chimp decided he wanted to drive himself or jump out the window — not uncommon — the chaos was instantaneous. "It was a trauma," says Falitz, who often rode shotgun. "There were no car seats or seat belts in those days, so you had to hold him tightly on your lap. Nim liked to grab the wheel." His chauffeurs played games with the chimp to keep him occupied, as well as to amuse themselves. When they drove through the Henry Hudson Parkway tollbooth onto the West Side Highway, Falitz would occasionally place the money in Nim's hand and have him reach out the window and pay the toll. The attendant's inevitable shrieks sent them into hysterics, relieving the tension in the car.

Finally, the Delafield team generated its own internal study to prove that Nim's vocabulary was growing more rapidly at Riverdale than at Columbia. Nim had even been observed alone in his room signing spontaneously to his dolls. They presented their statistics to Terrace and informed him that they would no longer transport the chimp to campus. Terrace had no choice. In his own book, he admitted that the staff forced him to back down. In effect, the classroom had been a cage for Nim, and he was far more productive when he had a modicum of control on his own turf. From that point on, Delafield became the undisputed center of Project Nim. The professor would have to come uptown to see the chimp, which he did only irregularly, and

mostly to shoot photographs with his Has-
selblad or escort a celebrity visitor on a tour.

One afternoon in 1977, word spread that
Kurt Vonnegut wanted to meet Nim. The
staff read (or reread) Vonnegut's novels,
preparing to meet the author, answer his
questions, and watch him interact with
Nim. When Terrace arrived with Vonnegut
in tow, Falitz happened to be on duty and
had the chimp tethered to her body as they
played outside. "Herb walked over to us and
introduced Nim to Vonnegut and totally
ignored me as if I wasn't even there," she
recalls. Falitz was always miffed by Terrace's
lack of respect for women. "We were all
invisible."

But Butler refused to be invisible and
often spoke for the whole group. She was
not afraid to complain about Terrace's
methods to his face or in the daily journal,
which was available to be read by anyone
on the Project Nim staff. At one point, according to Tynan, Terrace contemplated firing her. But staffing problems at Delafield
were so severe that there was no one but
Butler to hold the project together, and Terrace was forced to recognize that just lining
up four people each day to cover the chimp,
one-on-one, from 10:00 a.m. until 8:00
p.m. was a time-consuming, often impos-

sible job. Butler often took the unfilled slots — willingly. She also transcribed tapes, made sure staffers kept the house in order, and monitored Nim's day even when others were with him.

There were good reasons that it was hard to line up people to take care of Nim. By the time he was three, he was too strong to be physically dominated. He excelled at manipulating people, playing one off against another to his advantage, and if that didn't work, he was not averse to simply biting to get his way. The most harrowing parts of the day were known as "transfers," when Nim was handed off from one person to another at the end of a shift. Like many human toddlers, Nim didn't handle transitions well. A transfer required a carefully choreographed technique called "body to body," wherein whoever was minding Nim lifted him up and put him into the next person's arms and passed his tether to the newcomer's hand, while the departing person quickly exited through a door and locked it to prevent the chimp from escaping. Too frequently, Nim bit the newcomer to break the hug and then dashed out the door, running after the previous person, who often fled to the nearest bathroom, slammed the door, and locked it. (Butler once waited almost an hour in a locked room while Nim banged on the door.) Transfers were so fraught with complications that Nim's handlers analyzed them in the journals every day, reporting which techniques worked, which didn't, and why.

On January 6, 1977, Butler reported: "Transfer to Renee [Falitz] — almost b-b [body to body]. NC [Nim Chimpsky] was put down on floor. Renee took over as best she could without losing an eye. NC was being very aggressive." The following day, on duty again, Falitz had a grumpy chimp tied to her waist. Playing around at the top of the stairs, Nim leapt onto her head, scratching her face and bursting a blood vessel in her eye. This was just the beginning for Falitz.

Nim constantly challenged her more than he did his other trainers, apparently sensing that he could dominate her. After several difficult transfers, Falitz began having trouble putting Nim to bed at night. One evening, the chimp was playing happily downstairs when she decided to sneak upstairs and put something away in her room, off-limits to Nim. Nim, of course, heard her door open on the third floor and flew up the stairs in seconds to check it out. Falitz saw him coming and slammed the door closed to keep him out of her room and away from her cat. Nim proceeded to lock her in her own room. (Falitz, to this day, has no idea how he managed this, since she ordinarily locked the door from the inside but now could not unlock it.) She begged and pleaded and used her most seductive voice, finally cajoling him into letting her out, and then she managed to get him into his own bedroom. Falitz quickly — maybe too quickly — locked the door behind them. Nim, possibly annoyed that he'd been tricked into his own room, bit Falitz on the arm. She was furious. In the journal, she reported: "I started to beat him and then he bit my leg and got thru again." Hearing the all too familiar cries for help, Tynan came to her rescue, and eventually Falitz got Nim, screaming all the way, into his own room — alone — and locked the door.

Falitz was not the kind of person to give up, and this kind of abuse only made her more determined. Not only did she adore the chimp, but she found that the association with Project Nim opened all kinds of doors for her both professionally and personally. Falitz walked the chimp around the neighborhood, using him as a magnet to pick up interesting men. Nim, for his part, appeared to enjoy her company as well as the battle. But he continued to bite her, each bite a little harder. Falitz fought back, trying to show Nim that he could not slap her around. During various fights, she bopped him with a plastic bowling pin, smacked him, lectured him for hours at a time about his behavior, and refused him hugs and affection.

As hard as Falitz tried to dominate the chimp, nothing seemed to work, and Tynan worried for her safety. But some days Nim and Falitz were fine. Convinced the chimp loved her, despite indications to the contrary, she wanted to stay. "Had to peel Nim off me today," she reported in the journal. "He grabbed me and sucked my lips. Got a hickey on my neck." A few days later she wrote: "He sat on my chest and tickled me . . . bent over and smacked a kiss on my lips. Very bestial." When she played tag with Nim, "the pervert kept swatting me right on the ass." Many years later, Falitz concluded, "We had a contentious relationship. But I loved him to death."

Falitz's journal entries, like most other staffers' entries, were frank admissions, filled with raw feelings of anger, frustration, and affection toward Nim, who was becoming stronger and more destructive each day.

All his keepers, including Butler and Tynan, were troubled by the chimp's aggressive behavior toward humans, which was intensifying and becoming more difficult to control. Since none of them had any experience with other chimps, they had no way of telling whether this was "normal" or not. Their confusion was reflected in the journals. "He was a different chimp today," wrote Butler in the log. "I don't know who he is." After another alarming experience, Falitz wrote, "Nim kept asking for his head on a platter."

Says Johnson, "We were told we could throw him around a little bit, give him a toss, but never to hit him in the face, because in the chimp world, that was a sign of 'one of us is not going to leave here.' " Terrace had no idea how to handle Nim, and if there were behaviorists or trainers available who could have helped, he did not search them out to advise the group. One evening, after a difficult day in which Nim had been followed for hours with cameras, Terrace picked the wrong moment, despite warnings, to introduce Nim to a new volunteer named Ray. Ray left with twenty bite marks on his hands and arms.

On June 22, Falitz noted that Nim's behavior was off the charts, even by his standards. One minute he was calm and the next he was attacking her, "not nibbling but taking real bites and swiping at my face. Very hard to control. Kept pulling on the lead," which he was now wearing inside the house as well as outdoors. A few weeks later, Nim gave her a nasty bite on the hand. Determined as ever, she forced him to clean up her blood and bandage her wound. The chimp often became contrite after a bite, willing to do whatever Falitz asked of him. But he did not stop biting her. The following morning, on duty again, Falitz reported that Nim woke up "real grouchy and uncontrollable." When he took a swipe at her face, Falitz filled the bathtub with water and threw him in it. Then she locked him in a closet and left him there for an hour.

Nim grew to expect punishment when he misbehaved, but this did not deter him from daily tantrums and biting incidents. Days without bites were noted in the journal like holidays. The chimp frequently jumped out of windows, broke every lock he could reach, smashed furniture, and smeared walls with his feces. In the journal, his keepers called Nim "bratty," spoiled," crazy," "nasty," and "malicious" as his aggression became more of a constant. They continued to love him, but there was no denying that he was becoming too much to handle.

Some days Nim was such an angel and signed so fluidly they wondered if he had a split personality. But too often, the Master of Delafield acted like a confused and angry prisoner. His behavior seemed so bipolar that his keepers, especially Butler and Tynan, his greatest advocates, were losing patience with him and resorting to desperate measures. One night, Butler cracked him on the head with a frying pan in a furious effort to end a tantrum. It worked. But she worried about the day when nothing would work. There was no plan, and she knew they needed one.

Getting through the long, hot summer of 1977 was an ordeal. The temperature often broke 100 degrees, and the house was stifling. The ceiling fan barely cooled Nim's bedroom. Whether because of the heat or his circumstances, Nim gradually became withdrawn, not much interested in signing or anything else. In the morning, the staff had to wake him up from a deep sleep and drag him out of bed. The only good news for Nim was the return of Walter Benesch, on summer vacation from graduate school. Nim perked up at the sight of his old friend. But it was too hot to do much of anything other than stay outdoors in the shade, eat ice cream, and try to remain cool.

On July 28, Butler woke Nim up and decided to take him fishing at the pond on the Delafield property. Nim seemed hyper but manageable. Tynan took him from Butler after lunch — they had no problem transferring the chimp between them — and at five in the afternoon, Falitz took over from Tynan. That transfer was a nightmare. "One of those you wish didn't happen," reported Tynan in the journal. "Renee tied the lead on her belt. N was quiet, and when Renee signed Hug, N went to her. . . . But as he put his face next to her he opened up and chomped, gashing her face. I hit Nim hard in stomach to get him off her, then split, as Renee was hauling N into house to give him hell." There was a protocol for dealing with Nim's aggression. When he bit anyone, the victim had to respond on the spot, or otherwise Nim would bite as soon as he got close again. Tynan was following procedure, giving Falitz a chance to figure out what form of payback she wanted to exact. What he did not realize was that Nim had taken a chunk out of her face.

"I thought he was going to kiss me!" Falitz remembers. "So I didn't duck. He put his lips on my cheek and then boom — bit down full force. His jaw was so strong that he severed the nerves. I didn't have any feeling on the right side of my face. I dragged him into the house while I was screaming. I wasn't in pain, but I was scared to death."

An armoire with a mirror sat in the hallway outside Nim's room. When Falitz walked by, she caught a glance of her own face covered in blood. Steeling herself to appear calm, she managed to get Nim in his room, lock the door, and then call a cab, which she had the good sense to know would come faster than an ambulance. Tynan told the driver to go to the closest hospital, Montefiore, which happened by great good fortune to have a craniofacial clinic. As the only other person at Delafield that moment, Tynan had to remain at home with Nim, so he called Terrace and told him to meet Falitz at the hospital.

The emergency room doctors had never seen a chimp bite, and they lined up to get into Falitz's room and examine her face. The wound could not be immediately stitched up, for fear of infection, and she was hospitalized for three days of intravenous antibiotics. For the next three months, the tear needed to drain before the doctors could stitch up her face; plastic surgeries were still one year off. As soon as Falitz was released from the hospital, she returned to see Nim, for her own sense of closure, but she knew she could not stay on the project. Upset by the bandages, Nim immediately tried to tear them off her face. Tynan promptly came between them. It was just too dangerous for her to be anywhere near Nim. Falitz packed up her bags and left Delafield. She had no insurance to pay any of her medical bills, but Terrace saw to it that Columbia covered all her expenses.

In Terrace's view, life for Nim, and perhaps for himself, had gone downhill ever since Petitto's departure, and he had been unable to win any ongoing foundation support. In an unusual deal for a scientist to make, he signed a contract with the Children's Television Workshop (CTW), putting Nim to work on *Sesame Street*. CTW planned to install a hidden camera in Nim's bedroom and shoot the chimp for two whole days, waking up, getting dressed, eating breakfast, and going about his business. A day in the life of Nim would be edited down to provide a beguiling role model for toddlers just learning how to do those simple housekeeping tasks that Nim had mastered. But Tynan and Butler dreaded the whole prospect, fearing that he might fly into a rage when strangers invaded his privacy.

On August 6, Nim woke up to bright lights, cameras, and a crew shooting in his bedroom. Predictably, the touchy chimpanzee was not pleased. Butler got him up, into the bathroom, and outside as quickly as possible to let him unwind. "During the next two hours we had five fights," she reported. But she managed to keep him from having a tantrum, and the crew turned off the cameras at four o'clock. The day had passed without any serious incident.

That evening, Benesch and Nim were playing outside when they heard thunder rumbling in the distance. Frightened, Nim climbed into Benesch's shirt, poking his head out the neck. About thirty-five pounds, he could still curl up his body into a tight little ball. They were sitting on the front steps of the mansion around eight o'clock, Nim's usual bedtime, when Butler and Tynan drove up the driveway, returning home.

Nim was still nervous and wound up after the unusual experience of being filmed by a television crew, so Butler and Tynan decided to tire him out before putting him to bed. They took him upstairs to their bedroom, where he played with the cats while Benesch took an hour off. At nine o'clock Benesch returned to get Nim. But once in his room, getting him into bed was hopeless. Nim raced around the floor at breakneck speed clutching his blanket and pounding on the walls; Benesch, staying calm, just sat by the door, waiting for him to get tired. After thirty minutes, Benesch slipped out of the room, hoping Nim might settle down. But it was the wrong move. The hysteria escalated, with Nim pounding frantically on the door. Not sure what to do, Benesch called Tynan for help. The two of them were standing in the hallway, trying to figure out the next step, when they heard Butler screaming. Nim had somehow escaped from his room, gotten into hers, and attacked the cats he had been playing with a little while earlier. (The cats survived.)

Somehow, the two men managed to drag Nim into a small upstairs kitchen on the human side of the house. Benesch stayed with Nim as Tynan, outside, locked the door. Tynan laced some fruit juice with a tranquilizer and passed it, along with some oranges, back into the room, gingerly opening the door a crack. Nim refused the juice, but he started to quiet down enough that Benesch was able to put him into the harness and lead that Tynan tossed into the room. Together, Benesch and Nim walked downstairs as the chimp ate the oranges.

The storm had passed. They went outside for a breath of fresh air and started to relax. Nim signed "tickle" to Benesch, who obliged. They tumbled gently on the soft grass. A few minutes later, Nim was so tired that he signed "sleep" and Benesch took him up to bed. Looking around Nim's room for his escape route, Benesch was surprised to find the window still closed and intact. Then he saw a hole in the wall leading to the hallway, where the CTW crew had hidden the camera. When they left, they had covered the hole with a sheet of plywood, which was now on the floor. The hole had allowed Nim to escape.

Everyone was exhausted when the crew arrived the following morning. For the second day in a row, Nim awakened to bright lights and the purr of rolling cameras. Not surprisingly, Tynan found him in an edgy mood, but nevertheless managed to maneuver him through the morning. They headed for the pond to do some fishing, usually a foolproof activity for the nervous chimp. Benesch joined them and caught a fish, pleasing Nim as well as the crew. But during some play that followed, Nim became too mouthy, and Tynan knew the chimp was going to bite someone. As the cameras rolled, Nim started to bite him.

251

Tynan, one small step ahead of him, booted Nim hard in the rear — so hard, in fact, that he dislocated his toe and had to be rushed to the hospital. Nim was fine.

Benesch took over for Tynan from two-thirty in the afternoon, the time the incident took place, until ten o'clock that evening, with some relief from Terrace. But help from Terrace, even in a pinch, was a mixed blessing. Despite warnings, Terrace again insisted on introducing Nim to another new volunteer, who, like others before him, was bitten badly, this time on the face. It was a long night.

The following day, Benesch had the best time with Nim he'd had since returning to Delafield. The cameras were gone, and they went to the pond, where the fish nibbled on Nim's toes, much to his delight. Then they walked to the river, picking and eating berries as they went along.

In early August, Nim lunged for a young boy on the street and was pulled back just in time. He had scratched the boy but not badly enough to draw blood. Butler, who had herself been bitten twice in recent weeks, knew they were facing a crisis. "We were pretty much winging it on our own with Nim," says Tynan. "We would have tried anything to get more control over the situation, but we just didn't know what to do. We were still introducing new words, but it was just a numbers game." Although Nim's vocabulary was growing, it sometimes took his trainers two hours to get him to sign just one word. Butler, Tynan, and Johnson were not about to abandon the chimp; however, they knew that training new people to work with Nim made no sense. The hospital emergency room saw so many bite cases that, according to Falitz, the staff feared the department of health might demand that Nim be euthanized. "We were on rabies alert frequently. I wasn't the only one bitten," says Falitz. "Herb realized it was getting very dangerous. He was hiring twenty-year-olds who needed a place to live, instead of qualified people. Somebody was going to get even more seriously hurt."

Terrace gave himself a deadline. If he was unable to find serious funding by late August, he intended to end the project. By the third week in August, Terrace began researching places to send the chimp. But there was a problem. "Finished" research animals, including valuable chimpanzees, were hard to even give away. Project Nim had no exit plan. The psychologist did not want to be remembered for dumping this unique and by now famous animal in the wrong place. He too felt attached to the chimp, though not enough to keep him.

According to Terrace, Project Nim had ample data — mounds of it, in fact — in various media formats, which were in need of time-consuming analysis. He believed that the chimp had reached a plateau and that there was no longer any reason to generate more data. Nim had outlived his usefulness to the study. In fact, he was getting in the way of it. Dangerous and expensive, he had exhausted Terrace's patience. Terrace was tired of dealing with bites, broken windows, complaints from the staff, and the endless hunt for replacements. "I can't even begin to describe how consuming this was seven days a week," Terrace commented. "And I knew that it would only get worse exponentially."

One day Terrace gathered his staff for what they thought would be a typical meeting to discuss Nim's progress, problems at the house — the usual issues. In a dry and unemotional tone, as if he were announcing a routine change in the chimp's schedule, Terrace informed those present that Nim would be sent to live out his life elsewhere.

The news was so unexpected and hard to comprehend that the Delafield staff fell silent at first. Presenting it as a fait accompli, Terrace left no room for discussion. The psychologist didn't ask Butler or Tynan for their views about what to do with Nim, probably because he understood that they would never choose to part with the chimp. The suddenness of Terrace's pronouncement was confusing. Up until then, he had projected only his confidence in the experiment, not his doubts; nor had he ever mentioned the possibility of getting rid of Nim. Butler, Tynan, and Johnson well understood the problems they faced working with the chimp as he got older, but they had assumed that they, and Terrace, would find ways to surmount them. The alternatives for Nim were horrific to contemplate, and in almost four years of meetings, Terrace had never suggested that they might be necessary. Butler and Tynan blamed themselves for Project Nim's demise. They felt as if they had been inadequate parents and, as a result, they were losing their child.

Terrace wanted to do the right thing for Nim, but he didn't know exactly what that was. In the past, the ultimate disposition of his research animals had never been quite so troubling. At the end of the study, they were routinely euthanized if they could not be passed along to another researcher for further use. Having been raised as a human, Nim could hardly be thrown into a small cage in Columbia's biomedical facility, nor did Terrace want him to be euthanized. But he was far too problematic to remain in residence at Delafield under the current circumstances. Terrace had originally wanted to expand Project Nim and bring in additional chimps to keep Nim company and expand his research. Instead, after almost four years, he came to the opposite conclusion. Taking responsibility for even one chimp was more than he felt he could continue to do.

Terrace had only to do a little bit of investigation to know that the options for Nim were few and frightening. Therefore, it was not long before he put in a call to Lemmon. The New York psychologist had little respect for Lemmon as a scientist, but he knew that the IPS director understood chimpanzees, and he hoped that Lemmon would understand Nim's fragile state of mind and treat him gently. It never occurred to Terrace that Lemmon would not be thrilled to welcome the chimp back. After all, Nim was now famous, and his presence would raise the profile of Lemmon's research institute.

Back in Norman, Lemmon was surprised

to hear that after less than four years, Project Nim no longer needed its much-celebrated chimpanzee. But he was used to having his chimps bounce back to him as soon as they had nowhere else to go, and he agreed to give Nim a home. The graduate students around IPS, many of them working with Roger Fouts, wondered what had gone wrong in New York. Nim was returning to Norman before Terrace completed Project Nim, which suggested that the Columbia professor was having problems.

As Terrace was finalizing plans with Lemmon, the three staffers most attached to Nim — Butler, Tynan, and Johnson — continued to plead with him to expand the project rather than end it. Nim needed the comfort of his own species and would be happier and more cooperative if more chimps could be brought in as part of the study, they argued. They envisioned Delafield becoming a small chimp laboratory. As the three pillars in Nim's life, they were prepared to remain on the project for the long haul; Terrace would not have to scramble for a whole new staff as he did most summers, they assured him. As usual, Terrace ignored his staff's suggestions. He had come to the end of his rope.

In a last-ditch effort to save him, Nim's

The Project Nim team on the steps of Delafield

advocates plotted to kidnap the chimp and take him to Florida, where Butler's parents owned a piece of land. Butler intended to design and build Nim his own island, just like the one in Katonah. "We had everything we needed but money," she admits. "And no standing anywhere to raise any." The plan remained a fantasy.

Nim's September schedule filled up with video and photo sessions; *60 Minutes* came to do a shoot, and Nim behaved like a professional for the cameras, as if he knew he was giving his farewell performance. There were no problems. To mark the end of the project, Terrace planned a picnic at Delafield to which he invited all the teachers, employees, and volunteers who had passed through the doors of Project Nim. It was a chance to see the chimp for the last time. Stephanie, WER, Josh, and Jenny showed up. (Stephanie and WER were still talking and not yet divorced.) Laura-Ann Petitto came too. Jenny was bereft at the decision to send Nim back to a cage in Oklahoma. "It was like a Charles Dickens novel," she says. "We raised him to be a prince and then we sent him away to be a pauper."

Most of the key people in Nim's life gathered around him to say good-bye. A portrait of Terrace, Nim, and twenty-five of Nim's teachers taken on the mansion's front steps portrays them as one big happy family. Nim is sitting on Terrace's lap; Terrace sits next to Petitto. The photo shows him grinning and grabbing at Petitto as she cringes, leaning away from him. Butler stands tall in the back row, casting her eyes downward on the chimp. None of the La-Farges is in the portrait.

■ ■ ■ ■

In a test to prepare Nim for his imminent flight to Oklahoma, Butler and Tynan injected him with a new tranquilizer, a mixture of Valium and Sernalyn. It was a powerful sedative and put him to sleep for hours. The next morning, he was fine.

During one of their final days together, Nim signed effortlessly with Butler. She noted in the journal, "If all sessions were like this one Nim would never be sent back to Oklahoma."

On September 25, 1977, Nim was awakened at six in the morning from a deep sleep, wrapped in his favorite blanket, and injected (by a veterinarian, not a pediatrician) with the tranquilizer they knew would work. Tynan, Butler, and Terrace accompanied Nim aboard a private plane the psychologist had waiting for them at Teterboro Airport in New Jersey. Johnson remained behind at Delafield to clean up the mess and put the mansion back in order. He remembers weeping for hours while he picked up Nim's clothes and put all his toys in a box. The accoutrements of Project Nim were considered contraband in Oklahoma.

The plane took off at eight-thirty with the

unhappy group. In the middle of the flight, Nim woke up and began to shriek at the top of his lungs. Terrace, worried that the pilot would become alarmed, injected Nim again.

When Nim woke up in Norman the following day, he would find that he had fallen through the looking glass into a strange and unfamiliar place. Delafield was gone. He would no longer put his clothes on in the morning, brush his teeth, or get tucked into bed at night with his favorite blanket. Lemmon was going to teach him how to be a real chimpanzee.

■ ■ ■ ■

PART TWO:
THE INSTITUTE FOR
PRIMATE STUDIES:
NORMAN, OKLAHOMA

■ ■ ■ ■

Roger Fouts and Washoe in Norman, Oklahoma

Chapter 7
Meanwhile, Back
on the Farm

Herbert Terrace thought of the Institute for Primate Studies as little better than a breeding operation. In his view, "Lemmon's work did not even rise to the level of professional judgment." And Roger Fouts's work, which probably wouldn't have impressed him in any case, was not on the Columbia professor's radar. But Terrace actually had little understanding of IPS culture, as he had had only minimal exposure to it on his one visit there nearly a decade earlier. In 1968, when Terrace went to pick up Abe/Bruno, his first chimp, he had done a brief tour of the place but had found no reason to return. Now he assumed that when Nim was sent back, he would have a decent quality of life as a breeder, hardly the worst circumstance for a captive chimpanzee. Terrace imagined Nim being surrounded by like-minded chimps, many of whom had also been born at IPS and placed as infants in human homes, where they had learned a modicum of ASL. This was certainly a reasonable expectation, given that home-raised chimpanzees such as Nim were the stock in trade at IPS. The members of this group, all under ten years old and relatively human-friendly, made ideal subjects for the student research projects that flourished there.

In fact, Nim would have an opportunity to participate in these projects and to become far more than a breeder at IPS — which was a good thing, as he was never particularly interested in mating. By 1977, both Lemmon and Roger Fouts, along with their graduate students, were conducting a wide range of research projects, and regardless of their scientific validity, they certainly exceeded Terrace's reductive view of what went on at IPS. In what was clearly original research, Lemmon was closely scrutinizing the behavior of his chimpanzees through his Freudian lens and conducting numerous experiments to determine which elements were hardwired in the chimp brain and which were not. At one point, Lemmon designed an experiment to see whether the incest taboo was operative between female chimpanzees and their male offspring — a study that, not surprisingly, did not attract any funding. In an article that was never published but was presented at a scholarly meeting, Lemmon presented his findings: that the incest taboo *was* operative between captive female chimps and their male offspring. He went on to design another experiment to explore the Oedipus complex in his colony, but there is no evidence that he ever completed that project.

One of Lemmon's best-known studies set out to demonstrate that female chimps had autonomous clitoral orgasms. Lemmon, like most people who spend time around female chimps, frequently observed them masturbating to climax — but there were no data to prove it. In 1977, the year Nim returned, Lemmon and Mel Allen, one of his graduate students, were documenting clitoral orgasms in a number of adult and adolescent females. At the time, conventional scientific wisdom held that male animals enjoyed climactic ejaculations but that nonhuman females were not orgasmic. To prove otherwise, Lemmon adopted many of the same criteria that William Masters and Virginia Johnson had used in their landmark study on human female sexuality. The results of Allen and Lemmon's unusual but authoritative research were published in the prestigious *American Journal of Primatology,* which included the outré details of their methodology. Allen manually masturbated the chimps until their orgasms could be observed and measured. Detailed tables that mapped secretions, heavy breathing, grins, spasms, and other physical manifestations of primate arousal accompanied the article.

Roger Fouts took exception to the majority of Lemmon's Freudian experiments and found them to be not only inappropriate but often inhumane. Fouts himself, along with his students, focused exclusively on ape language, continuing the work that the Gardners had begun in Reno, using IPS's home-reared chimps.

There were two kinds of students working with the Norman chimps: those who belonged to Lemmon and those who belonged to Fouts. (A handful of others did projects for other OU faculty members.) Lemmon interviewed and approved each student who set foot on IPS soil, even if he or she belonged to Fouts. All of them, by necessity, learned to handle the chimps before they began to do research on them.

Lemmon's students researched chimp behavior; Fouts's students did language research, often repeating versions of the Gardners' experiments. Although Lemmon had little academic interest at the time in language acquisition, he viewed Fouts's program as entertainment for his chimps, who wanted as much attention as they could possibly get. Fouts's students kept them busy, a necessity in captivity, where boredom is a killer. Slow days at the farm produced jailbreaks or violent fights with blood flowing through the cages. Lemmon's single most important employee, Dwight Russell, nicknamed "Tiny," who lived on the premises, sewed up their wounds on the spot with a needle and thread. (He often bribed the chimps with cigarettes if he needed to get into and out of a cage.)

Lemmon's students and Fouts's students were like two competing teams, although the students got along far better than their captains, who were usually at war over one thing or another. Lemmon owned and controlled all the chimps, but it was Fouts and his students who spent hands-on time with the adolescents, often took care of them, and came to know them well. Fouts matched his students to the chimps based on their profiles and temperaments in an effort to ensure that no one — chimp or human — got hurt. Once the students gained some confidence, they were allowed to put their favorite chimps on leashes and to take them out for long walks in the countryside, where the chimps climbed trees and filled their bellies with wild berries. Fouts knew that bonding with a chimp was a prerequisite for doing one-on-one sign language work or any other research that required close contact with a subject. It was also a remarkable experience, unlike anything these students had done before. Some of them found the chimps too frightening and quickly dropped out of the program. Others returned to see their chimps every day.

Nim, of course, had the potential to shine in Norman, doing further sign language work. As far as Terrace was concerned, none of this research would be of any value to Project Nim or to any other rigorous experiment. But Fouts's students, while they had no interest in impressing Terrace, were very eager to meet Nim and see him sign, and excited about the possibility of using him for their own projects. First, however, Nim would have to learn how to survive behind bars, which is where all IPS chimps lived.

From Lemmon's perspective, moving the chimpanzees back and forth between comfortable human homes and crowded cement cages filled with their own kind was just business as usual. From the perspective of Fouts, who had to work with these animals, it was a nightmare. As one of his students put it, "The chimps returned to Norman and all went crazy." Whatever happened to Nim, he would have to prove himself user-friendly before becoming eligible for any research project, and he would also have to overcome Fouts's apparent resistance to using a chimp who was a celebrity — and therefore real competition for Washoe, his own star chimp.

The sign language experiments took place outdoors during the warm weather, or in an enclosed playroom inside a building called the Pig Barn, where the adolescents (plus Fouts's Washoe) lived in several large, interconnected cages that could be cut off from each other when necessary. These chimps were the live wires of IPS, energetic, eager to interact with humans, and exciting to be around, and this was the group Nim was slated to join, as they were his peers. Students referred to the Pig Barn as the "Insane Asylum," because the young chimps were so often frenzied. One day when the chimps were particularly wild, it turned out that they had broken out of their cages and eaten the apples stored in dozens of barrels kept in the building. The apples, from Lemmon's orchards, had fermented. Shit-faced drunk, the chimps tore up the place, and each other, with great glee.

The older chimps, who lived in another building, had fewer visitors and were no longer involved in any of the language projects. Even if they had been around humans their whole lives, they were just too dangerous and unpredictable to be handled. Most students dreaded even entering the adult building, where the chimps spat and hurled anything within reach, especially bodily fluids. Lemmon, however, often walked through the building to check on them — Pan, Wendy, Carolyn, and many others — as they were his top breeders and therefore most valuable animals.

Despite all the apparent chaos, language training did get done at IPS. Visitors, as Emily Hahn observed in *The New Yorker,* might walk through the research facility and see chimps casually signing to each other in their cages. The signers included Bruno, Terrace's warm-up chimp, who had blazed a trail for Nim in New York. Terrace had declined Lemmon's offer to take Bruno back after he returned from his sabbatical, which had made the chimp, fourteen months old, a candidate for a second human adoption. Lemmon preferred to keep his chimps in human homes for as long as possible. He sent Bruno out again, this time to a childless family in Tulsa, Oklahoma, that had been waiting months for a chimp. Tulsa was relatively close to Norman; Lemmon, or one of his minions, could easily visit Bruno to check up on him.

Whether or not Bruno's first placement with Terrace was successful is debatable; the chimp made barely any impression on Terrace or LaFarge — or the shape of Project Nim. But Bruno's second placement was a definite disaster. After two days of clinging nonstop to his new mother, Bruno let go of her only long enough to tear up the family dogs, two fully grown St. Bernards who had been keeping a respectful distance from the chimp. A few days later, Bruno attacked a neighbor's cow. The dogs survived, but the cow did not. Bruno's frightened new parents, who were unable to cope with their chimp's aggressive behavior, returned him to the farm after three weeks.

When discipline problems arose in surrogate families, Lemmon tended to put the blame on the parents rather than the chimps. (Terrace did the same thing in New York to the LaFarges.) After Bruno returned to IPS, Lemmon installed him in a cage in his own living room so that he could observe his behavior closely. At the time, Lemmon was collecting data on the effect of different rearing situations on the early development of chimpanzees; Bruno was one of Lemmon's case studies. For whatever reasons, the chimp was perfectly well behaved in Lemmon's house. Visitors too found Bruno to be exceptionally gregarious and bright. He appeared to be a well-adjusted, normal juvenile male. Based on his personal observations, Lemmon could see no reason to pull Bruno from the cross-fostering project. A month later, he sent the genial chimp to his third home, with a couple in Los Angeles who owned a pet store and claimed to have raised an uncaged chimp for ten years. He had died, apparently from an illness, and they wanted a replacement. Lemmon felt that since these people had more experience with chimpanzees than many of his more naive adopters, they would be ideal parents.

After only a few days, however, Bruno developed chronic diarrhea and refused to eat or drink anything. Nor would he allow his new parents to touch him. In a letter to Lemmon, his worried foster mother observed, "He just curls up and turns his face to the wall." She was willing to give him more time in hopes that he would come around. But soon after the letter arrived, Lemmon received a panicked phone call. Bruno had become so ill that he had been rushed to an animal hospital. Lemmon agreed to take him back directly from the hospital as soon as he was well enough to travel. He dispatched his assistant, Jane Temerlin, along with his son, Peter, sixteen years old and with a brand-new driver's license, to Los Angeles to pick Bruno up. The trip to the hospital took them three days. On their way home, Peter took over the wheel and Jane held the listless chimp, swaddled in blankets. To get him to eat, she prechewed bites of food and fed him from her lips. Bruno survived, and Lemmon decided to keep him.

Bruno seemed to be more comfortable at IPS than anywhere else. By the time Fouts arrived in 1970, Bruno was almost three years old, still small, and reliably well behaved around people. Fouts began teaching Bruno ASL along with a selected group of other chimps. The chimps were taught in one-on-one sessions with as few distractions around them as possible. Often, Fouts rewarded the chimps with raisins when they signed, a small but welcome treat for most of them. At first, Bruno had no interest in the wrinkled little fruits or in taking classes with Fouts. But one afternoon, Fouts turned on his cattle prod as a warning. When the rod began to buzz, Bruno repeatedly slapped his head in an energetic effort to sign "hat." It seemed that Bruno responded better to sticks than carrots (or raisins, as the case may be).

During the warm weather, Bruno and his chums, who consisted of the other adolescents working with Fouts's students, lived on one of three man-made islands in the middle of a pond behind Lemmon's house. After his arrival, Nim too spent time on the island. (One of the other islands was reserved for Lemmon's gibbons and the third for his monkeys.) The islands were accessible by a small boat that carried animals and supplies back and forth. The chimps had eaten all the foliage, turning the place into a desert, with only an African-style hut, called a rondeval, for shade. But there were no cages, so the island was as good as it got for the Norman chimps, and they are standard today at the more spacious chimp sanctuaries. Appealing as the chimp island was in many respects, its inhabitants sometimes found themselves missing the companionship of humans. As a result, the islanders often plotted to get back to the mainland. Getting off the island became the challenge, as if the chimps were competing on *Survivor* to get home. Chimps hate getting wet and do not swim. But this did not deter them from stealing the boat and rowing back to shore. The only foolproof way for a human — often Peter Lemmon in the evenings — to deliver food and still maintain command of the boat was to row close to the island and throw supplies to the chimps without docking.

One time Bruno commandeered the boat and made it back to shore. He then wandered over to a neighbor's house to join their son's birthday party. No one discovered that the boat or Bruno was missing until Lemmon received a hysterical phone call from the boy's mother. He calmed her down, went over to the party, held out his hand to Bruno, and walked him home.

Like Bruno, Mae, Lucy, and Ally (Nim's full brother, and soon to be a close pal) were vanguard members of Lemmon's cross-fostering project, who also became participants in Fouts's early signing classes. Having been adopted by three of the psychologists in Lemmon's inner circle, Mae, Lucy, and Ally grew up in what appeared to be normal, middle-class homes, and they were often seen doing normal, middle-class human activities. The three chimps were well known in Norman for making appearances in grocery stores, on campus, and in various places where parents typically took their children — including church. But they were never allowed to meet each other during the years they lived in human homes, as Lemmon wanted them raised in species isolation.

All three chimps seemed to particularly enjoy the company of humans. However, Mae, who had been adopted by Vera Gatch, had little interest in learning to sign or working with Fouts. When he showed up for her private lessons, Mae often insisted on turning them into a tickle party, where Fouts tickled Mae and she, in turn, tickled Gatch's dogs. But Lemmon had plans for Mae beyond whatever she might contribute to Fouts's language research. When she matured, at around eight years old, he intended to artificially inseminate her — while maintaining her species isolation — and compare her maternal instincts and child-rearing style with those females in an IPS colony who had been raised by their natural mothers. Would Mae's chimpanzee instincts kick in? Or would she imitate Vera Gatch, who had raised her from infancy? Either way, Gatch was thrilled by the prospect of "grandchildren."

Sadly, she did not get them. In the winter of 1971, Gatch went to California for a conference, leaving her own mother to care for Mae. Gatch had never left her "daughter," almost seven years old, for more than a few hours. Perhaps Gatch left too soon, before Mae was emotionally ready. Perhaps Mae never would have been ready. After only a few days without Gatch, Mae slipped into a deep depression, which had a drastic effect on her immune system. She came down with a high fever that puzzled her pediatrician and veterinarian alike. Her condition quickly grew worse, and in a panic Gatch flew home. But it was too late. "She died in my arms at the stroke of 3:00 a.m.," recalls Gatch. "I was devastated. It was no different than losing a toddler." In retrospect, Lemmon surmised that female chimps, more so than males, suffer terribly from separation anxiety and feelings of abandonment when left by their human parents. He believed that male chimps reattached themselves more easily to another human caretaker. Gatch had to agree.

Lemmon was surprised when Gatch refused a second chimp. But she had no desire to repeat the trauma. Gatch was particularly disturbed by the condition of species isolation for the chimps and did not want to raise another infant chimp apart from others. She thought it possible that Mae might have survived in the company of another chimpanzee, especially one who had been raised by her side. But two chimps in the same home would have been antithetical to Lemmon's research, specifically to his goal of teasing out hardwired behaviors from learned ones.

Gatch may not have agreed with all of Lemmon's protocols or conclusions, but she continued to support him and his research. She remained part of Lemmon's inner circle and on occasion introduced her own students into the group. Just as Lemmon had mentored Gatch, Gatch was mentoring a student-patient protégée too — a young clinical social worker named Polly Murphy (this name has been changed) who was hoping to follow in her footsteps and adopt a chimp baby. Murphy was in the process of getting her master's degree in social work when she first met Mae and became fascinated by chimpanzees. Around the time of Mae's death, Ally, Nim's older brother, who was born in 1969, suddenly became available. Like Bruno, Ally had been shipped off to a human home when he was just a few months old. The feisty male wore out his welcome in less than a year, and when plans were made to bring him back to IPS, Lemmon agreed to pass him directly on to Murphy. Murphy had been in line for a female infant, but she could not turn down this rare opportunity.

Murphy was in her twenties. She was Gatch's student and patient, but she socialized with Bill and Dottie Lemmon and on weekends could often be found at the farm, hanging out on the island with Bruno and his buddy Booee, another signer. Lemmon didn't screen his surrogate parents too thoroughly, but he had watched Murphy frolic with his chimps and thought she would do fine with Ally. Had Lemmon realized that she had a fierce independent streak, not to mention serious religious convictions, he might have placed Ally in a different home. Murphy, however, was completely besotted with Ally and with her new status as a chimp mom and a participant in Lemmon's important research. She took Ally everywhere she went and began teaching him to sign right away. Like his brother Nim, Ally picked up ASL quickly. Murphy taught him to make the sign of the cross on his chest when she pointed to a photo of Jesus stuck to the door of her refrigerator. She even brought him with her to church on Sundays; "mother" and "son" sat with other parents and infants in a separate "cry room" where the baby noise did not disturb the rest of the congregation. Murphy was proud of her baby and wanted to show him off. When she surreptitiously gave other mothers a peek inside her bundle, however, they were horrified. And Lemmon, when he discovered that she was raising Ally as a Catholic, was not pleased.

Lemmon read all about Murphy's activities with Ally in her diary, which she had agreed to keep and turn over to IPS. But Lemmon didn't want to read about Murphy in the local newspapers — he'd already had enough controversy in his life — and, moreover, didn't want his chimps attending Mass. The idea that Murphy was teaching Ally the concept of God, or even going through the motions, offended Lemmon's faith in science as well as his respect for the Bible. Lemmon was hardly a religious person, but he considered the Bible to be a great work of literature and could quote lengthy passages from the Old Testament. He frequently gave his chimps biblical names. Ally was originally named Balem, and Lemmon gave others such names as Ishmael, Menachem, Uriah, Ezekiel, Cain, Able, Hosea, and Zephaniah. Although adopters usually renamed them, when the chimps returned to IPS their names often reverted back to the original ones. (Balem had been renamed Muhammad Ali in his first home; Murphy kept part of the name for the sake of continuity but changed the spelling to Ally to erase any political overtones.)

Lemmon confronted Murphy, accusing her of moral bankruptcy, if not idiocy, and suggested that she stop taking the chimp to church. Murphy argued with Lemmon, explaining that Ally's religious training was purely symbolic, more a performance than a spiritual quest. "Ally was innocent," she explains. "He didn't need redemption." Young and rebellious, Murphy continued to bring Ally to church. According to her diary, one time when she was holding him in her arms, one of the priests spotted the chimp running his hand through her hair and fondling her breast. Murphy registered the look of disapproval on the priest's face but did not restrain the chimp, despite the fact that the church was becoming more important to her. She proceeded to have Ally "baptized" in a private ceremony at her home with the help of a friendly priest.

Fouts tutored Ally in ASL at Murphy's home. Murphy felt an immediate attraction to the engaging professor, and one afternoon the language classes moved into her bedroom. Concerned that Lemmon might disapprove of the affair if he found out about it through others and remove Ally from her care, she confessed all to the IPS director. To her surprise, Lemmon showed little interest. Recalls Murphy, "Bill's attitude about [sex] was, 'Just please don't do it on my front porch. But if you do — I'll just walk around you.' Everyone was screwing everyone." Murphy's missionary zeal toward Ally bothered Lemmon much more than her affair with Fouts.

Murphy's diary, surprisingly detailed, made little of Ally's religious training and more of the physical relationship that developed between her and the chimp. As Ally matured and began to make sexual advances toward his surrogate mother, she was not inclined to stop him. Murphy describes his blossoming interest in her breasts, and his willingness to please her with the use of a vibrator. She considered their sexual relationship, whatever went on, to be part of the ongoing research project. Vera Gatch's mother, who by this time was quite familiar with the world of cross-fostered chimps, once came to visit and walked in on Murphy and Ally kissing, their tongues snaking through each other's mouths as if they were lovers. Mrs. Gatch warned Murphy that Ally was going to get larger and harder to control, which would make this activity quite dangerous; one bite and Murphy could lose her tongue. But Murphy was not deterred. Lemmon had allowed, even encouraged, a sexually charged atmosphere to flourish around his chimps. It was all grist for his Freudian mill. In the 1960s, the sexual revolution and the outré therapies that went along with it burned through American culture like so many wildfires. By the 1970s, they had even reached Norman. The parents of Lemmon's chimps were just keeping up with the guru, for whom sexual permissiveness, whether it involved humans or chimps, was de rigueur.

Permissiveness in certain other areas was not acceptable, however. No one crossed Lemmon without suffering the consequences. Murphy's refusal to bow to Lemmon's wishes concerning religion resulted in her excommunication from the inner circle (though Gatch remained close to her). She was too dangerous, too hard to control. In Murphy's own words, "I was a loose cannon." Fouts also cut Murphy off, ending their affair and concluding Ally's ASL lessons, which made Murphy furious. She felt that Ally, an especially able signer, was paying a price for her sins. Meanwhile, as Ally became older and bigger, he was becoming more difficult to control. One day Murphy returned from work to find that Ally had completely destroyed her house; the furniture was in pieces, the cabinets were off the walls, and the walls themselves were badly damaged. She moved to a larger place in the country, closer to IPS, and built the chimp a cage in her garage. Ally's days of being close to his "mother" were coming to an end. His best friend was now a dog, who stayed by his side and slept with him at night. But Murphy couldn't bathe him anymore. He soon became too dirty to come into her house — and far too unpredictable.

In 1973, Murphy became engaged and wanted to have some human children. She still loved the chimp but could no longer cope with him. She arranged for Ally to return to IPS. Murphy and Ally had a slow, wrenching separation. Fouts, as a favor to Murphy, brought Ally to the farm for several visits, slowly introducing him to other chimps, and then brought him back to her at night. She was convulsed in tears each evening when Ally returned. Consumed by guilt, Murphy wanted the process to move more quickly. After a few days, she instructed Fouts, against his advice, to leave Ally at IPS. Ally had a devastating reaction to his abandonment. He suffered a full-blown panic attack that resulted in hysterical paralysis of his right arm; he stopped eating, pulled out his hair, and withdrew from everyone around him. Fouts and several students spent as much time with him as they could, trying to pull him through the trauma. They held him, tried to feed him by hand, and kept him company. Two months later, after much tender loving care, Ally finally recovered. It is impossible to know whether Ally would have done any better had Murphy allowed Fouts to take more time. Suffice it to say that when Murphy went to visit Ally six months after that, he was playing with another chimp and totally ignored her. Murphy wept but considered his attitude to be a positive result. She never saw him again.

Of all the chimps in Lemmon's cross-fostering program, Lucy, Mae's half sister, who was being raised by Jane and Maurice Temerlin, was the most precocious. She would later become famous not for her precocity, however, but because she was the only IPS chimp who, having grown up in a human home, was eventually released into the jungle. Generally speaking, the only captive chimps who had experience of the wild

Ally on the chimp island with George Kimball, the graduate student who worked most closely with him

were those who had been born there. In an unusual reversal, Lucy made the opposite journey, as a consequence of the choice made by her surrogate parents.

Over the years, the Temerlin and Lemmon families had become closely entangled as they followed the same paths. Maurice Temerlin had become the number one supporter of Lemmon's unbridled chimpanzee research, while Jane Temerlin had put her own academic career on hold to help Lemmon run IPS. Like the LaFarges, the Temerlins believed in the revolutionary importance of the research they were doing, which in their case was intended to lead to revelations about the evolution of the human psyche. They took on the job of raising their chimpanzee with the utmost seriousness. Lucy was the Temerlins' second attempt at cross-fostering; their first chimp had died at a young age in an accident. Like Nim, Lucy was integrated into every aspect of family life. And as far as anyone could tell, Lucy Temerlin was thriving in Norman, where she was the poster child for "humanized" chimpanzees, the prototype for Lemmon's research project.

Visitors deluged the Temerlins' home. The press, "experts" of one stripe or another, and the merely curious all elbowed their way through their front door, often to be met by Lucy herself. In 1973, the same year Stephanie LaFarge picked up Nim, Lucy's unique circumstances had been featured in *Life, Psychology Today, Parade, Science Digest,* the *New York Times,* and *The New Yorker.* On her first day in Norman, before Nim was placed in her arms, LaFarge was taken to the Temerlins' home and introduced to the poster child, then eight years old. Lucy was proof positive that the task of raising a chimp in a human home could be done. Or so it seemed to LaFarge and to many others who toured Lucy's suburban habitat.

Four years old at the time Fouts arrived in Norman, Lucy, like Ally and Mae, was an excellent candidate for sign language training. Since Lucy was not allowed to mix with other chimps (per Lemmon's instructions), Fouts made house calls to the Temerlins, where the chimp dazzled him, not so much with her aptitude for language or her intelligence but with her lavish and thoroughly humanized lifestyle. Wrote Fouts, "The Temerlins embraced Lucy as their own flesh and blood to an extent that went significantly beyond the Gardners' more arm's length parenting of Washoe."

Maurice Temerlin's book, *Lucy: Growing Up Human,* published in 1975, proudly revealed the details of the chimp's soigné existence. Lucy's lifestyle in Norman had never been kept secret, and visitors — chimp people, friends, patients, and colleagues — were welcomed into the house to watch Lucy holding court. A typical evening in the Temerlin home, not unlike in the Lemmons', began with cocktails. Lucy preferred gin and tonics during the summer and switched over to whiskey sours in the winter. At dinner, a sit-down affair with the family, Lucy drank whatever the Temerlins drank, including expensive French wines. "She never gets obnoxious, even when smashed to the brink of unconsciousness," wrote Maurice, revealing more about the chimp's alcoholism than perhaps he intended. At one point, he tried to wean Lucy off the good stuff and onto Boone's Farm apple wine. Assuming she would delight in the fruity swill, he purchased a case and filled her glass one night at dinner. Lucy took a sip of the apple wine, noticed her parents were drinking something else, and put her glass down. She then grabbed Maurice's glass of Chablis and polished it off. She finished Jane's next. Not another sip of Boone's Farm ever touched her lips.

Not everyone was impressed with Lucy or the peculiar circumstances in which she was raised, and the holdouts included Temerlin's colleagues in the OU psychology department, who had already helped pressure him out of the chairmanship of the department as part of the cleanup that swept Lemmon off campus. Lucy's growing notoriety only made them nervous. Notoriety is for rock stars, not for the men and women of science — or their research subjects. Of course, Terrace had shamelessly brought in all kinds of press to meet Nim too, but Project Nim had academic clout —

a much-published professor presiding over it, Columbia University, grants — whereas Temerlin was out on a limb with no safety net beneath him.

If Temerlin thought his tenure would protect his faculty position at OU, he was mistaken. The university was just looking for the right moment to fire him, and as things turned out, an incident occurred the year before the book was published that sealed the psychologist's fate. In 1974, Temerlin shot a pig that had mistakenly wandered off a neighbor's farm. To add insult to injury, he took the pig to the butcher to be cut up into chops. The butcher recognized the pig and informed its owner, who got into a nasty dispute with Temerlin over the incident. When news of the murdered-pig controversy reached OU, Temerlin was summarily dismissed. The administration had no more patience for his "hunting accidents" than it did for his countercultural impulses or his intellectual flamboyance.

When Temerlin's book on Lucy did finally come out, it only confirmed the suspicions of the OU administrators and faculty that the psychologist had lost his grip. There were alarmingly graphic accounts of Lucy's sex life, which made his relationship with his "daughter" hard to accept as any form of serious research. His writing style, more kiss-and-tell than academic, read like a lurid diary, and the accompanying photographs must have made a lot of folks in Norman nervous. In one series, Lucy was sitting on the living room couch flipping through the pages of *Playgirl* magazine while masturbating. The text explained, while additional photos documented, that Lucy eventually moved from pornography and manual stimulation to the direct application of a vacuum hose, which she found more effective.

As he made clear in the book, Temerlin was as thrilled by her orgasms as if she were a toddler taking her first steps. Temerlin also described Lucy initiating sexual activities with him, which was easy to believe, given the notoriously pansexual nature of chimpanzees. "Lucy attempts to mouth my penis whenever she sees it, whether I am urinating, bathing or having an erection," he wrote, as if he were an observer rather than a participant. Temerlin professed to have no sexual feelings for Lucy and to see her interest in him as completely normal — by chimp standards. So when Lucy ran into the bathroom and "caught the stream of [his] urine in her open mouth," he explained, he tried to suppress his "Judaic Christian up-bringing" and let the chimp have her way. For Maurice, Lucy's apparent desire to mate with the dominant male in her house was entirely predictable. For whatever reason, he was unable to tell her to stop.

Even after he was fired and after his book was published, Temerlin still had his private practice. Yet as he continued to focus on Lucy with such intensity that even his patients began to wonder about his sanity, his practice began to dwindle too. At one point, Temerlin organized a series of Esalen-style weekend workshops at his home, where Lucy was free to join the group at any time. (He had visited Esalen several times during the 1970s to take workshops for psycho-therapists, including one on Gestalt therapy.) During the sessions, he referred to Lucy, with some, but probably not enough, humor, as his "co-therapist." She romped around the room, jumping on the partici-pants and frightening some of them as they sat in a circle on the floor. Like Lemmon, Temerlin was expert at making people as uncomfortable as possible in order to exploit every ounce of anxiety in the room, but unlike Lemmon, Temerlin was not charismatic enough to get them to put up with his more extreme behavior.

As Lucy increasingly took over Temerlin's life, Jane began spending more time at IPS, where her organizational skills as well as her natural ability with chimps were highly valued. In the early 1970s, as IPS continued to grow apace, she was just what Lemmon needed. According to Peter Lemmon, "In the old vernacular, Jane was my father's secretary. But she was much more than that. She basically ran the operation." She did so for almost a decade, during its most successful period, success at IPS being measured by the number of chimps born, the number of graduate students the program attracted, and the amount of press generated. By all those standards, IPS was doing well.

Inevitably, working as closely and companionably as they did, surrounded by the high drama of chimpanzees, Jane Temerlin and Bill Lemmon began to feel a mutual attraction, and soon Maurice found himself lacking not only a job but a wife — and without much of a practice either. Nor did he have a future at IPS. Fouts, whether he intended to or not, had supplanted Temerlin in the IPS pecking order, and Jane had replaced them both. If Temerlin had expected to take over IPS when Lemmon retired, he now realized it would never happen. He held Lemmon responsible for all his troubles. The rivalry between the two men — over work, women, and chimps — finally turned them into mortal enemies. Says J. R. Morris, OU provost at the time, who knew both men, "Maury went from being the chief enforcer of the Lemmon 'cult' to becoming Lemmon's chief adversary."

Lemmon's friends frequently became his enemies, suffocated as they were in his closed universe of psychologists, patients, students, and lovers, where all these roles tended to be interchangeable. As the group grew ever more incestuous, Jane became the central figure, holding the place together. She left Maurice and moved into Lemmon's house, while Lemmon's wife, Dottie, moved out, renting an apartment in town. Dottie had no illusions about the man she had married or his affairs. The Lemmon soap opera was public. There were no secrets in Norman.

Although the Lemmons divorced, Jane and Maurice remained married, despite their complex liaisons and personal problems, not the least of which was their growing chimp daughter. What was to become of Lucy? More than other adopters, the Temerlins understood that adolescent chimpanzees became dangerous roommates. But they were determined to meet the challenge of raising Lucy. As she grew older, they had built her a rooftop, caged apartment, hoping to be able to contain her there when they had to leave her alone. (This arrangement eventually worked, though at first Lucy managed to escape every day by stealing a key to her new condo, which she kept hidden under her tongue, until the Temerlins finally caught on.)

Through all the Sturm und Drang that turned every day at the farm into a drama, Maurice and Jane still loved Lucy like a daughter, and they feared that if anything were to happen to them, the chimp could easily end up in a zoo or a research lab. Maurice refused to give Lucy back to Lemmon, convinced that he might harm her, even kill her, in an act of revenge against his ex-protégé. The battle between Temerlin and Lemmon had become so bitter that even Jane did not want to give the chimp back to Lemmon. At her core, her loyalty was to Maurice, their son, Steven, and Lucy. Eventually, she came to her senses, returned to Maurice, and straightened out her own house.

Nim would never meet Lucy because in 1977, a few months before he returned to

Norman, the Temerlins, back together again, made the agonizing decision to send her to a small chimpanzee rehabilitation program in Africa. Jane Goodall compared it to sending a pampered American teenager to live with an Aboriginal family. Regardless of whether this was the right decision or not, at least it came from the heart. When faced with the choice of sentencing Lucy to life in a cage or allowing her to experience the jungle for however long she might survive, they chose the latter. The Temerlins did everything possible to prepare Lucy for what would be an extraordinary transition. They acquired a second chimp, named Marion, and introduced Lucy to her own species in the privacy of their home; the two chimps were sent to Africa together. They also hired Janis Carter, a devoted graduate student who was on her way to becoming an expert on the species, to accompany the chimps to Africa and remain with them as long as feasible.

In Africa, Lucy struggled through severe separation anxiety and at least one grave illness, ultimately becoming relatively self-sufficient in a controlled reserve where her progress could be monitored. But her example did not pave the way for other captive raised chimps to be returned to the wild. Lucy's life ended with a poacher's bullet; only her bones were left behind, stripped bare. Shortly afterward, in 1987, the Temerlins moved to Oregon, leaving Oklahoma in the dust behind them.

*Bill Tynan, Nim, and Herbert Terrace arriving in Okla-
homa*

CHAPTER 8
CAPTIVITY

Filled with anxiety about his decision to end Project Nim, Herbert Terrace arrived at IPS on September 25, 1977, with a groggy chimpanzee still under the influence of the tranquilizers that had knocked him out for the long flight to Oklahoma. If Terrace had expected the red carpet, he was going to be disappointed. Lemmon's attitude toward Terrace had changed over the past few years. Though Lemmon had once been under the spell of the Columbia professor's reputation and status, hoping to share some of the glory and wealth generated by Project Nim, the IPS director no longer had any illusions about what he might stand to gain from Terrace's work. He had generously given Terrace two free chimpanzees and plenty of advice on what to do with them. In exchange, Terrace had excluded him from Project Nim, never listing him as a consultant on grants, a common courtesy between colleagues. After years of corresponding, as well as several face-to-face encounters, Lemmon had accurately concluded that Terrace had little interest in his research and even less in helping IPS, whether Nim was in residence or not.

Refusing to do the honors himself, Lemmon delegated the job of welcoming Nim — and Terrace — to Fouts. Fouts may have been curious to meet Nim, but he had also heard, and spread, rumors that the chimp was far too dangerous for much human interaction. Nim's reputation as a biter had preceded him in Norman. If Terrace had mistreated Nim — and Fouts believed this to be the case — he might not even be viable for more language work, however talented he was. Fouts may have had other reasons to be nervous about Nim, for Nim's reputation as an enthusiastic signer had also preceded him. If he became a star in Norman, it might be Terrace, not Fouts, who got the credit. Project Nim was making a big splash in New York, which could potentially drown out any acclaim for current experiments by Fouts and the Gardners. By some accounts, Fouts's animosity toward Terrace — a Harvard intellectual who entered the field with the expectation of dominating it — had already spilled over onto Nim before his arrival in Norman. "Roger warned us all about Nim," says Roger Mellgren, a psychologist who had joined the OU faculty in 1970 and taken an interest in Norman's signing chimps. "We expected Nim to be a real pain in the ass."

Still, Fouts knew Terrace would need all the help he could get just maneuvering Nim into a cage for the first time. It would be best for everyone involved, including Fouts, if this event went as smoothly as possible. Perhaps Fouts felt a modicum of sympathy for Terrace as he dropped off his chimp. Seven years earlier, when Fouts and Washoe first arrived in Norman, they had faced the same difficult moment. Fouts had wanted to go slowly with Washoe and protect her from the other chimps. But after a week, Lemmon moved in and took over the introductions, letting a male chimp into Washoe's cage when Fouts wasn't around.

While Lemmon "humanized" his chimps as early as possible and insisted they be raised in species isolation, he failed to empathize with their human-like traumas when they returned to Norman as adolescents or adults. He had no interest in dragging out the process of integrating them into the colony, regardless of the danger they might face. He pushed the new chimps hard, often placed them in risky proximity to each other, and was dismissive of critics who found his methods inhumane or cruel. Livid that Lemmon had interfered with Washoe, whom he considered to be his chimp, Fouts had the depressing realization that he had little authority at IPS. Moreover, Lemmon, as was often the case, had sized up Washoe correctly. She was perfectly able to fend off the attentions of other chimpanzees and did just fine. It was Fouts himself who needed to toughen up if he was going to survive daily interactions with Lemmon.

Despite his tangled relationship with Lemmon and his competitive feelings toward Terrace, Fouts cleared students and wanna-be chimpers off the farm in an effort to create a calm atmosphere in anticipation of Nim's arrival. He carefully selected Mac as the one chimp to whom Nim would be introduced before he was thrown into a cage with the rest of his peers. At the time of Nim's return, there was a fluid population of approximately fourteen chimps under the age of ten who were housed in the Pig Barn. A group of ten or more adults, including Carolyn and Pan, was living in the addition that was attached to Lemmon's house. Though Nim would be allowed a few days in a cage by himself, no chimp at IPS enjoyed that luxury for very long, and the faster new chimps made the transition to life behind bars with their fellow inmates, the faster they would move up the social scale. The Norman chimps functioned like a gang: new chimps entered at the bottom of the ladder and had to earn the right to move up, rung by rung. The chimps observed one another closely, judging one another's strengths, weaknesses, and sexual prowess. As Jane Goodall once said, if chimps had knives and other weapons along with the knowledge to use them, they would. At IPS, their handlers knew this and armed themselves with a variety of guns and prods.

When Terrace and Nim finally drove up to the fading pink house at IPS, it was late enough that all the chimps had fallen quiet. Terrace hoped to put Nim to bed somewhere safe before he woke up and began to see where he was and what was going on around him. If Nim felt threatened and became upset, it could take hours to calm him down, and after a sleepless night, he would be even more edgy the following day, an eventuality Terrace dreaded. Lemmon had left clear instructions for Terrace to put Nim into an empty cage, close the door, and walk away. He was to remove any remnants from his prior life, such as his favorite blanket or any clothes. If Nim was going to fall apart — and returning chimps, especially those raised in species isolation, inevitably did fall apart — Lemmon wanted it to happen quickly, so the IPS staff could start putting pieces of the chimp's life back together again. The students and staffers were accustomed, sadly, to watching the new chimps suffer, and did what they could to offer some consolation. Each chimp responded differently, but all of them took the initial shock hard. The question was not whether Nim would be traumatized but how long it would take for him to come around and how the other chimps would respond to him.

Once Terrace heard about Lemmon's plan for Nim's first night, he rejected it out of hand. He feared it might set Nim off like an alarm, ultimately making him more upset than necessary. The pampered chimp had never felt the cold hard surface of cement beneath him nor been left alone his first night in a new place. Terrace believed that when Nim opened his eyes in the morning, his first glance would be formative, establishing the chimp's attitude toward his new home. At the very least, he insisted on staying with Nim throughout his first night at

IPS. He wanted to be there when Nim woke in the morning.

Fouts must have felt some genuine concern for Nim, as even before Terrace arrived, Fouts had decided to ignore Lemmon's instructions and had set up a mattress on the floor of the Pig Barn, tucked into a hidden alcove, where Terrace and Nim could spend the night huddled together, outside a cage. Once Terrace arrived, Fouts also took the trouble to warn him to get Nim out of the barn early in the morning, before the other residents, all adolescents with the exception of Washoe, began their earsplitting shrieks for breakfast, a sound so disturbing that it might set Nim back for weeks. Fouts had witnessed several returning home-reared chimps, including Ally and Onan, Nim's older brothers, become terrified by the cries of the other animals. It would be far better for Nim if Fouts and Terrace worked together to ease the new boy into the scene, introducing him to Mac in the morning. The plan made sense to Terrace. He was grateful to have any place at all where he could stay with Nim. Now they just had to get through the night.

As the first light crept into the barn the following morning, Nim continued to sleep soundly, while Terrace, already wide awake, worried about the next twenty-four hours. So far, none of the other chimps appeared to have noticed them. Washoe herself slept right across a hallway from them in her cage, completely unaware of the campers nearby. (Fouts had convinced Lemmon to allow Washoe to live with the younger chimps, despite her age and size, as a protective measure for her. Unhappy as he was about giving Washoe any privileges, Lemmon had finally relented.) In the morning, as the chimp house began to come alive with hoots and calls for breakfast, Terrace watched Nim open his eyes. He gently picked him up and carried him outdoors, pleased that Nim had slept through his first night without incident.

Terrace tethered Nim to him on a loose ten-foot lead. They sat down under a cottonwood tree, where together they listened to the escalating commotion in the chimp barn just a short distance away. Nim's lead allowed him to move toward the sound at will and even peek into the building. Curious, but not too curious, he remained close to Terrace. The psychologist thought that Nim had caught Washoe's eye as they walked out of the building. Certainly, Nim must have known there were other creatures in the barn, but he may not have realized they were creatures just like him. Regardless, he appeared to be more interested than over-whelmed or scared by the crescendo of high-pitched shrieks. This seemed to bode well.

Joyce Butler and Bill Tynan had both insisted on accompanying Nim to Okla-homa, whether Terrace wanted them around or not. It is likely that he did not. But no one could have stopped Butler from remain-ing at Nim's side to help him face this sud-den, radical dislocation in his life. She had never let anyone take the chimp on even an overnight without her. From her perspec-tive, Nim needed her more than he needed Terrace. But Tynan and Butler had not been invited to IPS on Nim's first night, so they had to wait until the following morning to show up. They had spent the night in town with Charity O'Neil (now Charity Rowland), one of Fouts's graduate students. O'Neil had been working with several chimps — Vanessa, Jezebel, Kelly, Mac — on language training with moderate success. Though she did not believe that chimps needed, for any reason, to learn ASL, O'Neil fully understood the emotional at-tachments that could develop between humans and chimps. She tried to reassure her visitors that Nim would survive the transition. But Butler and Tynan were inconsolable. "They could hardly speak," recalls Rowland. They were dreading the moment when Nim would be caged and they would have to walk out the door and leave him behind. Butler had broken what Fouts would later describe as the first commandment of the behavioral sciences: "Thou shalt not love thy research subject."

That first morning, Butler and Tynan arrived at the farm with a picnic breakfast of cereal, yogurt, fresh fruit, and juices. Nim, still tethered to Terrace, greeted them with his usual exuberance. Surrounded by his friends, munching on his favorite foods, Nim was in high spirits, but Butler worried that this breakfast might be his last familiar meal. Terrace, on the other hand, felt a glimmer of optimism. The following day, a camera crew from the Children's Television Workshop was scheduled to arrive from New York to film Nim's first encounter with a member of his own species. Never one to miss a photo op, Terrace hoped Nim would make a speedy transition and, if things went really well, sign to the other chimp while the cameras were rolling. Terrace wanted to construct a happy ending, one that would please the young audience of *Sesame Street* — and himself.

Butler and Tynan had never been inside a primate research facility. They were shaken by what they saw, but they worked hard to conceal their fears from Nim. Planning to stay in Oklahoma for as long as Nim needed them, they had imagined Nim in an environment where he would be mostly uncaged, receive lots of human attention, and be slowly integrated into the colony over a period of months. But the stench of IPS and the cages full of chimps hit them hard. Nim was headed for a devastating trauma — and there was nothing they could do to prevent it. Sitting in the sun as the gibbons sang and the chimps hooted in the distance, they tried to relax, knowing that would keep Nim relaxed. They kept Nim close as they spotted Fouts, tethered to another chimpanzee, approaching slowly.

McCarthy, "Mac" for short, was small and mild-mannered. Like every chimp in Norman, he had a poignant backstory. Born somewhere in West Africa in 1971, he had been orphaned in the jungle and had fallen into the hands of an American woman working for CARE in Liberia, who bottle-fed him for more than a year. But then she became engaged to a man who was unwilling to share his bride with a clingy chimpanzee and she had to figure out what to do with Mac, who she knew would never be able to survive in the jungle. "McCarthy is a very hard child to give up and I love him like a baby," she wrote to Lemmon, hoping he might agree to take the chimp and find him a new human family. Because news of Lemmon's unique colony of home-reared chimpanzees had traveled around the globe, he frequently received such letters from surrogate parents who were desperate, for one reason or another, to place their infant chimps in Norman. The fantasy, shared by many "mothers" who gave Lemmon their chimps, included a happily-ever-after ending.

In April 1973, Mac arrived in Oklahoma packed inside a small cargo crate. He was sixteen months old, deathly ill, and visibly traumatized by what must have been a terrifying journey alone. (At the time, some dealers insisted on shipping chimps in twos so they could comfort each other; otherwise, they frequently died in transport.) Having agreed to find Mac another human home, Lemmon nursed him back to health for two months and subsequently placed the young, personable chimp with a couple in Wichita, Kansas, who had read about Lemmon's chimp adoption experiments in *Life* magazine. Psychology students themselves, they

Mac at IPS

were eager to help Lemmon with his research by taking notes on Mac's development. They had already completed a class in ASL and were ready to teach the chimp to sign. But like so many others, they soon learned to their dismay that raising a chimpanzee is not like raising a child. In Kansas, Mac's student-parents found him disobedient, frequently sick, picky about food, and too rough with people. "Can chimps be taught to treat people more gently?" they plaintively asked Lemmon in a letter that included a long list of other questions. Overwhelmed, they returned Mac in less than a year, albeit with a small vocabulary of signs and detailed notes on his progress.

Mac had been twice abandoned by humans, which Lemmon felt was sufficient. There would be no more adoptions. Over the next few years, the resilient young chimp settled into a social group in Norman and learned to live with his own species. Lemmon lent him out only one more time, to a colleague in Oklahoma for a short behavioral study, but Mac came home sick and was diagnosed as malnourished. Apparently, he had refused to eat monkey chow, the staple diet in most facilities, but not at IPS, where meals were not only nutritious but homemade and apparently tasty. Unlike Nim's relatives Ally and Onan, who were among the more dominant males in the colony, Mac got along with both humans and chimps. Fouts knew that Mac would attempt to make friends with Nim rather than challenge him.

At their first sight of each other, Nim froze while Mac began jumping up and down, hooting with excitement, a polite invitation to play. Not feeling the least bit social, Nim leapt behind Terrace. Undeterred, Mac continued to approach; when he got too close for comfort, Nim struck out at him with his arm. The psychologists introduced some games, hoping the chimps might engage in parallel play. But Nim would have none of it. Repeated efforts failed completely, and after a few hours Terrace and Fouts agreed to take a break and try again later in the afternoon.

Trying to keep him in a positive frame of mind, Tynan and Butler went off with Nim to explore the grounds during the break. They too were a little frightened by the other chimps, but they liked Fouts, largely because he was so much better with chimps than Terrace. They hoped that Fouts might actually look after their much-loved boy and give him some special attention.

The next meeting, a few hours later, did not go any better. Terrace tickled and cajoled Nim and bribed him with candy in hopes he would interact with Mac. But Nim wasn't interested. He maintained a physical distance from Mac, and there was nothing any of them could do to bridge it. At the end of a long, tense day, Nim was facing his first night in a cage.

Lemmon had assigned Nim to one of the four larger cages in the adolescent barn. These cages often housed three or four chimps, but Lemmon agreed to allow Nim

315

to have the space to himself for the first few days. Washoe, Mac, Onan, Ally, Vanessa, Kelly, and several other juveniles would be in the cages around him, Mac the only familiar face among them. But getting Nim to go into any cage for the first time would require enormous patience — and a plan. Terrace refused to just pick the chimp up, throw him into the cage, and try to lock the door before Nim realized what was going on. He wanted Nim to enter his cage by himself, hoping to avoid a tantrum later. First, however, he had to get Nim to walk into the building, something Nim did not want to do. Terrace kept the lead as loose as possible and casually walked inside the barn, but as soon as Nim's feet touched the cold cement floor, he ran back outside, as far as his lead would allow. The pattern was repeated over and over. Had Lemmon been watching this routine, he would have scoffed at Terrace's subterfuges.

Then Terrace asked Tynan to go into the cage and play for a while, pretending that he was enjoying himself. Reluctantly, Tynan agreed. He went in and began swinging from the ceiling and jumping up and down, making lots of noise, as if he were a chimp. Nim ran into the cage to be with his buddy. Tynan sat with him for a few minutes and then, as soon as Nim was distracted, zipped out the door, which Terrace slammed closed and locked. A second later, Nim went ballistic, screaming and bouncing off the walls of his cage. Tynan walked out of the building weeping. He felt as though he had betrayed Nim. The terrible feeling he had at that moment remains with him still.

That night, in a fit of rage, Nim tore the cap off an exposed water pipe on the ceiling of his cage. The cap had been in place for more than ten years, despite the efforts of countless other chimps to remove it. A torrent of water poured out the open end of the pipe, while the chimps shrieked and hooted in terror. The commotion woke up Lemmon. Fuming, he ran to find his ever-reliable employee Tiny, known to be a mechanical genius, and the two of them managed to cap the pipe. Lemmon went back to his house and called Terrace, waking him up to complain about the incident. Terrace, upset by the call, offered to drive right over to the farm and help. Lemmon refused the offer; he was going to bed. He just wanted to rattle Terrace and make sure he lost some sleep.

Terrace called Butler and Tynan in the morning and told them the news. Worried about Nim, they rushed over to the farm.

When they arrived, the CTW crew was already setting up video equipment. The sight of cameras infuriated Butler. And even Terrace, distressed by Nim's destructive behavior during the night, suggested that the crew pack up their cameras and come back in a few weeks when Nim might be more settled. But there was no denying CTW, especially when the crew had flown halfway across the country. They set up in a field and waited for Nim and Mac.

Terrace found Nim sleeping in his cage. When he opened his eyes, he greeted Terrace affectionately, the anger and distress of the previous evening apparently forgotten, at least for the moment. Eager to get Nim out of his cage, Terrace opened the door and took him out into the sunlight where his friends, and another human breakfast, were waiting. Nim could see the camera crew milling around but, given the general strangeness of his new surroundings, it did not seem to bother him. Mac and Fouts were there as well. As the cameras rolled, the chimps approached each other warily, while their respective handlers cheered them on as if they were watching a tennis match. Terrace maneuvered Nim so that he accidentally bumped into Mac, touching him for the first time. Suddenly, the two chimps began to tumble with each other the way only chimps can, as if they had known each other their whole lives. It was a milestone, caught on film. With some coaxing, Nim and Mac even signed a few words to each other, to everyone's delight.

Terrace left that evening for New York. He had obviously not spent enough time at IPS to acclimate Nim, but he had seen enough to reassure himself that Nim would survive. Tynan and Butler knew they had to leave soon too; it was crucial that Nim make a complete break with his past. But, less convinced than Terrace of Nim's resilience, they decided to remain one more day. The following morning, Butler and Tynan fed Nim breakfast, as they had done before, and took him for one last walk. Nim seemed to be in better shape than they were. Tense and miserable, they wanted to make the break quickly and cleanly, but when it came time for them to leave, Nim leapt into Butler's arms and refused to let her go, as if he knew exactly what was about to transpire. Tynan tried to peel Nim off her body and entice him away with treats. Nothing was working. Nim clung to Butler as if he were an infant. Then Lemmon, never the sentimentalist, appeared out of nowhere with a cattle prod and removed Nim from Butler's arms in milliseconds. He only had to use the prod once.

Butler and Tynan drove away heartsick, leaving Nim in Fouts's arms. They didn't want to see any more.

Bob Ingersoll and Nim at IPS

CHAPTER 9
BECOMING A NORMAN CHIMP

Robert Ingersoll arrived at IPS a few hours before Butler and Tynan parted with Nim, just in time to watch the chimp nestling in their arms, signing with them, and tenderly reciprocating their affections. Contrary to his advance press, Nim struck Ingersoll as a sweetheart. He looked as though he would be fun to be around and still small enough to manage physically. Most surprising to Ingersoll, his signs were fluid and natural, in contrast to those of the other Norman chimps, including Washoe. He instantly decided he wanted to get to know Nim.

Ingersoll was one of a handful of undergraduates in the psychology department who were allowed to study chimpanzees with Fouts. Fouts's chimp program at IPS was primarily for graduate students, but Ingersoll and a few others who were passionate about chimps had managed to slip into the group. For Ingersoll this was a life-altering opportunity. A Vietnam-era veteran, Ingersoll was stationed in Miami when he was run over by a drunk driver, hospitalized for seven months, and then discharged. He was happy to be alive — but lost. He was married to Gail Williams, who had also been in the military, and who had brought him back to live in Norman, her hometown, where they both enrolled in college on the GI Bill. Never particularly engaged by any of his studies, Ingersoll wore his hair long, smoked a lot of pot (like everyone else he knew), and had little ambition. His salvation — until he met up with the chimps at IPS — was the Grateful Dead. He still recalls the day his interest in chimpanzees began, two years before he first met Nim. It happened quite by accident, in 1975, when, at loose ends, he ambled into Fouts's classroom and heard him give a lecture about his work. Fouts showed some footage of young chimps signing with him — chimps who were living on a farm located right in Norman — and told stories about them while imitating their sounds and movements, much to everyone's amusement. Ingersoll was riveted. He wanted to meet the chimps in the flesh and sign with them, just as Fouts was doing. Ingersoll believed he had found a mentor — and a subject meaningful enough to hold his attention.

Ingersoll is not the kind of person who dips his toe in the water before diving in. He is passionate, often angry about a multitude of injustices in the world, and rarely without strong opinions. An Irish working-class kid from Boston, he is devoted to the Red Sox and occasionally travels all the way across the country for a game. His devotion to primates runs even deeper. On that morning as he sat in Fouts's class, something clicked inside his head. It felt almost like a physical sensation. Only hours later, he declared himself a psychology major, and Fouts sent his new recruit to get a TB test, mandatory before setting foot on IPS soil. (This was to protect the chimps, who are particularly susceptible to the disease.) A few days later, Ingersoll and his wife, also eager to meet the amazing chimpanzees, drove out to the farm.

Immediately upon getting out of their car, Ingersoll and Williams were accosted by Vanessa, a young, gregarious chimp out for a stroll with Gary Shapiro, a graduate student working with Fouts. Home-fostered, like most returning juveniles at IPS, Vanessa had been born in Africa and purchased through a dealer, Safari Imports, by a couple in Waco, Texas, who raised her as their daughter for almost one year before filing for divorce and giving the chimp to Lemmon. She had grown up taking bubble baths and swigging Dr Pepper. At the farm, she bonded with Mac and picked up sign language from him so readily that Lemmon wrote to Vanessa's foster parents to inquire whether they had taught her any ASL. They had not.

Vanessa greeted the newcomers with classic chimp enthusiasm. She grabbed Williams's purse, rummaged through it, and then leapt into her arms, trying to open all the buttons on her blouse. Ingersoll, captivated, rescued his astonished wife and took her home. She never spent much time at the farm after that (they were divorced a few years later), but Ingersoll could not keep away. For whatever reasons, he found himself in these primates.

Fouts used to tell students, "You either have an instinct for chimps or not." He and Ingersoll both had it. Most people were terrified of chimps when they came into close contact with them, but Ingersoll enjoyed their company. Soon acknowledged as one of the more proficient handlers, he was among the few undergraduates who managed to get Lemmon's blessing and become part of the fabric at IPS. As Ingersoll handled the chimps for graduate students during their experiments, he became interested in pursuing his own advanced degree and gaining the clout that went with it. Within months, he was spending so much time at the farm that he knew all the chimps by name and they in turn knew his. One afternoon Washoe used ASL to ask him his name. Then she made up a sign for Bob: the index and middle fingers rubbed along the right eyebrow. Ingersoll liked it and taught the younger chimps to sign his name the same way. He was gruff and dominant with the chimps, which he felt he needed to be to compensate for his short stature. (Large men, such as Tiny and Lemmon, tended to have more immediate command over the chimps.) But he also felt a genuine affection for them.

There was a constant turnover of students at IPS. Some left almost immediately because they were appalled by the noise, smell, danger, or stereotypical signs of depression (rocking, self-mutilation) that some of the chimps displayed. But Ingersoll thrived in the chaos and drama that surrounded the animals. He had found not only an intellectual focus for his studies but a social life. Fouts's students, the "chimpers," hung out together, partying into the night with their professor. They smoked dope, emptied kegs of beer, and spent hours talking about the chimpanzees. Like many of his fellow students, Ingersoll became enthralled by Fouts's notion that the chimps were highly intelligent animals who deserved our respect, and that by teaching them to communicate with us in a common language,

IPS graduate students and chimps during the early 1970s. Bottom row: Rick Budd (holding Kelly in place), Charity Rowland (with Vanessa), Gary Shapiro, Tom Dickey, Janis Carter (Mac in lap), Unknown, Diana Davis (holding Jezebel), and Marci, current head chimp keeper. Standing: Unknown, Jeanne Roush, Mel Allen, Unknown, Richard Forney (Onan on shoulders), Janette Wallis, Pete Burch. ("Joe" sign is a stand-in for Joe Couch.)

the chimpers would have the opportunity to break through the usual species barrier between humans and animals. Fouts and Washoe had transcended the objectifying relationship between scientist and research animal, and the students were expected to do the same as they forged personal relationships with the Norman chimps. No one, including Fouts, had any idea what chimpanzees were really capable of doing or thinking. But Fouts was on a mission to find out. Ingersoll bought in to Fouts's every word and was eager to sign on. It all made sense to him, and like most of the others on Fouts's team, he was convinced it was groundbreaking research.

Ingersoll had been at IPS for a year when Nim returned to Norman. Despite Fouts's warning to stay away from Nim, he couldn't wait to see him up close. All the students had read up on Project Nim, mostly through articles in the popular press, and understood the chimp's potential to raise the bar for the entire field. A few of them, including Ingersoll, had watched Nim with Butler and Tynan, slurping up yogurt and behaving like an angel. "Nim still had his baby teeth," says Ingersoll. "He was hardly a menace." As Falitz knew, those teeth could inflict quite a lot of damage, but Ingersoll, like most of the OU students in Fouts's language study projects, had far more expertise in handling chimps than any members of the Project Nim team, and the celebrity who had landed in their midst would present them with no challenges they hadn't previously encountered.

Nim's age and diminutive size automatically made him eligible for the best IPS had to offer — human companionship, walks through the woods, outings on the chimp island during warm weather, and a place in Fouts's language program. But he would have to become acclimated to IPS before Ingersoll or anyone else could introduce him to these activities. Nim's first days alone, without the comfort of Butler, Tynan, or Terrace, did not go well. Cringing in the back of his cage, he became severely depressed and refused to eat. Alyse Moore, one of Lemmon's employees, made sure he did not starve. She fed him by hand, introducing him to monkey chow (considered a snack food at IPS) and the Radcliffe diet (homemade loaves of meat, grains, and vegetables). The food was healthy but a far cry from pizza and soufflés. At least as distressing as the new dietary regimen was being in a cage with other chimps; he had no idea how to respond to them. Though he had played briefly with Mac out on the grass, the hierarchical world inside the cage was intense and frightening for a newcomer, and Nim did not yet know how to negotiate for a position. When the other chimps reached out with their hands in a normal greeting, Nim bit them. (He also bit Moore, who, according to a graduate student to whom she described the incident, severely whipped him with a prod; he never bit Moore again.) Having never spent any time with other chimps, Nim failed to understand their vocalizations, and when they struck him, instead of fighting back, he became upset and lapsed into passivity. Onan, Nim's full brother, was his first friend — and protector. Caged together with a few others, they became inseparable, as Nim gradually learned to communicate with his fellow chimpanzees.

Onan had had his own rocky initiation into chimp communal life the year before, after the four years he had spent living in a human family. Lemmon had handed Onan off when he was thirteen days old to a wealthy couple in California who had a big house, no children, and a large swimming pool. When they sent him back to IPS, Onan immediately sank into a terrible depression and nearly died. His savior was a

Bob Ingersoll with Nim and Onan, dressed for cold weather

new graduate student named Richard Budd, known as Rick, who arrived at OU around the same time that Onan did, in 1976, to pursue a master's degree in experimental psychology. Budd wanted to work with Fouts and his famous signing chimpanzees. On Budd's first day in Norman, Fouts drove his new recruit out to the farm and introduced him to Onan. Budd was shocked by the chimp's emaciated, miserable condition. Onan had not been back for long, but he had already pulled all the hair off his arms and legs, and he wasn't eating enough to stay alive. Onan, like Nim, had worn clothes, consumed a human diet, and never met another chimpanzee. Fouts assigned the chimp to Budd, hoping that his new, enthusiastic student would help Onan get through his emotional trauma. Budd had one month before his classes began, and he took the assignment seriously: he went to the farm every day and spent about six hours at a time with Onan, taking him on long walks and letting him climb trees. Still small enough to be cuddled and held, Onan got the affection he needed from Budd. The two became close, and Onan began to cheer up and accept the conditions of his confinement. Budd gave the chimp a routine — and a decent life for a young chimp in captivity.

After several months, Onan's hair began to grow back and he started to interact with other chimps, even taking part in sign language work. Budd began an experiment to see if a chimp could learn to sign from images of objects, rather than from the actual objects. Apparently, Onan learned more quickly from pictures. Budd used his work with the chimp for his thesis. (The acknowledgment page refers to Onan as his "chimpanzee son.")

Unlike Onan, Nim never pulled out his hair or became dangerously ill after his return to IPS; according to Ingersoll, Nim also never took any savage beatings from other males, who greeted some newcomers with brutality to make the pecking order clear. After about two months, he started to come to the bars at the front of his cage when approached by people. He frequently signed to them, asking to go out or for a drink — anything to get their attention. Students, handlers, and even Fouts noticed Nim's unusual ability to communicate.

Contrary to Fouts's warning, the sophisticated New Yorker was no more difficult to handle than any of the younger chimps. They would soon learn that Nim was a rascal and knew how to get around people, but he certainly didn't pose the kind of danger Fouts had led them to expect. Ingersoll feels that Fouts's negativity toward Nim had little to do with the chimp: "Roger saw Nim as competition for Washoe. That was his main concern and it colored his attitude toward Nim." Fouts may have turned his students against Terrace, whom he considered a Skinner clone who had wandered into the wrong field, but he couldn't control their feelings about Nim. Captivated by Nim's overt charm and his skillful, relaxed use of signing vocabulary, the students couldn't wait for the opportunity to use him in their sign language experiments. Washoe had a large vocabulary, but no one took her out of the cage unless Fouts was present; she was older, more difficult, and too valuable. (Even Fouts worried about taking her out after he hadn't done so for long periods of time, fearing that he would not be able to manage her.) Nim was available, begging for attention — and famous. He was also well versed in the activities that the students themselves enjoyed: he smoked cigarettes, requested joints, and chugged beer. He signed constantly to get what he wanted and learned rules quickly. Mellgren recalls that it didn't take Nim long to become a regular IPS chimp — "a real Okie."

Having overcome the trauma of his transition to IPS much more readily than Onan and a number of the other chimps, Nim, not shy, promptly revealed his talents. Ingersoll, like others, began using ASL with Nim. "We had never seen anything like Nim," he says. "He spoke for himself." The other chimps responded when asked to sign and were often rewarded when they did. Nim initiated conversations. He signed spontaneously to students to attract their attention. Ingersoll did not start out collecting data on Nim with any rigor, but the atmosphere encouraged him to take the possibility of his own degree more seriously. Fouts may have had little interest in having

Terrace's chimp excel in Norman, but Ingersoll didn't have the same axes to grind as his professor. Moreover, he developed a genuine closeness with Nim.

Whether he liked it or not, Nim came to understand that, at the end of the day, he lived in a cage. Mac and Onan were in the same cage with him, along with an easygoing female named Lilly (brought to IPS by Alyse Moore), who spent much of her time on the outside socializing with students. Nim was not an avid breeder, but he and Lilly would have one offspring together, a female named Sheba, born in 1981. (Lemmon sold Sheba, when she was still an infant, to the Columbus Zoo.) Washoe, Ally, and a fluctuating group of other adolescents lived in the same building, in separate cages, a few of which could be opened and linked together. Many of these chimps had learned a modicum of sign language in their adoptive homes and subsequently from Fouts. So Nim found himself surrounded by signing chimps and by students who were generating a multitude of language experiments.

The ape language program had become part of the OU psychology department with Fouts's arrival in 1970. Over the next decade, Fouts won the esteem of his colleagues. His classes were packed with graduate students from around the country, and his own research had the potential to attract substantial grants. Fouts also excelled at teaching students how to be around the chimps and manage them sufficiently well to conduct research projects with them — not a simple task. The rare opportunity to work closely with these compelling animals was an inducement for graduate students to choose OU. The program promised genuine excitement in the form of cutting-edge research, meaningful results, and access to the unknown world of interspecies communication. And Fouts, the charming ambassador for the chimps, was a magnet for new students. The psychology department backed the ape language curriculum with genuine enthusiasm as they watched their new professor's popularity grow.

Fouts did not demand much academic rigor from undergraduates. He encouraged them to spend as much time as possible with the chimps, gave them credit for merely clocking hours at IPS, and had them design their own experiments. As a result, some of the wackiest projects ever executed in the name of ape language research were done for Fouts's classes. One of the most inventive was the first one designed expressly for Nim. The project was rooted in Fouts's philosophy about chimps, which his more ardent students had fully embraced. In Fouts's words: "Most scientists tend to think of chimps as large white rats to be experimented on. We look at them more as colleagues." Robert Ingersoll and Dave Autry, another chimp-crazy undergraduate under Fouts's wing, took the idea rather literally and decided to explore it. In a reversal of the usual roles of chimp and teacher during sign language instruction, they wanted to see if Nim could teach a human to sign. The two young men were friends, and by this time, they had frequently taken Nim out on long walks (occasionally accompanied by Onan), unhooked him from his lead, and watched him climb up into the top branches of the trees and disappear. During these walks, Nim signed to Ingersoll about where he wanted to go next, when he wanted snacks or tickles, or when he felt too tired to walk. Autry had not yet learned to sign. He would be Nim's first student.

Autry and Ingersoll conducted the experiment over the course of several ordinary afternoons, during their usual walks with Nim, to emphasize their view that language, for both humans and chimps, occurred more naturally in *real* situations, rather than artificial settings such as a classroom. (Opportunities to show that Terrace had misconceived Project Nim were never overlooked, and Autry and Ingersoll's observations of Nim's behavior on their outings with him had only reinforced their belief that signing happened more frequently when it was done spontaneously, rather than in response to demand.)

Ingersoll encouraged Nim to sign with Autry during these walks. Autry noted every sign and tried to comprehend it in context. According to Ingersoll, Autry picked up twenty signs from Nim in just six hours.

To Terrace, Nim's significance lay in the data he had generated. Once Terrace and his team had collected enough, they were finished with the chimp. Ingersoll, on the contrary, was convinced that Nim himself would become critical to any discussion of sign language and the long-term development of the field. Well trained by Fouts, he was intent on developing a serious relationship with Nim that would be for life. Ingersoll admits that there was also an opportunistic element in the relationship. Attaching himself to Nim, just as Fouts had attached himself to Washoe, might lead to a degree and a few published articles.

Ingersoll asked Lemmon to invest in video equipment. The Gardners had taped Washoe signing, and Ingersoll planned to do the same with Nim. Lemmon had a weakness for new toys. Despite his lack of enthusiasm for the ape language studies, he bought the equipment. Ingersoll spent months shooting Nim doing whatever Nim did — walking in the fields, playing with other chimps, climbing trees, finger-painting — while simultaneously making a special effort to catch his signs on camera. Other students couldn't help but notice Nim, who was frequently outside his cage. Rick Budd, who was fond of Nim, recalls, "We could see that he was a real signer. You could talk to Nim. You could say, 'What do you want to do?' And he would sign, 'Rick tickle Nim.' And I'd sign, 'Tickle where?' And he'd sign, 'Tickle here,' and then he'd point to some place on his body and crunch up and wait to be tickled." Most of the young Norman chimps, taught by Fouts's students, signed one or two words in response to a question; they did not enter into dialogues. Nim's immersion in language from infancy through his first four years had paid off in a rough "fluency," an ability to use his signs more proficiently than the other IPS adolescents, who had been trained in infrequent sessions and returned to their cages. (Nim's proficiency would deteriorate over time once he was no longer immersed in a signing environment.)

At one point during 1978, Fouts assigned an energetic new student named Chris O'Sullivan to Nim. The match made sense to O'Sullivan. "We were both from New York and we both liked sunglasses," she says wryly. O'Sullivan had the gumption to be around the Norman chimps, but she also had academic credentials. She had studied linguistics at Yale and made the effort to learn some sign language prior to her arrival in Norman. Perhaps of even greater interest to Fouts and Lemmon, O'Sullivan had Hollywood contacts. She had spent time working as a production assistant in Los Angeles, where she had met numerous actors, including several working chimpanzees, and her uncle was Budd Schulberg, who wrote the novel *What Makes Sammy Run?* and the screenplay for *On the Waterfront.* Screenwriter Robert Towne had whetted the Oklahoma psychologists' taste for the entertainment business when he came to IPS while doing research for *Greystoke: The Legend of Tarzan,* which would come out a number of years later. Lemmon, hoping that Towne would make his film right at

IPS, offered him the use of one of his islands for the movie, along with his chimps. Though both Lemmon and Fouts had Hollywood ambitions, their motivations were different. Lemmon was desperate to find new sources of income for IPS, while Fouts thought he himself had star potential. According to O'Sullivan, Fouts wanted to play the part of Tarzan in *Greystoke* and had his students, just for fun, shoot some footage of him pounding his chest and hanging out with a Cheetah-like youngster. In the end, *Greystoke* was shot elsewhere and Fouts was disappointed. Nevertheless, his first exposure to celebrities and Hollywood's largesse had made him long for more.

O'Sullivan liked the film world, but she had little doubt that scientific research was far more intellectually challenging than making a movie would ever be. Fouts actively recruited her for his graduate program, and though she was initially skeptical about the idea that chimps could "talk," she agreed to give the program a try. An ideal candidate for ape language studies, she came well versed in language theory and had even taken a few classes from the master himself — Noam Chomsky. Fouts expected her to bring a new level of sophistication, as well as her scholarly contacts, to his ongoing research with Washoe.

O'Sullivan agreed that she might be able to make a significant contribution to the work. She arrived in Norman filled with optimism about her return to academia. She felt important — she had been singled out, wooed by Fouts, virtually begged to make the move from California to Oklahoma. Fouts promptly introduced her to the chimps, and she spent time with all three brothers — Nim, Ally, and Onan. In her words, "Onan was a chimp's chimp, while Nim was a human's chimp." He got along better with people, and she found him more amusing to be around than some of the other chimps. O'Sullivan was very fond of Ally, but Nim had the biggest vocabulary and reputation, which made him a natural for her first language experiments. Using the celebrated Nim Chimpsky in any experiment, even for research on a dissertation, might attract some attention and help get a scholarly article published down the line.

O'Sullivan set out to investigate a few of the countless smaller questions that pop up with regularity when chimps and humans converse. For instance, one project examined turn-taking behavior during signing sessions. O'Sullivan wanted to find out which species interrupted the other more frequently and how it affected the results of the research. No one was surprised when she demonstrated that humans interrupted the chimps far more often than the reverse. Other experiments focused on how Nim's social context affected his ability and willingness to sign.

O'Sullivan may have done more actual research with Nim — which was work from a chimp's point of view — than any of the other students, which could be the reason that Nim bit her badly one afternoon. There was nothing extraordinary about the occasion. As she had often done before, she went to fetch Nim for a project; he was on the island with his buddies and she brought him back to the mainland in the boat. For whatever reason, Nim was not in the mood to sign. When O'Sullivan insisted that he work, he became irritated, but she kept pushing him. O'Sullivan had taken her shoes off. When she decided to put them back on and walk away, Nim chomped down hard on her foot. The skin was not broken, but she was badly bruised and in pain. Her foot began to swell. Before going to the hospital, she took fifteen minutes to chastise Nim and let him know that he had hurt her. (It turned out to be a fracture.)

He repeatedly signed "bite" to her. O'Sullivan had no idea whether he was trying to apologize or tell her that he wanted to bite her again. For a student who was trying to prove that chimpanzees understood and used language coherently, this was a discouraging moment. She realized that she had no way to know for sure what he was trying to communicate.

O'Sullivan's initial optimism about Fouts's research was beginning to fade. "Fouts had more instinct than intellect," she says. "Signing was irrelevant to chimpanzees. You either had a relationship with them or you didn't." She describes Fouts as a "believer," not a scientist. "I wanted to be a scientist, not a member of a cult." But Fouts had plans for her. He enlisted O'Sullivan, a self-described Chomskyite, to collect data from Washoe and Ally, hoping to shed light on their comprehension of syntax and grammar. O'Sullivan watched Fouts trying to teach Washoe and Ally, caged together, how to distinguish prepositions from one another — the difference, for example, between "on" the box and "in" the box. This was the start of the long march toward demonstrating grammatical structure and chimps' ability to use language the way that humans do — a goal similar to Terrace's.

O'Sullivan, however, was not only starting to have her doubts about the intellectual content of ape language studies but was also troubled by the way Fouts worked with the chimps. She had learned, mostly from Fouts, to view Skinner and his protégé as the enemy because of their rigid training methods, which did not appear to be propelling the language acquisition experiments any further. She had assumed that the learning at the farm would be more integrated into the chimps' whole social experience, rather than confined to discrete training sessions. But her assumptions had been naive, based mostly on a video that Fouts showed recruits, which portrayed him working with uncaged chimps in outdoor rural environments and on Lemmon's island. When she arrived in Oklahoma, O'Sullivan soon learned that only a few social groups of adolescents made it out to the island during warm weather, while most of the chimps lived in crowded cages that they rarely left. Now she saw that, as she puts it, "Fouts was training them in a rote way — in a Terrace kind of way."

As she took notes on training sessions with Washoe and Ally, O'Sullivan became progressively more disillusioned. Her romantic ideas about working closely with free-roaming chimps had certainly faded, but more disturbing to her was her feeling that the data she was collecting were not impressive. She believed the data proved that the chimps were confused — nothing more. Washoe and Ally thought that "in the box" was one word for "box." Fouts had O'Sullivan run the trials over and over, hoping to get better results. In the end, none of the material was publishable. Moreover, O'Sullivan began to question the practice of using chimps in research at all. Fouts believed his work was humane, but O'Sullivan was no longer sure she agreed. If the chimps were so intelligent and social, what were they doing locked up behind bars?

Then O'Sullivan suddenly had an eye-opening opportunity to watch Terrace drill Nim on his vocabulary right at IPS. The professor returned to Norman in 1978, prior to publishing his results on Project Nim. He had received periodic reports from Lemmon on Nim's progress. Lemmon had casually mentioned, probably to irk Terrace, that Nim was still signing, and was signing more in Norman than he had in New York. Terrace wanted to see what was going on with his own eyes. As it happened, CTW also wanted more footage of Nim. The chimp's first meeting with Terrace, after one year, promised to be an emotional reunion. Butler and Tynan were not invited to return. Says Tynan, "Terrace wanted all Nim's attention."

Fouts selected O'Sullivan to be Terrace's host during his visit to the farm. To her surprise, Terrace arrived with a detailed plan: he wanted to go out into a field and hide behind a tree, then leap out and surprise Nim, as if they were playing a game. The cameras would be set up and running.

Oddly enough, Terrace's hide-and-seek method worked brilliantly. O'Sullivan described the scene in her diary: "When Nim was about ten feet away . . . Terrace came out from behind the tree. Nim screamed! He gamboled over to Terrace and threw his arms around him for a *long* tight hug, screeching with excitement. He unbuttoned Terrace's shirt and groomed his chest hairs; he took off Terrace's shoe, put it on his own foot, and stretched the leg up like a female model." But, in typical chimp fashion, Nim lost interest in Terrace a few minutes later. The professor had to work to get Nim's attention again, by begging, cajoling, and finally pouncing directly on top of him for a rough tickle. Nim was ecstatic. There was nothing he liked better. O'Sullivan had never seen or heard Nim laugh so hard. He was obviously thrilled to see his old friend.

As they sat together for half an hour, while Terrace conducted a short language session, the cameras rolled. Nim produced nineteen signs, naming objects as they were removed from a box, one by one, just as he had done in his Columbia classroom. Terrace counted the words, visibly thrilled each time the chimp signed correctly. They were together for less than an hour. Terrace flew home the same afternoon, explaining that he had to rush back to teach a class in New York. But he finally had a sense of closure on Nim. "I was sure that he would do well without me," Terrace wrote in his book. "But I on the other hand would always miss Nim." This was the last time the psychologist ever saw him.

O'Sullivan had observed the entire lesson hiding behind a truck so as not to disturb the scene. Her conclusions about their session were mixed. She was appalled by Terrace's rigid method of working with Nim, which she believed was not conducive to any meaningful learning, yet she could not deny that they had worked well together. Nim had given an extraordinary performance, signing with efficiency and clarity, and was clearly elated by the surprise visit. O'Sullivan knew she had just witnessed a highly successful, coherent signing session, one that was more organized than the usual sessions in Norman. Terrace had gotten clear results, mostly without rewards.

O'Sullivan and another graduate student, Carey Yaeger, designed an experiment to test the effectiveness of Terrace's methods with Nim. In weekly sessions, the two graduate students took Nim from his cage (with the help of Ingersoll or Autry), sat him down as if in school, and, one by one, removed objects from a box and asked him to name them. Forcing Nim to be attentive and preventing him from moving around, they drilled him on word after word. After several sessions, Nim became so annoyed that he refused to work at all. O'Sullivan and Yaeger concluded the Terrace-like sessions. In part two of the experiment, they observed Nim's language during the course of his average day at the farm, as he went for walks and communicated with Ingersoll and Autry. They noticed that Nim was more cooperative and signed with greater frequency. Their results were eventually published in a collection of essays put together by the Gardners, who appeared eager for any scrap of research that undercut the authority of Project Nim and Terrace's methodology.

O'Sullivan was critical of both Terrace and Fouts. She believed the two men were making the same mistakes. They were too focused on grammar, syntax — and Chomsky. O'Sullivan also felt that Fouts was too busy competing with Terrace. Fouts had used Terrace as a whipping boy while promoting Project Washoe and his own work. And he was just as competitive with Lemmon as he was with Terrace, constantly struggling to maintain control over the chimpanzees in his studies. O'Sullivan wondered whether her professor had simply been blinded by ambition, to the detriment of his work.

However, if Fouts could rethink his academic agenda and head in a new, more original direction, rather than simply trying to beat out Project Nim, O'Sullivan thought he had a chance to make a significant contribution to the field. Fouts would never be an intellectual giant, but he was dedicated to chimpanzees, and he had one major asset — Washoe.

With Washoe as the main subject, Fouts was about to begin what he believed would be the most significant experiment of his academic career in Norman.

Nim sitting outside at IPS

CHAPTER 10
THE FALL OF IPS

Roger Mellgren took a genuine interest in Fouts's signing chimpanzees. Mellgren had a background in animal behavior, experience with laboratory rats and pigeons, and expertise in experimental design. Having arrived in Norman the same year as Fouts, he too was a member of the faculty of the OU psychology department, and the two men became fast friends, affectionately referred to by the students as "Roger Chimp" and "Roger Rat." Fouts invited Mellgren to the farm to observe the talkative chimps, and together they made several visits to the Temerlins' home to see Lucy before she was shipped off to Africa. Mellgren had initially been reluctant to buy in to his colleague's obsession with signing chimps, but after watching Fouts communicate with them, Mellgren became a believer. There was definitely something unusual — and fascinating from a scientific perspective — going on in Norman, whether it was truly language or not. Mellgren respected Fouts's dogged dedication to ape language, as well as his long-term commitment to Washoe. Few scientists held on to their animals at the end of the experiment, and even fewer viewed their research subjects as highly intelligent creatures with complex emotional lives, feelings, and sensitivities to their surroundings. Fouts was cut from a different cloth. The connection he felt to Washoe was *real,* yet he wanted to do serious scholarly research.

Mellgren knew little about chimpanzees, but over time he began to feel intellectually challenged by the nearly impossible task of proving that the interspecies conversations he had observed were authentic. The chimps appeared to be communicating to each other as well as to Fouts. Mellgren joined what Chris O'Sullivan described as "the cult" and agreed to serve as a sounding board for Fouts as he developed an ambitious new experiment for Washoe, one different from any the Gardners had ever done.

The project would have to stand up to Project Nim to win significant grants. But Fouts thought his current idea was more promising than anything Terrace had accomplished with Nim. Because Fouts was a virtual novice in the academic world, he required the help of an experienced grant writer to produce a proposal good enough to get noticed and be moved to the top of the heap. Academic proposals are long, dry, carefully researched documents. Mellgren, more familiar with the demands of scientific research than Fouts, knew how to generate a strong, theoretically sound document. Fouts asked him to write the proposal for the Washoe study and offered him the title of co–principal investigator, although the experiment, like Washoe, belonged to Fouts.

Mellgren spent months conceptualizing and designing the new project with Fouts. They eventually submitted a fat proposal to the National Science Foundation (NSF). In 1978, much to their delight, the NSF made them an initial award of $187,000. If the data were properly handled and the results were convincing, the grant would be Fouts's ticket out of Norman. He and his chimps would be far more appealing to another university if they arrived with funding. Like other promising scientists, Fouts hoped to have his own research institute someday — independent of William Lemmon.

The essential purpose of the study, in Fouts's words, was to see "whether or not chimpanzees would transmit sign language across generations." Fouts intended for Ally, Nim's brother, to father an infant with Washoe. Then Washoe would be put in an environment where she would be encouraged to teach the infant to sign. But the experiment was not as simple as it appeared. Even if Washoe did teach her offspring to sign, Fouts and Mellgren had to prove it. Less savvy about chimps than Fouts and less biased in their favor, Mellgren was nonetheless optimistic. As always, collecting reliable and convincing data would be the greatest challenge, but Mellgren was a cautious and meticulous scientist who felt that he could design the experiment to compensate for the obvious problems.

The Washoe project did not consider the question of whether or not chimpanzees could learn to sign. Just as Terrace had taken that as a given, based on the Gardners' work, Mellgren and Fouts also assumed that Washoe was signing, regardless of whether or not her "language" conformed to Chomskian criteria. Chomsky, for the moment, was cast aside. Mellgren and Fouts were not going to search for transformational grammar in the infant's signs — the signs themselves would initially suffice. The project might evolve over years and generations as the chimps developed their own vernacular and the scientists investigated its authenticity and meaning.

The experiment was flashy and intriguing enough that Fouts was confident he could launch his career with it. But he had one significant problem: Washoe and Ally lived on Lemmon's property, and cutting the IPS director out of a major project going on in his own institute, especially when funds were involved, was virtually impossible. Nonetheless, the co-investigators did not invite Lemmon to participate.

Language had never been a burning interest for Lemmon. Nor was he impressed with the quality of Fouts's research or his attitude toward primates, which from Lemmon's point of view verged on advocacy. But the imminent arrival of a sizable NSF grant changed everything. He was determined to get a piece of it. In Lemmon's view, he had been paying Washoe's bills for almost ten years, because it was the $50,000 a year that OU gave IPS that supported the chimps for Fouts's program. But the chimp population had grown during those years, expenses had gone up, and Lemmon needed more money. Increasingly, he was having to pay the farm's bills out of the income from his private practice. To generate additional income he had gotten some small state grants to run a clinic for convicted sex offenders (specifically peepers and incest abusers) at the Institute. A few of them helped with the chimps and interacted with students, all of which Lemmon considered part of the therapeutic experience — although it was not without risk. One student was attacked and nearly raped at knifepoint but managed to talk her way out of the situation.

Lemmon wanted Fouts to contribute funds to the farm, but now Fouts was obtaining grants for his own experiments and leaving Lemmon out of the equation. This was particularly galling to Lemmon because Fouts was just starting out, while he himself had been trying for years to tap into the main vein of government support for the chimp research he wanted to do and been consistently turned down. Naturally, he resented Fouts's success and believed that his fixation on Washoe was more neurotic than scientific. Worse, he predicted that Washoe would never be an adequate mother, which would kill the experiment before it launched. Whatever one thought of his research, Lemmon was one of the world's most successful breeders and was considered by others to be an expert on reproduction and the maternal instinct, able to distinguish the "good" mothers from the neglectful, unwilling ones without fail. When the latter gave birth, he removed their infants quickly, to ensure the babies' survival.

Lemmon took sadistic pleasure in torturing Fouts by disparaging Washoe. The IPS director occasionally referred to her as "the bitch" to students, especially when Fouts was around. Fouts took every insult personally. He seemed to feel an almost paternal investment in the chimp's personality. Washoe may have had a reputation for being hard to handle, but the farm was filled with tough-as-nails adult females. Washoe was hardly any different. Fouts constantly defended her honor, insisting that she would make an ideal mother.

But Fouts did worry that Washoe might not get pregnant or that she would somehow not be able to deliver, which would put his grant at risk because the grant proposal had designated three chimps — Washoe, Ally, and their offspring — as the family unit under scrutiny, and the NSF would not release a penny until the three chimps were in place. The decision to specify a traditional family group may seem strange, since the nuclear family is hardly a model for chimp society, and males have little to do with raising their offspring in the wild. But Fouts and Mellgren thought it wise to have two chimps who signed to each other for the infant to observe, and they had chosen Ally as the father because he was an active breeder and a proficient signer and he and Washoe got along well together.

Washoe and her intended mate had shared a cage for five years, off and on. The two chimps had a sexual relationship that was so well established that they had even been observed copulating through the bars on an occasion when they were in separate cages. Moreover, Ally had already impregnated Washoe once. Their first offspring was a male named Cleveland — named after Cleveland County, where IPS was located, just as Washoe had been named after the county where the Gardners lived — but the infant had died at birth in 1976.

In May 1978, Washoe became pregnant again. Fouts promptly removed Ally to a cage opposite her, hoping the distance between them might encourage the chimp couple to sign back and forth to each other, thus keeping their ASL skills sharp. To further encourage the chimps to sign, neither Fouts nor his students spoke around them — they signed exclusively. Fouts hovered over Washoe like a nervous and expectant father; he took her for walks in the woods, fed her treats, and made sure other chimps were kept at a distance. Lemmon, ever critical of Fouts, felt he was spoiling her, which would only make her harder to please. He and Fouts argued endlessly about Washoe, the grant, chimps, and whatever else Fouts happened to be doing. With Lemmon questioning his competence at every turn, Fouts became increasingly nervous about Washoe's safety and his own ability to control the project. "Bill had this attitude that the sign language program was getting too big for its britches," says Mellgren, who watched the drama unfold from the sidelines. "He didn't like playing second fiddle to someone who wasn't even taken seriously." Students tried to remain aloof from the dispute. They were devoted to Fouts but preferred to focus on the chimpanzees, their dissertations, and their own lives. Instead, they watched their professor fall apart as Lemmon walked all over him.

Not needing an invitation to meddle in Fouts's work, Lemmon waited until Washoe was pregnant and then, bypassing Fouts, quietly convinced OU to release $5,000 of the grant directly to IPS. He would use the funds to rebuild Washoe's living quarters to make them more spacious for the coming family. Fouts was infuriated. He had drawn up his own plan for the new enclosure and intended to build it himself. Moreover, he knew that Lemmon had no desire to pamper Washoe with plusher accommodations; it was purely an opportunity to demonstrate Fouts's powerlessness and take over the first chunk of money. Fouts was not even consulted before the funds were released to IPS. The incident was a turning point. Fouts began to avoid IPS whenever possible. He let his students take care of Washoe, while he stayed away, planning his escape strategy.

On the morning of January 8, 1979, a student on duty (Washoe was monitored around the clock) noticed that there was blood and water on the floor of Washoe's cage. She was about to give birth. The student called Fouts at home and he rushed to the farm. The infant was born at 11:57 after four hours of labor. Nim was watching the action from the sidelines with about twenty other chimps. Fouts named the baby Sequoyah, after the famous Oklahoma Indian who had invented the Cherokee alphabet.

Within hours of the birth it quickly became apparent that mother and child were not bonding. O'Sullivan, who was there, recalls that Washoe "would hold the baby for a little while and try to nurse her, but then the nursing would hurt and she'd put the baby down. We were giving her beer because we had read all the La Leche material — it helps the milk flow — but it wasn't going well. We knew it."

Far too soon after giving birth, Washoe put Sequoyah down on the cold cement floor, rejecting him, when she should have been keeping him warm and close, nursing him into life. At one point, Fouts took the baby into his own arms and held him at his chest, showing Washoe how to breast-feed him, hoping she might mimic his gestures. He badly wanted this baby to survive and to remain with Washoe. But she was clearly not interested in, or perhaps not capable of, feeding her baby. Worried that Sequoyah might not survive, Fouts decided to remove him from the cage.

Fouts and his wife, Deborah, took Sequoyah home for the night. The baby had a fever; he required fluids intravenously and through a bottle all night long. In the morning, Sequoyah was doing well and Fouts returned him to Washoe, hoping that her maternal instincts would kick in and that she would take over. But Washoe refused to feed him — and, worse, refused to give him back to Fouts again. Now he had a bigger problem. Fouts was forced to anesthetize Washoe before he could safely remove the infant from her cage.

Diana Davis, a graduate student who was close to Fouts, took the baby home and became his primary foster mother, assisted by several others, including Ingersoll. Like a human baby, Sequoyah needed to be held continually and fed on demand twenty-four hours a day. Thanks to La Leche, he was actually breast-fed. A little sac filled with milk was attached to a thin tube, like a straw, which brought the fluid right to the nipple; the infants sucked on the nipple and never noticed the tube, which delivered the milk. The milk was the real stuff, donated by local lactating mothers who had agreed to participate in the project and pump their milk, and picked up every morning by students on their way to IPS. Human breast milk had far more nutrients than formula, and Fouts wanted to do everything possible for the infant.

When Sequoyah began to improve, Fouts decided to return him to Washoe again. After all, if he became too attached to Davis instead of Washoe, it might jeopardize the mother-infant bond — and the grant. It was

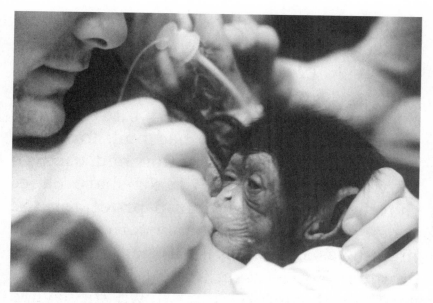
Sequoyah during a La Leche feeding with Bob Ingersoll

even possible that Washoe might completely reject the baby if Fouts waited too long. Davis disagreed. She wanted to keep Sequoyah until he was a little bigger, better able to hold his own. O'Sullivan sided with Davis. But according to her, Fouts thought Davis was becoming too attached to the baby and had inflated her role as his mother out of proportion. Although it was a tough call, giving Sequoyah back to Washoe as soon as possible did seem to make sense. Fouts, who knew Washoe better than anyone else, overruled Davis and O'Sullivan and returned the infant to his mother's cage.

There are several versions of the events that led up to the disaster that occurred on March 8, 1979, when Sequoyah was less than three months old. Washoe, Ally, and Sequoyah had been moved into the new enclosure that Lemmon had built for them. It was hardly ideal. Lemmon had used an inexpensive metal with razor-sharp edges that he considered chimp-proof for the walls. Fouts was justifiably furious — the metal was obviously treacherous for the chimps. Fouts assigned all his available students the job of filing down the jagged edges, by hand, until they were smooth. It was time-consuming, physically taxing work. Before it could be completed, Sequoyah cut his foot on the wall and the wound became infected. According to Fouts, at the same time, Lemmon intentionally let the propane gas run out in the building and there was no heat for the chimps. Sequoyah, already weakened by infection, died of pneumonia. Fouts blamed Lemmon for the infant's death.

But there is another unhappy story about Sequoyah that Fouts omitted from his book. Eugene Linden tells it in *Silent Partners*, published in 1987. Linden, a science reporter who took an early interest in ape language, spent time at IPS during the

1970s and hung out with Fouts, his students, and some of the chimps. According to Linden's sources, the infant's death was related to abuse he suffered at his mother's hands. Washoe's weapon of choice was a toothbrush that someone left in her cage, which she apparently jammed down Sequoyah's throat. The toothbrush was a legacy of Washoe's days with the Gardners, who had taught her to brush her teeth at night; she continued this practice at the farm with a toothbrush she was given every evening, which was supposed to be taken away when she finished. But one day shortly before Sequoyah's death, Ingersoll arrived at the chimp barn for his morning shift and saw three inches of toothbrush protruding from the infant's throat. He persuaded Washoe to bring Sequoyah over to him so he could extract it without entering her cage. No one will ever know whether Washoe was trying to brush her baby's teeth or hurt him. But either way, Sequoyah had a very sore throat and subsequently contracted pneumonia, from which he died.

According to O'Sullivan, who was one of several students monitoring mother and infant in round-the-clock shifts, Fouts fully understood that Washoe might harm her infant, as captive chimps are prone to do, often because of depression. "We had a little cap gun that we were supposed to use if we saw Washoe abusing Sequoyah," she recalls.

But the problems between Washoe and Sequoyah might well have gone beyond a captive chimp's postpartum depression or the failure of her maternal instinct. O'Sullivan suggests that the chimp had ample reason to resent her new baby. The design of Fouts and Mellgren's protocol dictated that once the infant arrived, none of the humans in Washoe's world were allowed to sign directly to her, thereby ensuring that Sequoyah saw no signs other than Washoe's and that any sign language he learned would be exclusively from his mother (and presumably from Ally too). But signing was Washoe's only mode of communication with humans. Once she gave birth, all the people she regularly signed to refused to sign back, leaving her isolated with her newborn infant. She must have felt as if she had been rendered invisible. According to Linden, Fouts would occasionally sign to Washoe, mostly because he felt sorry for her, but only when Sequoyah was sleeping. Like O'Sullivan, George Kimball, another graduate student working closely with Fouts, believed that the study had conditioned Washoe, however inadvertently, to resent

Sequoyah's intrusion into his mother's life. It was another glaring example of researchers ignoring the emotional needs of their chimp subjects.

Lemmon did not intervene, but he told at least one student that Washoe had killed her infant. For decades, he had observed female chimps mothering their children, noting how they held the babies, fed them, even looked at them. If a mother began to fail her infant or if an infant was unable to properly cling or breast-feed, Lemmon removed the baby from the cage, often saving his or her life. Babies did die at the Institute all too frequently, but only after Lemmon had gone to heroic lengths to save them. Fouts had done his best for Sequoyah — short of asking for Lemmon's help. And that may have been a terrible mistake, as Lemmon did have a gift for keeping infants alive.

Only six months after Sequoyah died, Lemmon had occasion to demonstrate the extremes he was prepared to go to in order to save IPS's newborns. On August 26, 1979, Carolyn, Nim's mother, produced her fourth set of twins: Zebediah and Ezekiel (Zeb and Zeke), born one and a half months early, weighing 3 pounds and 2.6 pounds, respectively. Carolyn, an experienced and devoted mother, held them both to her but seemed to be favoring the larger infant, possibly because she instinctively knew that he was more likely to survive. Lemmon, worried that both twins were too small to breathe on their own, immediately took them from their mother and placed them in an incubator, on loan from a hospital, where they were given oxygen and intravenous fluids. If the twins survived, they would not go back to Carolyn; Lemmon was designing his own language experiment for them.

Zeb and Zeke's first days were an uphill battle. The local media, called in on day one, followed their progress, dramatizing the details of their struggle for life. At three and one half weeks Zeb suddenly needed a transfusion. Lemmon and Mel Allen, his devoted research assistant, rushed Zeb to the neonatal unit of the children's hospital in Oklahoma City. Allen, a universal blood donor, provided the blood, becoming the first human (at least in Norman) to donate blood for a primate transfusion. Lemmon convinced Oklahoma City's Children's Memorial Hospital to donate human milk for the chimps to drink, and volunteers (both male and female) took turns breastfeeding the babies (La Leche style, of course) twenty-four hours a day. One of the twins now had human blood running through his veins, both were drinking human milk, and soon Lemmon would place them in a human home for his research. It would be hard to get more human than that. Zeb and Zeke, unlike Sequoyah, began to thrive. Lemmon became a local hero.

Painfully aware of Lemmon's negative attitude toward Washoe, especially after the death of Sequoyah, Fouts grew more paranoid, convincing himself that the IPS director might try to poison his valuable chimp. Lemmon, eager to twist the knife, publicly threatened to sell Washoe — and Fouts with her. According to Mellgren, Lemmon was joking, but if he was, Fouts didn't think it was funny. He longed for the day when IPS would be so far down on his résumé that it might actually drop off the page. He was desperate to get out of Norman. But first, he needed Washoe to become a mother again.

According to Fouts, Washoe kept signing to him to return Sequoyah, apparently confused or maybe just unconvinced that her baby had died. (She might well have observed Lemmon taking healthy babies from their mothers.) Eager to please his chimp, not to mention meet the criteria for his grant, Fouts began searching for an infant that Washoe could adopt. Breeding her again seemed far too risky. In 1979, Fouts located a chimp at the Yerkes Center. Loulis, a ten-month-old male, was the son of a chimp who had undergone experimental brain surgery there. Yerkes agreed to loan Loulis to Fouts for his experiment. (Years later, Fouts paid $10,000 to keep him.) Diana Davis, the student who had so devotedly mothered Sequoyah, drove to Atlanta to pick up Loulis and bring him home, even though she and several of the other students working with Fouts "had doubts about the ethics of taking the infant from its natural mother, whatever her condition, and delivering him to the questionable affections of Washoe," according to *Silent Partners* author Eugene Linden. Fouts had railed against Lemmon's practice of separating young chimpanzees from their mothers for any reason apart from saving their lives. But now that it suited his own purposes, he was apparently willing to do the same.

In any case, the adoption was a success. It took only a few days before Loulis began hugging Washoe, turning her into the mother he badly needed. Surprising everyone, Washoe reciprocated. Fouts's new experiment could now get off the ground, and with it his academic career.

When he had first arrived in Norman, Fouts had been so penniless that Amway schemes looked appealing. Ten years later, he had a respectable grant and the means to support his own chimps, and he intended to remove them as soon as possible from Lemmon's property and Lemmon's oversight. Fouts knew that as long as Washoe and Loulis lived at the farm, Lemmon could control his access to them, and thus his funds. In secret negotiations with OU, Fouts arranged for Washoe, Loulis, and Ally to move off the IPS farm to an area on the university campus known as South Base — the very place where Lemmon's Psychological Clinic had once been located. Unlike IPS, South Base did not have a facility designed for chimpanzees. So Washoe and family had to spend their days warehoused in cages with no acreage to roam. Whatever the chimps may have made of their new accommodations, Fouts must have felt a palpable sense of relief as he enjoyed his hard-won independence. Big Brother was no longer watching.

Infuriated by Fouts's ploy, Lemmon demanded all three chimps back, arguing that the Gardners had given Washoe to *him*, not Fouts. Even Loulis, Lemmon argued, had been released to IPS and Lemmon's care. Fouts must have expected a battle, as Lemmon would have refused to give him a bag of monkey chow, let alone one of his chimpanzees. Taking Ally, in particular, was a brazen act of theft; Lemmon had bred him and clearly owned him. But Fouts felt he needed the chimp for his study. Ally had been written into the NSF proposal, and Fouts hoped to keep him and Washoe together. It was wishful thinking. After the screaming stopped and negotiations began, Fouts agreed to return Ally to IPS. In exchange, Lemmon relinquished his claims on Washoe and Loulis.

Although Fouts had moved Washoe and Loulis to campus, beyond Lemmon's reach, his troubles were not quite over. He still had to produce accurate and believable data for the NSF. Just as Terrace had compiled a vocabulary list for Nim, Fouts kept one for Loulis, but of course Loulis learned from Washoe, not from humans, or so the theory went. But could Fouts prove that Loulis had acquired the words from Washoe? As expected, documenting conversations between chimps was nearly impossible, no matter what Fouts tried. Mellgren worried that their methodology would not stand up to scrutiny. Every language researcher who worked with chimps faced a methodological catch-22. The work could not be done unless the researcher had a relationship with the chimpanzee, that is, had established a certain level of trust, but that relationship created bias, which made the results suspect. If ever a field of study confirmed Heisenberg's uncertainty principle, in which the observed is influenced by the very fact of observation, it was language acquisition in chimpanzees. But Fouts was undeterred. He had correctly predicted Loulis's ability to pick up signs from his "parents," and every addition to the infant's vocabulary caused a corresponding increase in Fouts's optimism. Mellgren, however, who was a stickler for accuracy, was less sanguine. His reputation was at stake as well, and he was not willing to compromise it for anyone.

Discussions about how the data were obtained, processed, and recorded were often heated. Mellgren and Fouts did not always agree. One student recalls a brawl in a bar between them over the accuracy of the record keeping. As the story goes, Mellgren had become livid after hearing rumors that Fouts was exaggerating the success of his results. "The data didn't make sense," O'Sullivan says. "One person would note that Washoe signed twenty times to

Loulis in an hour and another person would record only three signs." According to O'Sullivan, a decision was made to put a lockbox by the chimps' cage. Students would put their notes into the box when they completed their shift. Only Mellgren had a key, and he took charge of tabulating the data. Mellgren says he does not recall a barroom brawl or a lockbox, but he certainly remembers the difficulties they faced. "We never got the data to convince anybody of anything," he says, "and it was all very frustrating."

The science they were generating was indeed questionable, even by the standards of Fouts's own students. O'Sullivan kept a diary in which she accused her professor of milking his data in the media. "Roger lied. He plain lied," she wrote. "[He is] giving false data to the scientific community." She and her friend Carey Yaeger, another graduate student, worried that their degrees would be meaningless if the academic community viewed Fouts as a fraud. They began to openly question the value of the whole project and whether or not they wanted to even be associated with it. When O'Sullivan heard Fouts spouting statistics about Loulis's vocabulary during a live radio interview, she wanted to grab the microphone from him and shout, "It's all a hoax!"

O'Sullivan lost all her respect for Fouts. Since joining Lemmon's Freudian research on chimps, which had turned her stomach from day one, was not an option either, she switched to the sociology department — focusing now on humans, not chimps — to finish up her Ph.D. Rick Budd left Norman and went on to law school. Others, including Ingersoll, stayed and continued to work on whatever projects they could find that involved the chimps.

Meanwhile, on November 23, 1979, Terrace published the long-awaited results of Project Nim in *Science* magazine, an event Fouts must have been anticipating with dread. It was indeed a disaster, and posed a real threat to the continuation of Fouts's own work, although not in any way he could have anticipated. In a bizarre turnaround, instead of announcing a breakthrough in chimp language acquisition studies, Terrace characterized Project Nim as a failure. He went even further, lambasting the entire field. Terrace concluded that Nim was not speaking, nor were any of the other chimpanzees who appeared to be. They were just mimics, making fools of the scientists chatting with them. In effect, Terrace had written an obituary for ape language research.

Terrace's complete reversal was entirely unexpected, given the constant fanfare that had surrounded Project Nim. He had collected a huge amount of data over a relatively short period of time, and for years he had claimed to have discovered patterns in the order of Nim's signs, patterns that were rudimentary at best but that still amounted to what could be viewed as a grammatical structure. True, Nim did not make sentences or use proper ASL gestures, but in the past Terrace had said that he could show that Nim drew from a vocabulary of more than one hundred signs and used them to communicate. Proving even this much would be significant. In addition, Terrace had stated that he had compared his data on Nim with studies done with human children and found them similar; like Nim, children begin learning language by picking up single words, proceed to combinations, and eventually create simple sentences that are not unlike the ones that Nim had made. Nim had occasionally put three or four signs together, and in these moments Terrace believed he had captured the chimp proactively using what he regarded as *language.* Project Nim's archive had twenty-seven thousand examples of Nim's multiple sign combinations, a sample of more than sufficient size on which to base what promised to be groundbreaking conclusions. At this point, even if the Gardners had the data, they had not published any on Washoe's combinations of signs, which made Terrace's findings potentially more momentous. Everyone watching expected the professor to trumpet his success, to announce that Nim Chimsky had become the first chimpanzee to have internalized a human language structure.

But in the *Science* article, Terrace asserted that his data had unraveled before his eyes. He found no evidence that Nim had any comprehension of what he signed. By responding to his teachers' cues, he often got the signs right and had managed to master individual words, but he had no ability to string them together in any meaningful way, which is one of the hallmarks of human language. Terrace concluded that unlike children, who put words together in increasingly complex structures and learn to express themselves more and more richly as they begin to form sentences, Nim combined signs only to emphasize words, rather than to form new constructions to express his thoughts. Terrace had to concede that Noam Chomsky was right and Skinner wrong: language is exclusively inherent to humans and cannot be taught to other species.

After years of crowing about Nim and his achievements, Terrace seemed almost humble as he admitted his error. The chimp had duped the professor; Nim's vocabulary, which amounted to approximately 150 words, was a chimera. Terrace's doubts about the accuracy of his results had come at the final hour, when Richard Sanders, a student assigned the task of scrutinizing the videos taken during Nim's classroom sessions, noticed a problem that could not be easily dismissed. Nim's teachers introduced new signs by repeating them, over and over, until Nim accurately made the same gestures; more often than not, Nim went through a number of words before he finally signed the correct one. When he did, his teachers responded with enthusiasm, then moved on to the next word. That was very troubling, for it seemed obvious to Sanders that the teachers were inadvertently cueing the chimp that he had landed on the right response. Terrace had planned to use these tapes to show the process by which Nim learned to *comprehend* signs. But instead, the tapes contained glaring evidence that the trainers had unconsciously biased the learning sessions.

Terrace could not ignore the evidence from the tapes, which appeared to him to be proof positive that Nim failed to understand sign language. Terrace had focused exclusively on the number of words Nim signed correctly, which was high. However, his vocabulary meant nothing unless the psychologist could prove that Nim understood the signs he was using and could combine them in expressive, creative ways. In the end, Terrace became convinced that his highly intelligent chimp was a mimic, nothing more. His vocabulary was "pure drill," Terrace told the *New York Times.* "Language still stands as an important definition of the human species."

Terrace's argument was cogent. The structures and patterns that he had painstakingly tracked and originally described as "language" were undermined by the bias that he had inadvertently built into his own experimental design. Indeed, Project Nim could be used to prove that language acquisition, at least in the manner that Terrace had framed it, was a dead end, undeserving of further investigation. As Terrace told a reporter, "Nim fooled me."

In an unusual move for any scientist, but especially for one known to be as conservative and calibrated as Terrace, he wrote a more personal, book-length account of Project Nim, simply titled *Nim,* published the same year as the *Science* article, and intended for a more popular audience. In this version of Nim's story, his vocabulary grows like a beanstalk, regardless of the turmoil all around him in the LaFarge home and then at Delafield. Like a doting father, Terrace looks on with pride at Nim's accomplishments while contending with incompetent babysitters, the fury of surrogate mothers, the threat of homelessness for Nim, and years of writing laborious academic proposals. *Nim* is a patchwork of memories, scraps of science, charts, and photographs, much of which contradicts the author's conclusions in *Science.* But the book was easy to dismiss as anecdotal, fueled by emotions that have no place in science. In the end, only the research results summarized in an academic publication had any authority.

Now that the veil had fallen from his eyes, Terrace leapt into bed with his adversaries; he used his research to batter other practitioners in the field. Fouts and the Gardners fought back, trading insults with Terrace, arguing that his failure had been his own. He had not attracted the necessary grants; he had been unable to handle his own chimpanzee, provide Nim with consistent teachers, or compensate for cueing in his experimental design. Worst of all, he had ended the study far too early to get significant results; at the very least, Terrace's about-face was premature. Then there was the inconvenient fact that once Nim had learned to sign, he often initiated conversations with humans. Didn't that count? The Gardners had an entirely different, less restrictive definition of language. "If you use the same criteria [as Herb Terrace used on Nim] to judge human children," Allen Gardner told the press, "you'd have to conclude that they don't have language either."

By his own admission, Terrace had failed to build in safeguards against bias — double-blind studies, masks worn by the handlers to prevent inadvertent cueing — as the Gardners, among others, were careful to do. In retrospect it became apparent that Fouts and Mellgren might have been guilty of some of the same experimental sins that Terrace had committed. Washoe and Nim had led virtually parallel lives. Both had been raised in human environments and relegated to cages at roughly the same age in Oklahoma, where Fouts, or more often his graduate students, drilled them in

ASL using food rewards. "It's almost impossible not to misuse operant conditioning techniques in this context," Mellgren concluded years later, when the reality and the frustrations of these projects had become obvious to everyone involved. Mellgren had frequently observed Fouts and his students enthusiastically reinforcing the chimps each time one of them made a correct sign. Everyone in the field faced the same methodological problem and strove to overcome it. As Heini Hediger, an influential zoologist, once said, totally eliminating the Clever Hans effect was analogous to squaring the circle: it was impossible.

A chorus of skeptics, emboldened by Terrace's apostasy, drowned out protests from the Gardners and their protégés. At an influential conference at the National Science Institute, called "The Clever Hans Phenomenon: Communication with Horses, Whales, Apes, and People," Thomas Sebeok, a prominent biolinguist, suggested that all ape language researchers, with the exception of Terrace, join the circus rather than the academy. Terrace's former opponents, seeing that he had now come over to their side, warmly and publicly embraced him. Says LaFarge, "Herb got more bang out of calling Project Nim a failure than he would have had he called it a success."

As far as Fouts and his colleagues were concerned, the sooner Project Nim was swept under the rug, the sooner the whole field would recover. In his own publications, Fouts would simply write Nim and Terrace out of the history of meaningful language acquisition studies. Project Nim was a mistake — not critical to the field. Nim's failure only made Washoe's success, which Fouts never questioned, more significant. In *Next of Kin,* Fouts describes Terrace as a virtual animal abuser, treating Nim as if he were "a rat in one of Skinner's operant conditioning chambers." This, of course, was far from true. And Fouts had no reliable research of his own, at least not yet, to counter any of Terrace's views on sign language. But Terrace *had* made one unforgivable error: he had used the inadequacies of his own experimental design and training methods as grounds for concluding that all primates were incapable of using language.

The violation of the integrity of the animal was another issue Terrace's experiment raised. Project Nim, as it turned out, was far more radical in its concept and design than Terrace, or anyone else at the time, understood. Just the notion that a chimpanzee could be raised in a human family and treated as if he were a human child was a potentially troubling concept for most scientists. Before language studies were in vogue, experiments that focused on animal behavior or cognition kept the research subjects locked in their cages. Removing the chimp from the laboratory — and the cage — opened many minds to the possibility that animals should have rights, including the right to legal protection from research. Terrace had, in effect, liberated a chimpanzee from the usual chains of science. Had he declared Project Nim a success, he might have further advanced the idea that chimpanzees were sentient beings, in some fundamental way our kin. Such an idea was rife with implications, and ahead of its time. Terrace effectively nixed it, along with Project Nim.

While Fouts was struggling to collect convincing data on Washoe and Loulis, an accident occurred that put an end to chimp studies at OU. Dr. Karl Pribram, an esteemed neurosurgeon teaching at Stanford University, had come to Norman to dedicate a new wing at the local veterans' hospital. The author of *Language of the Brain* (1971), he had become intrigued by Fouts's work and wanted to meet his remarkable chimps.

There are several different accounts of what happened next. According to Eugene Linden's version of events, Pribram arrived at Washoe's cage while one of Fouts's assistants was feeding her through the bars. The doctor, who had been doing research on primates for thirty-five years, offered to help, as he wanted to interact with the chimps. But when Pribram handed Washoe some strawberries through the bars of her cage, she bit down hard on one of his fingers.

In Fouts's version, Washoe merely held Pribram's finger in her teeth. The neurosurgeon hurt himself by pulling back in alarm and scraping his finger against a sharp wire in the cage.

Ingersoll, also there, claims that Washoe bit Pribram and then he rammed his hand against the side of the cage.

Pribram's own version is that when he arrived at the cages with Fouts, he fed some fresh strawberries to Loulis through the bars while Washoe watched. He turned to reach for more fruit, extending one hand while leaving the other in the cage: "Washoe dashed from the back of the cage and rammed my hand onto the sharp extruded metal of the cage," he says. "Blood spurted from my finger and Washoe signed, 'Sorry!

Sorry!' "

Pribram's hand had been cut to the bone. He was rushed to the VA hospital, where he had been scheduled to speak, was admitted as a patient, and later gave his dedication lecture from a wheelchair, with IVs in both arms. Soon after, he flew home to California, where it was discovered that gangrene was setting in, and he went through three more surgeries. He lost the tip of his finger but never stopped working, even while his finger was still healing; when he performed surgery, he cut off the finger of his surgical glove to make room for his bandaged finger, and then covered it with a condom.

Whatever actually happened, OU felt the sting of liability. Pribram, or rather his insurance company — a distinction Pribram still makes — sued Fouts, OU, and OU's board of regents for millions of dollars. Pribram wanted the university to pay, not Fouts. He felt that the university had failed to provide adequate caging for the chimps on South Base.

Three months later, as unresolved legal issues continued to swirl around the case, Fouts quietly resigned from OU and accepted a position at Central Washington University in Ellensburg, where he would be able to continue his study of Washoe and

Loulis. He packed up his chimps and moved them out in the dead of night; Dave Autry and another student, Allen Hirsch, went along to assist with the animals. Fouts abandoned the rest of his students, leaving them high and dry in the middle of the year. The signing program in Norman was over. Fouts's stealthy exit and the mess he left behind him on campus seemed to confirm the complaints against him. OU was besieged by local animal rights groups protesting Pribram's presence on campus in the first place. They argued that Pribram was a vivisectionist who had been cutting up primates for decades and that he owed them a pound of flesh, or whatever Washoe had managed to get from his finger.

Lemmon must have enjoyed watching Fouts's reputation in Norman go down the drain like so much sewage. But IPS, which was already in trouble, would go further downhill without him. Lemmon had never been able to attract outside funding or find any colleagues who could tolerate working with him for long. Once Fouts was gone, he had even fewer resources. His national reputation as a breeder had already eclipsed his authority as an academic. By 1981, fifty-three infants had been born at IPS and many more had passed through its cages.

But despite his well-deserved authority on the subject, a handbook he had written on the care of captive chimpanzees, for which so many of his colleagues in research facilities and zoos were clamoring, had not found a publisher. Lemmon was getting older, still smoking several packs of cigarettes a day, and had not managed to find anyone who could take over the farm, nor cover its finances. He had divorced his wife and Jane Temerlin had abandoned him, which left him very much alone and in terrible financial straits.

Yet again, Lemmon renewed his efforts to develop research projects that might attract media attention and financial support. At around the same time that Fouts was sneaking out the back door, the sign language project Lemmon had been planning for Carolyn's twins was about to begin. Now three months old, Zeb and Zeke were thriving in the IPS nursery, a newly erected prefab building that was built for twenty-four-hour care of infants and their surrogate babysitters. Soon the twins would be moved into a human home, where Lemmon could begin collecting data on them.

Alyse Moore, one of Lemmon's employees, who had been part of the team that saved Zeb and Zeke, and before that had been the person who hand-fed Nim during his traumatic early days at IPS, wanted the job as their mom. Moore had first driven her trailer up the IPS driveway two years earlier. She and Lilly, her six-year-old chimp "daughter," had been looking for a place to park their home. Lilly, who later became the mother of Sheba, Nim's only offspring, slept in Moore's bed, ate meals at the table with her, and was virtually inseparable from her. As Lilly got older and larger, Moore worried about their future together. Where do you go with an adult chimpanzee? Most landlords don't even allow a dog. Moore was just the kind of person that Lemmon liked. She was tough and could handle chimps, and in return for being allowed to park her trailer on the property, she was willing to help care for his growing population of transient chimps. There was only one catch: Lemmon insisted on treating Lilly like all the other IPS chimps and wanted to move her to a cage. Moore agreed. But no one, with the possible exception of Lemmon, was ever surprised to find Lilly in Moore's trailer at the end of the day, where a small group of students liked to relax and smoke pot. Lilly smoked with them and would roll the joint herself if the others were too slow about it.

Tiny, Lemmon's farm manager, who became Moore's companion, could also be found in her trailer at the end of the day. Putting Zeb and Zeke in their care gave Lemmon easy access to them whenever he wanted it, because they were right in his own backyard. Lilly even helped Tiny and Moore take care of the twins by giving them their bottles. A few weeks later, another infant named Naomi, born one month before Zeb and Zeke, was rejected by her mother, a female chimp named Peggy. Lemmon immediately removed Naomi from Peggy's cage and gave her to Moore too. The three adorable babies snuggled together on the couch like a litter of puppies.

To Lemmon, the babies presented a unique research opportunity. When they were old enough, he planned to teach two of them two different sets of signs; the third one, on the other hand, would not be taught any signs at all. "Then we watch them like a hawk to see which signs are transferred from whom to whom," he explained to a local reporter. It sounded like a game show — and everybody wanted to watch. The premise of the experiment put it in direct competition with Mellgren and Fouts's plans for Washoe, and it might well have finished first. But it never happened.

Two months after the three infants moved into the trailer, it burned to the ground. According to the fire department, a burner on the kitchen stove ignited some grease on the wall. Zeke and Zeb, five and a half months old, and Naomi, four and a half months old, were all killed. Moore, Tiny, and Lilly were not at home at the time. The local press covered the tragedy, omitting one detail: when Tiny returned to the trailer, the chimps were still alive, so he took out his gun and ended their suffering.

Other chimps had died over the years, but the accidental deaths of these three infants, who had all struggled so hard to survive, was particularly devastating. Lemmon's cross-fostering experiments were running amok. The research was not making any headway, and the suffering that both chimps and humans experienced was taking its toll. Separating newborns from their natural mothers was agonizing enough, but then the infants proceeded to break up human families and destroy homes, after which they were dumped back in Norman, where they went through terrible trauma before adjusting to life in a cage. The cycle to which Lemmon had devoted his career caused untold misery. While it did leave a legacy of students who became accomplished primatologists, in the end there were few scientific breakthroughs in Oklahoma, from either Lemmon or Fouts.

In the 1960s, Lemmon had purchased his first chimp for $500; by the 1980s, he was able to sell baby chimps — to researchers, circus trainers, and even the occasional couple who simply wanted to raise a chimp — for $10,000 each, though he was sometimes willing to settle for less. However lucrative they were, chimp sales did not generate enough money to keep IPS going, and circumstances became even more dire when OU warned Lemmon that his budget was about to be terminated. In preparation, the university hired an outside veterinarian, an expert on primates, to assess the physical facilities at IPS, while lawyers examined its legal ties to the university. According to J. R. Morris, provost at the time, the veterinarian's report claimed that the farm did not meet minimum standards provided by the U.S. Department of Agriculture (USDA) for research animals. Morris argued that the university could not justify using state funds to bring IPS up to code. (This is the reason that universities often give when they want to dump researchers and their animals.) All OU funding for IPS was terminated in 1981.

According to Ingersoll, conditions at the farm were not significantly worse than they had ever been, but Lemmon no longer had resources to pay for day-to-day maintenance, hire adequate staff, and make necessary improvements. Tiny had held the place together, but in 1980, he was driving home to IPS in his truck and was hit by a drunk driver and killed on the road. Lemmon never replaced him.

Lemmon remained determined to save IPS. He made what would be his final efforts to find funding, using his infants — before they were sold and taken to their new owners — for several new projects. In one, he rated each newborn on a behavioral assessment scale that had been developed by the popular pediatrician Dr. T. Berry Brazelton for parents to test their babies. The simple procedure involves exposing newborns to various bells and rattles while observing their physiological responses. With human children, the experiment takes about twenty minutes and can be done in the normal course of changing a diaper. With chimps, the infants had to be separated from their mothers — never simple — before the test could begin. By this time Lemmon was working closely with Pat

Crown, a woman who took on the position as Lemmon's assistant (and later became his lover). Lemmon and Crown selected three infants to be tested. Unfortunately, according to Ingersoll, Crown mixed up two of them, returning a male to the mother of a female and vice versa. Both infants were killed. If this account is true, it was a terrible, inexcusable error, and a clear indication that IPS was disintegrating.

Since the founding of IPS, Lemmon had never allowed his chimps to be used for any invasive biomedical research. (In his view, behavioral research was not invasive.) The standard IPS contract he used for buying and selling chimps stipulated that none of them would be used for medical research. But Lemmon could no longer afford to stand on principle.

In desperation, Lemmon turned to the pharmaceutical industry, the one place where adult chimps remained a highly desirable commodity. (Infant chimps were more highly valued than adults, because few people or institutions, apart from research laboratories, wanted the older, larger, more aggressive animals, who were expensive to keep and often difficult to handle.) As the species most closely related to humans, the chimpanzees had a value as human surrogates that was rising as fast as the profits of the drug companies. "There seems to be almost no medical condition that has not been explored with primates," wrote Deborah Blum in *The Monkey Wars*, a thorough exploration of the use of primates in research. Blum estimated that in the early 1980s, forty thousand primates (monkeys and apes) were living in laboratories.

Lemmon wanted his entire colony of chimps to stay together. He believed that whatever happened to them, they would take comfort in each other and continue to breed, making them valuable — as a social group — to any laboratory. Lemmon had never considered the small group of signing chimps within that colony, which of course included Nim, to be any different from the others. He could see no reason to make that distinction now.

As a last-ditch effort, Lemmon bid on a contract from Merck to test a hepatitis B vaccine. He hoped to keep his animals and do the study at IPS. But after a great deal of wrangling, Merck turned Lemmon down. He could not compete with the larger biomedical facilities around the country, all of which had some form of institutional support. Everything that made IPS moderately hospitable to chimps — the social life, time outdoors in the fresh air, and high-quality food — apparently made it less desirable for drug trials. But if Lemmon could not bring the drug trials to Norman, he could send his chimps to the facility where they were going to happen.

Lemmon quietly offered the majority of his adult colony, approximately thirty chimpanzees out of a total of around forty, to the Laboratory for Experimental Medicine and Surgery in Primates (LEMSIP), owned by New York University, which had won the enviable contract for the hepatitis trial. Hepatitis B is not terminal, although it can lead to liver cancer or cirrhosis. Lemmon considered the study to be one of the safest; if his chimps were used, they would be injected once with the virus and would only have to have their blood drawn periodically over the course of just one year. He hoped his chimps would then be used as breeders, nothing more, as they were known to be one of the most productive colonies in the country, and all labs, including LEMSIP, needed breeders. Whatever happened after the study would be out of his hands; LEMSIP would own the chimps. Even if Lemmon had wanted them back, he couldn't have afforded them. Once his chimps left Norman, the IPS director would never see them again or be able to track their where-abouts.

Dr. James Mahoney, the staff veterinarian from LEMSIP, came to Norman to meet the chimps and talk with Lemmon about the colony and the sale. An Irishman with a lilting brogue, Mahoney had a genuine interest in all animals and a reputation for taking excellent care of his chimpanzees. He had traveled around the world to various facilities — wherever chimpanzees were in residence — administering care and often saving their lives. Mahoney appeared to have more in common with the affable James Herriot than with the average vivisectionist. However, inside LEMSIP, he had to make life-or-death decisions on a daily basis. The chimps were in constant danger of being infected by a terminal illness or undergoing painful experimental procedures. Mahoney had no illusions about his work. He sought to achieve a balance in his life by shuttling back and forth between the worlds of medical research and rescue, always striving to keep his lab chimps alive long enough to retire them, at the end of their service, to any safe haven that would take them.

Lemmon believed that Mahoney would take good care of his chimps at LEMSIP and that eventually they would escape routine needles and biopsies. Still, Lemmon of all people knew the risks at LEMSIP. The laboratory constantly took on new medical projects in its own facility and sent chimpanzees to other labs as they were needed. A deal with LEMSIP was a potential death sentence for each and every chimp.

"He just couldn't go on," says Peter Lemmon in his father's defense. "He couldn't do it anymore, and he had no other choice." The fact that Lemmon liked Mahoney and believed that the amiable veterinarian would do his best for the Norman chimps helps to explain why he allowed them to go to LEMSIP. Also, other facilities were known to be — and were — worse than LEMSIP. But even by Lemmon's standards, this decision was controversial, and he knew it. He hoped to get the chimps out of Oklahoma before the story broke in the local papers and all hell broke loose.

As Lemmon sorted through his chimps, making decisions about which ones to keep or sell, he generated a list for LEMSIP. It included Pan and Carolyn, who had been faithfully reproducing for IPS since the 1960s. The list also included four younger chimpanzees: Bruno, Ally, Onan — and Nim.

OU chimp leaflet

401

Chapter 11
Inside LEMSIP

In 1965, New York University had hired Dr. Jan Moor-Jankowski to create the first primate medical research laboratory in the state, which became LEMSIP — the Laboratory for Experimental Medicine and Surgery in Primates. Groomed at NIH, and a leading expert in immunology, the Polish aristocrat was a brilliant scientist, an award-winning humanitarian, and a memorable character. He was known for his bespoke suits, his flashy Mercedes, and, more important, his ironclad integrity. Born in Poland in 1924, he joined the army to fight the Nazis at the tender age of fifteen. By 1942, both his parents were dead and Moor-Jankowski found himself incarcerated in a Warsaw prison. In one of his earliest escapes — there would be many — he slipped away from the guards, hidden by a blizzard of bullets, during a violent uprising by Jewish prisoners. The young soldier went underground to join the resistance, where he gained a well-earned reputation for fearlessness. At one point during the war he was shot in the leg and his knee was shattered. In need of immediate surgery, he impersonated a German officer and demanded to be taken to a hospital. As the story goes, he mumbled in German even as he came out of the anesthesia.

At LEMSIP, Moor-Jankowski used his international connections to obtain contracts from private companies around the world. These contracts, along with additional support from NYU, paid the bills. According to science writer Deborah Blum, Moor-Jankowski developed a sophisticated method for primate blood typing and innovative techniques for freezing blood, and did "remarkable work on the chemistry of pregnancy." Moor-Jankowski easily attracted top primate virologists in the field to his lab, where they used the chimpanzees to create a hepatitis B vaccine. He worked closely with Dr. James Mahoney, the veterinarian in charge of LEMSIP's primates, who had a team of assistants and veterinarians working for him. It was Mahoney's job to maintain a large pool of healthy primates (approximately 300 chimpanzees, 100 macaques, 165 marmosets, 15 baboons, and

8 squirrel monkeys) from which he selected individual animals for each experiment. But in the main housing unit, the chimps had no fresh air, natural light, or access to each other, which turned their incarceration into a grueling experience. Some became ill and were either retired or euthanized after their first trial, while others went on to the next experiment, and then the next. Mahoney and his staff managed to keep most of the animals alive and in decent health, but there were always some who did not survive the suffering and deprivation.

LEMSIP, along with its inmates, was all but invisible to the outside world. New York University (NYU) had established this research lab miles away from its New York City campus, in Sterling Forest, an affluent suburb, where residents were more preoccupied with dinner parties than with what went on inside the local research lab. From the outside, the place looked more like an unadorned corporate headquarters than a prison for primates. Deborah Blum, who had an opportunity to tour it, found the facility surprisingly accessible. "There is nothing fortress-like about LEMSIP — no barbed wire, no alarms," she wrote in *Monkey Wars.* But the bland exterior belied its grim interior. Nim and the other chimps from Norman were on their way to a cement prison where there were no windows to look through (or break) and no way out.

By the early 1980s, as Moor-Jankowski focused on hepatitis research at LEMSIP, primates, especially chimpanzees, were considered optimal surrogates for vaccine studies. Biomedical labs such as LEMSIP developed their own breeding programs to ensure a constant supply of "fresh" animals for whatever study came through the pipeline. So LEMSIP had pulled off a coup by acquiring the Norman colony of chimps, proven breeders who, with few exceptions, had been exposed only to behavioral experiments. Not only were they healthy and virus-free, but many had been raised by humans, an obvious advantage in a research laboratory where hands-on procedures such as shots, blood draws, and biopsies were business as usual.

In order to supply each research project with test subjects, Mahoney kept a list of available chimps (those coming off one experiment and healthy enough for another, and youngsters old enough for their first experiment) and matched individuals to experiments, a process he once described, with his customary frankness, as "giving them the kiss of death." The research itself, again according to Mahoney, was nowhere near as hard on the chimps as the terrible social isolation that went with it. Mahoney says it took him a full year to convince MJ, as Mahoney called Moor-Jankowski, to create a nursery for the infant chimps, in order to give them an opportunity to socialize at a young age, and hence the possibility, no matter how slight, of getting out of LEMSIP in decent psychological shape. MJ considered the nursery a luxury, not a necessity, and there were few luxuries in LEMSIP. Some baby chimps might stay with their mothers for a few years, but once they went into research they might never see them again; the separations were heart-wrenching. Mahoney wanted the adolescents held back from research until they were at least seven years old, and he did what he could to tuck them away in obscure corners of the facility for as long as possible.

If Moor-Jankowski and Mahoney had conflicting views on the quality of life inside the laboratory, it may have been because Mahoney knew the chimps as individuals, while MJ focused on the research, not the animals. MJ had not one doubt about either the quality of care for the chimps at LEMSIP or the significance of the research done on them. Lemmon believed that LEMSIP was superior in every way to some government facilities, which were known to house primates in far worse conditions, and perhaps it was. But LEMSIP was still a biomedical testing lab: the chimps inside were expendable, and many of them would die there. Nevertheless, with an equanimity born of his belief in the value of the research projects he presided over, MJ took calls from reporters and candidly discussed the research under way (without revealing the names of contractors) and sometimes even invited them to tour the facility. He was proud of LEMSIP and boasted about it to animal activists. According to one well-known story, when the group People for the Ethical Treatment of Animals (PETA) tried to bring some humorous attention to the not-so-funny misery of research animals, the organization sent MJ two hundred coconuts. Not missing a beat, the LEMSIP director graciously accepted the gift and made a show of handing them out to the chimpanzees with great enthusiasm. Sparring with PETA in the press amused MJ, who was convinced not only that his chimpanzees were not suffering but also that they were serving the interests of the medical establishment — and hence those of the human race.

William Lemmon shipped out the first batch of chimps to LEMSIP on December 2, 1981. He planned to send several more groups over the course of a year, as cages became available for them at the facility. The first chimps to leave were the oldest, most dominant males: Pan, Bruno, Booee, Onan, Pablo, and Tiger. Their departure would significantly reduce the wear and tear on the small staff and the cages in Norman. Lemmon managed to keep all his plans and negotiations with LEMSIP quiet.

Keeping any secret in Norman, especially one as consequential as this, might be considered an accomplishment. But once Fouts left IPS, and the Institute lost its OU funding, it became ever more remote from campus life. With few new students arriving and only a handful of chimpers remaining, there weren't many people to report on what was happening at the farm. Thus, Lemmon was able to send the first group of chimps away from Norman without any fanfare. Nim and Ally were scheduled to leave in six months, part of the second shipment to be trucked to Sterling Forest.

Chimps frequently trickled out of IPS as Lemmon traded or sold them, making the mechanics of these deals — veterinary checks, transport, paperwork — routine. But he usually sold off chimps one or two at a time, not in large groups. Inevitably, one of his most devoted graduate students, who had worked at the farm for several years, noticed that the arrangements Lemmon had made for the first shipment were unusual. A bright young woman who was devoted to the animals in her care, she quickly deduced that Lemmon was selling off the bulk of the colony to LEMSIP and leaked the news to a few friends, including Bob Ingersoll. No one in Norman felt more loyalty to the chimps than Ingersoll. He had been trained to treat them with respect and to communicate with them as if they were human. Ingersoll thought of them as his friends, not pincushions for medical experiments. The decision to sell them off for a hepatitis study seemed so reprehensible to him that he had trouble believing that Lemmon could do such a thing. Incredulous, Ingersoll went to the farm and confronted Lemmon. Lemmon, not considering himself accountable to a hot-tempered student, simply banished the uppity chimp-lover from IPS property. Ingersoll was relieved that he didn't get shot.

The uppity chimp-lover was not easily

silenced, however. He spread the news, called the press, and began to organize a protest to immediately stop the flow of chimps out of Norman. He and a few others developed a doomsday plan: if Lemmon went through with the rest of the LEMSIP deal, they would sneak onto the farm, dart the chimps, and put them all down. In their view, LEMSIP was a fate worse than death.

The plan never materialized. Instead, Ingersoll and his buddies called the press, and on May 2, 1982, a local Oklahoma paper broke the story. The details were sketchy; the exact number of chimps sold, whether they had already been shipped, how they would be used, what kind of care they would receive, and what might happen to them in the future were all questions that remained unanswered. The university blamed inflation for its decision to stop funding IPS. Lemmon, for his part, defended LEMSIP, arguing that the chimps would be safe there; LEMSIP had signed a contract with IPS agreeing not to use the Norman chimps in any invasive surgery or terminal research. According to Lemmon, the chimps would be kept together and used primarily as breeders.

Ingersoll continued to send out press releases, the first of many over the next few years. In his mind, OU was responsible for the sale of the chimps. Unlike Lemmon, the university had the resources and finances to save them. Moreover, OU students had used the chimps for years in their experiments, and he felt that the university therefore had an obligation to pay for their care. Ingersoll lambasted administrators for their lack of ethical standards. He stood on street corners, passed out leaflets, and wrote letters. But he was merely a thorn in their side. The university was determined to put its involvement with primates in the past.

Chris O'Sullivan, still in Norman, was no chimp activist, but the LEMSIP news upset her to the core. Although she had nothing but contempt for Lemmon, she had felt for his chimpanzees from the first day she arrived in Norman. Since she knew her way around Hollywood and the media, she contacted a friend at CBS and pitched the story: a group of unique, ASL-trained chimpanzees had been sold for medical research and were about to be injected with an experimental vaccine. O'Sullivan mentioned Nim Chimpsky and suggested that the reporter give Herbert Terrace a wake-up call.

The reporter reached Terrace in his office at Schermerhorn. It was June 1982. Most likely Terrace had not thought about Nim for several years. He was finished with signing chimps, ape language researchers, and the endless drama and debate still swirling around them. But Terrace was horrified by the news. Nim was on his way to LEMSIP, located in Sterling Forest, less than an hour north of Columbia University and even closer to the Delafield mansion.

Terrace had been in biomedical labs. He knew that once Nim entered the medical research system, he would probably be lost forever. Chimpanzees were shipped from one facility to another following the flow of research dollars. Tracking any animal was virtually impossible for outsiders. Terrace had been preparing to leave for a conference in Europe; he canceled his trip.

The quality of life at LEMSIP was so poor that the Norman chimps, born outside the biomedical system and arriving as adults, must have had tremendous difficulty making the transition. Nim and the others were housed in claustrophobic individual cages that hung from the ceiling in two rows that faced each other. Since their feces dropped through the floors of the cages, it was not necessary to clean them. The chimps could see each other across the room, but they could never leave their closet-sized, five-by-five-by-six-foot cells or touch each other. One visitor described the cages as no bigger than refrigerators. Short by seven and a quarter inches, the cages failed to meet even the minimum USDA standards, which were barely adequate but better than no standards at all. Mahoney, no doubt, made a difference for the chimps, but there was only so much he could do under the circumstances. According to Mahoney, MJ wanted to improve the facility, but to gain those seven and a quarter USDA-mandated inches required purchasing new cages and making structural alterations to enable them to fit the existing space, which would have cost more than NYU was willing to spend. The university had flatly refused to pay the bill. Mahoney himself felt that the USDA infractions were the least of the problem and that even if the cages had conformed to regulations, they would still be too small. He wanted to see more significant changes in the accommodations, which would give the chimps more space as well as time to socialize with each other. But the budget had no funds for such improvements.

The technicians at LEMSIP who took care of the chimps noticed Nim right away. "There was something different about his body language," Mahoney explains. Nim was used to signing when he wanted something, and continued to do so at LEMSIP. The technicians reported to Mahoney that Nim and other Norman chimps were signing to them. The gestures baffled the technicians. They had no idea what the chimps were trying to say, but they knew the chimps were trying to say *something.* Thus began the inevitable controversy over whether or not Nim was different from other primates incarcerated at LEMSIP. "Hard Times for Bright Chimp," read the headline in the *Boston Globe,* which broke the story in the national press; the NBC evening news picked it up, and millions of viewers debated the ethics of socializing a chimp in a human family, teaching him ASL, and subsequently dumping him in a lab as the subject of a hepatitis experiment. Nim Chimpsky was once again a household name.

Terrace was also back in the press, where he was quite comfortable. Although he had given up custody of the chimp and declared Project Nim a failure, he had trusted Lemmon to keep Nim safe in Norman for the duration of his life. Caught off guard and distraught over Nim's predicament, he rallied a few of the chimp's old teachers, including Stephanie LaFarge and Laura-

414

Ann Petitto, and then, to his credit, spearheaded the campaign to get Nim released from LEMSIP. Terrace was not an activist, but he was angry, and not shy about using the media. He jousted with MJ in the press, hoping to seize the moral high ground, and with it control over Nim's future. MJ rarely lost an argument. He was witty, fast on his feet, and used to being in charge. But he had never had a celebrity chimp like Nim in residence and was not prepared for the political drama that ensued.

Describing Nim's rearing and socialization and the goals of Project Nim, Terrace argued that Nim was far more sensitive than the average captive primate. "Terrace himself says this chimpanzee is only a mimic," MJ countered. Eager to separate Nim's syntax from his survival, Terrace shot back: "Just because he can't create a sentence doesn't mean he should be subject to these tests."

Most reporters were more interested in Nim's point of view than in MJ's. "What would Nim say to all this?" one journalist asked Terrace. " 'Out' is one of [Nim's] signs," responded the professor, who suddenly had no problem suggesting that the chimp's signs had meaning.

In a conciliatory gesture, Mahoney put

posters on the cages that explained a handful of ASL signs, so at the very least the techs could learn to understand Nim and the other signing chimps. But it was too little, too late. MJ had underestimated Terrace's tenacity as well as Nim's vast appeal, which had been captured and exploited by the media almost since birth. The spectacle of Nim trying to talk or sign his way out of a hepatitis laboratory could not be simply dismissed. MJ's insouciant attitude toward his chimps, and Nim in particular, played like callousness in the press. Nim had been at LEMSIP for only a short time, but as each day went by, the pressure on NYU to do the right thing mounted. After a request from Bob Ingersoll, Jane Goodall wrote a letter to NYU deploring the fact that animals who had been raised in human families were now languishing in a medical research lab where they "were subject to life imprisonment and in all probability, much pain and fear." Nim, Ally, Onan, Pan, Kelly, Mona, Booee, and Bruno, among others Lemmon had sold to LEMSIP, had all spent a few of their early years in human homes.

Whether the human-raised "talking" chimps would do better or worse than others under the harsh conditions at LEMSIP was a question that could not be answered without considering the plight of all research animals. The press went right to the heart of the matter. "Do animals suffer needlessly?" asked Robert Reinhold in the *New York Times*. Yes, the public wanted safe vaccines, but the idea of testing them on an animal who had grown up on the Upper West Side with a family and had retained enough ASL to use it wherever he was living — New York, Oklahoma, or LEMSIP — was deeply disturbing. Reinhold concluded, "These chimps are almost human." Whatever "almost human" actually meant, in scientific or any other terms, it was an apt description of the public's perception of Nim. Human hands had carefully molded his infant psychology, and the chimp had relatives — people who thought of him as family. "It's like seeing your child sold for medical experiments," Laura-Ann Petitto told a reporter. "I just don't think Nim is going to survive."

Moor-Jankowski reassured the public that the hepatitis serum would not kill the chimps; the vaccine had been developed at the Pasteur Institute in France, where it was already being safely given to humans. But that was beside the point. After all, Terrace had provided evidence to suggest that Nim had a mind and a heart as well as a body and that they too required sustenance. As Mahoney and even MJ himself well knew, the injections were far less dangerous than the quality of life within LEMSIP. The chimps suffered from the invasive physical procedures, but the emotional toll, the depression that resulted from their isolation from their peers, was even more excruciating.

Nonetheless, MJ and Mahoney held their ground. The two men did not always agree about the fate of animals in the laboratory. On several occasions, Mahoney had quietly taken sick animals home at night to nurse them back to health and then failed to return them to LEMSIP. In effect, he operated his own witness protection program, which was offered to selected animals who would not have survived otherwise. MJ apparently never noticed the missing animals, nor did anyone else. If there was any paperwork required, Mahoney did it himself, covering his tracks; there were far too many animals in LEMSIP for anyone to count heads. But Mahoney did not want to let Nim go. He worried that if Nim and the others from Norman were shipped out of LEMSIP, they might end up someplace even worse. MJ had other concerns. Allowing even one chimpanzee to elude the system on moral grounds would open the floodgates.

However, MJ's stonewalling backfired. Just as he must have feared, Nim quickly became the poster chimp for protests against the inhumane treatment of all chimpanzees in medical facilities and elsewhere. Advocates suggested that chimps required more protection in both the laboratories and the wild (whatever was left of it). They insisted that the entire species was far too intelligent and human-like to be exploited for medical research; there were other methods to test the vaccines without using live animals. The Humane Society of the United States made a futile attempt to negotiate for custody of Nim. Terrace had his own plan: he proposed retiring Nim to a zoo called Lion Country Safari, located in West Palm Beach, Florida. But MJ scoffed at this. "I sent some chimpanzees there once several years ago," he said. "One of them was bitten in half by a hippopotamus."

Despite his quick-wittedness in countering Terrace and the press, the LEMSIP director was in trouble. He had managed to keep animal advocates at bay for almost twenty years, but this was about one chimp in particular, a very famous one with friends in the media, and Nim's supporters were not giving up. As Nim sat in his cage, waiting for his turn to be infected with the hepatitis serum, protesters marched back and forth in front of NYU waving placards and chanting slogans. The spectacle kept the case in the public eye. NYU's attorneys, unimpressed by the controversy, saw no legal reason why Nim should be released. MJ dismissed all the fuss and predicted that it would soon die down. In his world, all chimpanzees were created equal. There was no room for exceptions.

Henry Herrmann followed the story in the *Boston Globe.* A Boston attorney who had always liked a good cause, he wondered about Nim's legal rights — that is, if he had any. Born in Belgium, Herrmann had come to the United States with his parents, docking at Ellis Island before settling in Queens. Over the years, he had studied philosophy in graduate school at Columbia, considered a career in marine biology, and ended up with a law degree. He had done some legal work for the New England Anti-Vivisection Society, the oldest organization of its kind in the country, and he was familiar with the dismal world of biomedical research. Herrmann is not against all research on animals, but he saw no reason to use this particular

420

animal for that purpose. Like Terrace, he believed that the chimp deserved better. Two days after the story broke, Herrmann picked up the phone and called the professor. He had no agenda and no hourly fee, which made his offer hard to refuse. "I wasn't asking for any bananas upfront," he quips. Nor did he ever get any later.

Now represented by counsel, Nim raised the specter of legal liability for NYU. MJ was not the least bit intimidated. He stonewalled Herrmann, refusing to discuss Nim's case or even take his calls. Herrmann realized that MJ had no intention of ever releasing Nim. "He was totally unreasonable," says Herrmann. The attorney contacted the dean of the medical school, who turned out to be much more receptive. As a first step toward resolving the deadlock, NYU agreed to withhold Nim from the hepatitis study until both sides reached an agreement about his future. In return, Herrmann told the press that NYU (as opposed to LEMSIP) was also concerned about Nim's well-being and was fully cooperating with an investigation. For the moment, Nim was protected from the needle. Herrmann had collected letters of support from dozens of children who had watched the chimp grow up on television. He told reporters,

"This case is not just about the vaccine. It's about a unique and highly socialized animal who deserves more. Allowing this to happen to Nim is like selling Bambi for dog food. How would that play on *Sesame Street*?"

Once Herrmann had his foot in the door, he moved quickly to force it open. He contacted the American Society for the Prevention of Cruelty to Animals (ASPCA), located in Manhattan, and made a formal complaint of animal cruelty against LEM-SIP. The ASPCA agreed to investigate the charges, despite the fact that the agency had never taken a case based on psychological rather than physical cruelty. Humane officers began an investigation that, depending on what they found, could result in a possible raid. "We prepared to break down the door and grab the chimp," says Herrmann. It was a backup plan, to be used only if all else failed.

Herrmann launched his most innovative battle in court. He began with the premise that the usual USDA standards (not that LEMSIP met them) for laboratory animals did not apply to Nim because of the peculiar circumstances of his upbringing. The attorney declared that Nim was sui generis, in a class by himself, and therefore could not be treated in the same way as other research chimps. He prepared a habeas corpus petition on his behalf, hoping to bring him into the courtroom. "The question would be, 'Does Nim feel cruelly treated?' And the judge would have to allow him in court to get an answer." Sign language interpreters were not unusual in a courtroom. But proving that Nim was sufficiently compos mentis to testify on his own behalf would be more challenging. Herrmann intended to put Terrace on the stand to testify that Nim's IQ was higher than that of some mentally disabled human beings who had been granted their day in court. At long last, Terrace's data would be useful to Nim.

But questions remained. How would Nim take the oath? Herrmann had a plan. He found a precedent in an early-nineteenth-century case where the judge had personally deemed the witness reliable and waived the oath. To do this the judge would have to meet Nim and assess his ability to communicate.

Meanwhile, back in Norman, Ingersoll relentlessly kept the pressure on OU. He spoke with Herrmann as often as possible, implored Roger Fouts to become involved, and spent long hours raising funds for a new sanctuary in Florida for all the Norman chimps, not just Nim. Fouts, for whatever reasons, was reluctant to speak out initially. But according to Ingersoll, a long list of prestigious judges and politicians all wanted to help.

The list of supporters included Thelma Doelger, a notable philanthropist who, with her husband, Henry Doelger, had a particular passion for rescuing primates. Over many decades, the Doelgers had quietly funded sanctuaries around the country that cared for retired research animals. Thelma took a particular interest in Nim's case. She had personal contacts on NYU's board of trustees — and no qualms about using them. Doelger made a few highly effective phone calls to insist that LEMSIP immediately release the notable chimp. Cleveland Amory, another prominent figure in the animal protection movement, also weighed in to support Nim. Amory had his own contacts at NYU, and a reputation for going to great lengths to rescue animals. He too contacted some of the trustees, calling them in the middle of the night to put them on notice that they would not get much sleep until Chimpsky was out of LEMSIP.

The amount of pressure on NYU, from all sides, had not been anticipated. MJ and various university administrators received hundreds of letters and calls, students were demonstrating on the streets of New York and Oklahoma, and questions concerning the ethics of Nim's incarceration were making news. The personal calls to NYU trustees seemed to push the school closer to taking action. MJ had been insistent on keeping Nim, regardless of the consequences. But with the controversy escalating and no end in sight, NYU made the decision to override its LEMSIP director. Despite MJ's objections, NYU initiated negotiations with OU — not Lemmon or IPS — to give Nim back.

The struggle was soon over. OU's chief counsel called Herrmann and told him, "Tell your client he can walk."

Nim had been in LEMSIP for less than one month and had not been injected with any serum. Although he never had his day in court, this was probably fortunate. The judge, according to Herrmann, was overheard saying to a clerk, "If you think I'm going to be the first judge in the United States to hear testimony from an ape — you are fucking crazy!"

Nim's advocates were victorious, but the crucial question of where he would be sent next remained unanswered. Herrmann proposed that they agree on a sanctuary that would guarantee Nim's safety for the duration of his life. This required some consensus on who actually owned Nim and had the authority to make such a critical decision. OU claimed that Lemmon owned all the Norman chimpanzees, including Nim; the university had never housed them and did not want to take responsibility for them or have a say in any decisions concerning their future. The simplest and fastest solution, which appealed to both NYU and OU, was to return Nim to IPS. Herrmann argued vociferously against this decision but finally agreed on the condition that OU continue to discuss further contractual protections for Nim. It was risky, but NYU wanted Nim out of LEMSIP as fast as possible. So did Herrmann. During the final negotiations, Herrmann says, "I had their ear, so I got Ally thrown in as a traveling mate at the last minute. It was the best deal I could make."

On June 22, 1982, Nim and Ally were loaded on a truck bound for Oklahoma. The two chimps slipped back into Norman without a welcome party. They had left in secrecy and returned without attracting much attention. Ownership of both chimps reverted to Lemmon, regardless of his plans for them or the stability of IPS. Herrmann continued to implore OU attorneys to write up a contract with Lemmon, which would ensure some protections for Nim and Ally, as there was no reason to think that Lemmon would not sell them again. But OU had no legal obligation to the chimpanzees and therefore no interest in them.

Bob Ingersoll was thrilled to have Nim and Ally back in Norman (although Lemmon would not allow him on IPS property to see his old friends). And he wanted the university to make amends for what it had done by erecting a bronze statue of Nim on campus. He considered the chimp a hero. But he wouldn't rest easy until all the chimps Lemmon had shipped off to LEMSIP were returned. Ingersoll continued to blast university officials for their callous indifference to the fate of the rest of the OU chimps. Twenty-four of them remained in Sterling Forest. The group left behind included Bruno, Terrace's warm-up chimp and Josh Lee's rambunctious playmate. (Bruno was one of the first chimps to be injected with hepatitis serum. He would eventually die in LEMSIP, too sick to be moved elsewhere.) Ingersoll could name all of them, and he was on a mission to get the whole group sent home. Refusing to end his protest, Ingersoll temporarily dropped out of school and opened up a shop in Norman called Jungle Jim's. The store was a hippie haven that Ingersoll decorated to look like an authentic African hut. Inside he sold tie-dyed clothes, beaded jewelry, woven tapestries, handmade sandals, and large posters with images of wild chimpanzees. Jungle Jim's was more than a shop — it was a place for young students to hang out with their friends and make their own tie-dyed T-shirts on a table in the back. Ingersoll might hand them some propaganda on their way out, a flyer or one of his articles. The store became the headquarters for his local "Save the OU Chimps" campaign. OU was hardly impressed by the ex-student's persistence. University officials declined to take his phone calls and ignored his letters and demands for an audience. They continued to maintain that the chimps were Lemmon's property and therefore his problem.

The controversy further blackened Lemmon's reputation, if that were possible, and it was anybody's guess what he might do next. Lemmon's health was deteriorating after a lifetime commitment to smoking, and Dorothy Lemmon, who resided in the same house with him although the two had been divorced for years, had been diagnosed with lupus and become severely depressed. Meanwhile, Pat Crown, Lemmon's new assistant, was taking over both IPS and its director.

Crown handled the media for Nim's homecoming, spinning the story to generate as much good press as possible for the beleaguered Institute. Local reporters wanted to know if Lemmon was so destitute that he would be forced to continue selling off chimps to LEMSIP. Crown assured them that Lemmon would never do that, but her assurances had little credibility. The flow of chimps from IPS to biomedical laboratories quietly continued. There was no media circus because no one ever found out what Lemmon was doing until it was too late. Ingersoll continued to write letters of protest and generate some support for the Norman chimps, but with Nim no longer at the center of the drama, getting anyone to listen was more difficult.

Six months after Nim and Ally's return, Lemmon sold Ally and two adult females (Harmony and Debbie) to the Buckshire Corporation, a biomedical warehouse in Perkasie, Pennsylvania. Ally and the others were spirited out of Norman before the press could get hold of the story and precipitate another rescue attempt. Ally had been raised much the same as Nim and had a substantial vocabulary of signs. Fouts had once wanted Ally and surely would have purchased him from Lemmon had he been given the chance, but months passed before chimper activists became aware that he was missing. Ally was not the first chimp that Lemmon had sold to Buckshire, nor would he be the last. But selling Ally to another medical research facility after he had survived the LEMSIP fiasco was a truly spiteful decision. It was revenge, plain and simple — Lemmon's way of getting back at Fouts and at all those who had dared to interfere with his master plan.

Buckshire was a warehouse for primates — no frills. The chimps were sent out for research to other labs, over and over, and used for blood and tissue banks. Some private labs drew the line at cosmetic research and toxicology studies. Buckshire did not, and as a result it was well known to animal activists. In 1994, an undercover operation by PETA would result in a thirty-eight-page report filled with alleged abuses and disturbing videos of traumatized chimpanzees, and eventually a USDA investigation of the facility. Under intense pressure from animal protection groups, Buckshire began retiring its "used-up" chimps to sanctuaries. But that was too late to help Ally, who would never make it to any sanctuary. Although Ingersoll and others searched and searched, they never found Ally again. He would be moved from facility to facility until he became sick enough to warrant euthanasia, on June 12, 1992, at the White Sands Research Center, a biomedical laboratory in Alamogordo, New Mexico.

Nim, however, was still safe from Ally's fate. So far, his celebrity protected him. Even Lemmon understood the outcry that would have greeted his sale to Buckshire or a similar facility. Nim remained at IPS, sitting unhappily in the back of a cage, while Lemmon figured out what to do next with the famous chimp. When a zoo offered Lemmon $25,000 for Nim, it got his attention, but the bids had just started to come in, and Lemmon was apparently in no rush. Nim was his most valuable chimpanzee. Lemmon waited patiently to see what use Nim might be to him. The chimp might attract all kinds of people — and offers — to the farm, and Lemmon, whether he admitted it or not, was in desperate straits.

■ ■ ■ ■

PART THREE:
SANCTUARY:
MURCHISON, TEXAS

■ ■ ■ ■

Cleveland Amory at a book signing for The Last Resorts, *published in 1952*

CHAPTER 12
THE BLACK BEAUTY
RANCH

Cleveland Amory, born in 1917 into an aristocratic Boston family, grew up in a mansion that rivaled Delafield. Surrounded by servants, formal gardens, and luxuries that most children only dream about, Amory yearned for the one thing he did not have: a dog. His parents finally relented when Amory was eight, and Brookie, a beguiling Old English sheepdog, joined the family. Brookie and Amory were inseparable. It pained the young boy so much to be apart from his dog that one morning, ever the optimist, he brought the shaggy mop to school and stuffed her under his small wooden desk, hoping she might not be discovered. His teacher immediately ordered him to take the dog home and leave her there.

Brookie was, by Amory's own account, his first true love. Formative as this relationship was, Amory also had two human relatives who had much to do with his eventual dedication to the mission of animal welfare. His favorite aunt, a woman named Lu Crehore, frequently picked up strays off the streets, one by one, turning her house into a lively menagerie. And Amory's great-great-uncle George Thorndike Angell, who died several years before Amory was born, had devoted his life to the protection of dogs, cats, and horses. A leading Boston attorney and philanthropist, Angell was the founder of the Massachusetts Society for the Prevention of Cruelty to Animals (MSPCA), one of the most venerable organizations of its kind. He also published the first American edition of a then little-known book from England called *Black Beauty,* written by his friend Anna Sewell. (The book was originally published in 1877, and it was the only one Sewell wrote; she died of hepatitis five months after its publication.) Sewell's goal was to expose the rampant cruelty toward working horses in England. Angell, a great admirer of the book, added his own subtitle to the first American edition, *The Uncle Tom's Cabin of the Horse,* and, under the auspices of MSPCA, handed out free copies in the streets of Boston. Many years later *Black Beauty* would make an indelible impression on Cleveland.

Amory followed in his father's footsteps as far as Harvard and then fled Cambridge for New York, where he began an illustrious career as a prolific author, columnist, television commentator, and radio pundit, known fondly as the "Curmudgeon at Large." Hardly the usual activist, he galvanized the animal protection movement with style and humor rather than rhetoric. "Dining with Cleveland is like going to a party with a combination of Sheridan Whiteside, W. C. Fields and Aunt Bee," wrote one acolyte. He snarled at the rich and defended the helpless, while at the same time managing to cultivate an impressive list of celebrities to bring media attention to animal cruelty. By the time Nim Chimpsky hit the national news, entrapped in a biomedical laboratory, Amory was easily the most celebrated animal advocate in the country. He wasn't a bomb thrower (figuratively speaking) and did not fit the rabid activist stereotype, but when he launched a rescue mission it rarely failed.

With great fanfare, Amory took on the most difficult, often hidden issues of animal abuse and turned them into popular causes. He had a natural instinct for publicity, a way of approaching people and issues that attracted an audience far beyond the narrow parameters of animal advocates. He also had vast resources: money, media access, and an address book filled with the names and phone numbers of the power elite. By the 1950s, he had harnessed all of his energy to the animal welfare movement, which had never had such a well-connected advocate and consequently had been languishing in obscurity. When Amory joined the board of the National Humane Society (eventually the Humane Society of the United States, HSUS) in 1960, six years after it had opened its doors, he helped put that organization on the map. But Amory was a leader, not a follower. When HSUS refused to take a public position against hunting — all hunting — he quit in disgust.

In 1967, Amory founded his own non-profit, the Fund for Animals, which was not beholden to benefactors, political agendas, or abstract issues — just animals. The Fund, as it is called, grew into a national advocacy organization with offices in New York and Washington, D.C. From its inception, the Fund went after hunters, whether they were shooting deer in the woods or clubbing baby seals for their fur in Newfoundland. (Amory showed a graphic clip of a seal hunt on the *Today* show, where he was a regular commentator, and was summarily fired.) He regularly enlisted his famous friends — Mary Tyler Moore, Henry Fonda, Princess Grace of Monaco, and Doris Day — to help popularize the injustices of routine cruelty to animals in research laboratories, the fur trade, and wherever else they were being slaughtered. Then he began rescuing them.

Amory's rescues, often captured on camera, were sensational dramas that played out like Hollywood movies. One of his most spectacular rescues began in 1979, a few years before Nim's trauma at LEMSIP, when the Bureau of Land Management (BLM) was about to destroy hundreds of burros at the base of the Grand Canyon. The burros were the descendants of animals who had been abandoned once the gold rush was over. They had been multiplying ever since, and beginning in the 1920s, despite attempts by humane organizations to put a stop to the practice, the BLM had been periodically rounding them up and shooting them to keep their numbers under control. Amory found the government's policy unacceptable, and he vowed to do something about it. He saw no reason for the burros to be hunted down and killed, rather than moved somewhere where they could live out their lives in peace. This, of course, was easier said than done. The complex logistics of getting them out of the canyon were so challenging that the inventive rescuer had to spend months coming up with a plan for an airlift and putting together a team of cowboys that might successfully carry it out. One key person was a talented roper named Dave Ericsson, who agreed to go down into the canyon and lasso the burros. Once captured, the burros were secured in individual slings that were designed to dangle from the base of a helicopter. On the spot, at the bottom of the canyon, Ericsson and the pilots devised a double sling to carry mothers and babies together, so that frightened youngsters did not have to fly through the air alone.

The plan worked — the helicopter pilots managed to take out about twenty-six burros a day, and the cameras rolled, documenting this daredevil operation for an audience of millions. The rescued burros were airlifted to the top of the canyon and then trucked to a nearby corral on Native American lands — not National Park Service property — on the bank of the Colorado River. "We generally had much better relations with the Indians than we had with the Park people," Amory wrote. But Amory was still on a learning curve. He was not pleased when the Indians suddenly began charging the Fund large holding fees for the burros and other fees for incidentals, including parking charges each time a vehicle pulled up to the corral.

Dangerous and expensive as it was, the rescue implicitly demonstrated Amory's belief in the inherent value of every living creature. Once Amory rescued the burros, however, he didn't quite know what to do with them. He had hoped to find adopters for these causes célèbres, but there were far too many of them and the adoption process would take too long. Amory previously had been searching for a sanctuary property, mostly for companion animals, and now he decided that what he needed was a ranch that would be suitable for burros. He found eighty acres two hours east of Dallas in Murchison, Texas. The land was inexpensive, not too far from where the burros were stashed, and available. (It was also surrounded by thousands more acres that would eventually belong to Amory.) So Amory bought it and hired a small staff to care for the burros. Thus the Black Beauty Ranch, named in honor of his favorite book, was born.

The burros had found a permanent home, and Amory had provided an unexpectedly happy ending to a horrendous story. All the

publicity introduced the public to these affable creatures, many of whom were docile,
like pets. Burros, which come in all sizes
and colors — shades of gray, brown,
dappled white, spotted — have an uncanny
natural charm. The easygoing, big-eared
creatures nuzzled the hands that fed them,
and some were so tame that they wandered
freely around the ranch, greeting cars as
they pulled through the gates. Their endearing qualities made the answer to the question of whether or not burros deserved
protection crystal clear. The whole operation, during which 577 burros were transported to Texas, took two years to complete
— and made Amory a hero. But the burros
were only the beginning. Now Amory had a
sanctuary, a place where many kinds of
abused animals — from the exotic pet trade,
circuses, petting zoos, research laboratories,
and canned hunts — could find a haven for
the rest of their lives.

Black Beauty boasted acres of flat grassy
meadows, rolling hills, and several small
ponds, perfect for all varieties of hoof stock.
But Amory had no idea how hot and inhos-
pitable the landscape could be. Drought
years would require supplemental feedings
for the more than a thousand horses, buffalo, and other large animals who eventually

came to live there. Amory became fond of quoting General Philip Henry Sheridan, who once said, "If I owned Texas and Hell, I would rent Texas and live in Hell." Nonetheless, after initial growing pains, Amory turned Black Beauty into one of the few widely respected sanctuaries for multiple species in the country.

When the uproar over Nim's sale to LEM-SIP appeared in the press, it inevitably caught Amory's attention. He stewed over Nim's situation, contacted Terrace, and eventually decided to take an active role in extricating the chimp from his plight, even though he was aware of the implications of singling out Nim and ignoring the rest of the chimps. "I am not one of those people who believes it is right to experiment on some animals and not others," he wrote in *Ranch of Dreams,* his book about Black Beauty Ranch. Amory would have preferred that no animals end up in places such as LEMSIP, but he had no moral qualms about drawing the line at Nim. This chimp *was* different. Amory argued that using Nim as a garden-variety research animal was a particularly inhumane way to thank him for his previous service.

Amory was not in the loop of the legal negotiations between NYU and Nim's advocates, but, having made his interest in the case clear both to Terrace and to the NYU trustees he had contacted about Nim, he tracked the chimp's progress in the news. When Nim was suddenly released by NYU and returned to Oklahoma, Amory knew there was still cause for concern. So long as the chimp remained in any research facility, he would not be out of danger. Amory's interest in Nim only grew stronger with his release from LEMSIP. Now he wanted to meet the chimp and see with his own eyes the conditions in which Nim was living at IPS. Wondering if a known animal advocate could get in the front door of IPS at such a sensitive moment, Amory put in a cold call to Lemmon. Always unpredictable, the director got right on the phone. They chatted about their common interest in animals, and Amory expressed a desire to meet the famous chimp. Lemmon asked when Amory would like to visit. He responded, "How about tomorrow?"

A few days later, Amory was on a private tour of IPS, listening to Lemmon describe his own research in excruciating detail. The encounter between the two men had all the earmarks of a high-stakes poker game, with Nim's life as the pot. Amory feigned a keen interest in Lemmon's every word and kept his mouth shut. A few hours went by without Lemmon's even mentioning his famous guest. In fact, he introduced Amory to all the remaining chimps except Nim. For his part, Amory played down his interest in Nim and encouraged the director to elaborate on his dreams for the future of IPS. After a congenial morning spent wandering around the farm, Lemmon and Amory went out for a long lunch. At the end of the day, Lemmon casually asked his companion if he wanted to see Nim. Amory agreed to take a quick look.

Amory found Nim sitting in the back of a crowded cage, looking despondent. Several adult chimps were milling around him. When he caught Nim's eye, Amory was convinced he saw misery. He thought the other chimps seemed menacing, and he wondered why Lemmon wasn't making more of an effort to protect Nim. Amory, of course, knew nothing about what captive chimpanzees required or how to interpret their behavior toward each other. But it was obvious that IPS was not an ideal place for any animal. The place looked run-down and now, unlike a decade earlier, there were no enthusiastic students around to amuse the chimps. In Amory's words, what he saw on the visit "galvanized into a desire to have [Nim]."

At this point, Nim had become no more than a sideshow attraction for Lemmon. He referred to Nim derisively as "Half and Half." (Although it was meant as a cynical commentary on the chimp's public persona and on Project Nim, the moniker would stick and be used fondly, not derisively, at the next stage of Nim's life.) Amory offered to buy Nim on the spot and bring him to Texas. He invited the psychologist to visit the Black Beauty Ranch before he made a decision. Lemmon agreed to come.

A few months later, Amory showed Lemmon around the Texas ranch. According to Amory, the IPS director was especially impressed by the variety of species that Amory had gathered in one place: by 1982, horses, bison, giraffes, zebras, and a few water buffalo had joined the burros. Lemmon agreed to sell Nim to the Fund for $7,500. Amory rarely paid for an animal, but he would have done anything to get Nim. Certainly, Lemmon could have sold Nim for more to a zoo; he'd already been offered more than three times that amount. But, in an uncharacteristic move, he made a decision that benefited the chimp.

The deal was signed before Herrmann,

Nim's chief counsel, heard anything about it. "We were making some headway for Nim with OU," says Herrmann. "But Amory grabbed him and preempted the process." Ingersoll and Herrmann were both infuriated by the decision. Herrmann deeply resented what he described as "Amory's awesome ego." Ingersoll wanted Nim to live out his life at Primarily Primates, which was also in Texas and which in his view was a more appropriate sanctuary, since Black Beauty had no chimps and Amory and his staff had no experience with them. In typical fashion, however, Amory had failed to consult any of the people who had helped extricate Nim and Ally from LEMSIP and who had continued to attempt to influence Nim's fate. Amory rarely worked with others when he did not have control over them and the situation. Unlike Ingersoll and Herrmann, however, Herbert Terrace and Stephanie LaFarge were thrilled by the news. They considered every day Nim remained in Norman to be risky. Black Beauty Ranch may have had no other primates, but it was a sanctuary; presumably the animals there would be safe forever. Amory was the highest-profile rescuer in the country. Now he would have the most famous chimpanzee.

In his eagerness to get Nim out of Oklahoma, Amory had his ranch manager, Jerry
Owens, build a cage for the chimp as quickly
as possible. It was modeled on the ones at
IPS, with no more than small inside and
outdoor areas, both built on cement, and
was dark and gloomy. No one at the ranch
understood much about the physical or
psychological needs of chimpanzees or other
primates, much less of this particular, highly

*Nim alone in his cage at Black
Beauty*

448

unusual newcomer. Amory believed he was doing the right thing, but as the person who raised every penny for the ranch, he was also concerned about the budget.

On April 3, 1983, Nim was loaded onto a truck, alone, and driven to Texas. Almost ten years old, he was not yet fully grown and appeared deceptively approachable to anyone unfamiliar with the species. Nim must have been frightened at being moved to yet another strange place. There were no familiar faces, either human or simian, to greet him in Texas. Nevertheless, upon arrival, he looked people directly in the eye and scanned their faces, anticipating some form of communication. There wasn't much. During those first few days, the ranch staff talked more about him than to him. Amory had described him as "the smartest animal in the world" but had not suggested that his employees learn any ASL to communicate with him. In fact, the staff at the ranch regarded signing, and all behavioral research, as a form of abuse and assumed that Nim would not want to sign if given the choice. No one, including Amory, understood that Nim routinely signed because it was the way he had learned to talk to people. In fact, he always looked for people who knew some ASL and was thrilled when he found them. When Nim gestured to the ranch hands at Black Beauty as they passed by his cage, hoping for a response that never came, it wasn't long before he became sullen and dejected.

The chimp's unhappiness was obvious. When staffers tried to get near him, he lashed out and tried to hurt them. They referred to him as "Half and Half" and meant it affectionately, aware of how human-like he was, but they were also frightened of him. Luckily for Nim, Jerry Owens, the manager of the ranch, lived with his wife in a small farmhouse on the property close to the chimp house, and she took it upon herself to learn a few words in ASL, which she taught to the others. Eager for human interaction, Nim enthusiastically signed with her and with whoever else on the staff made the occasional attempt to communicate with him.

Amory lived in New York, not Texas, and was removed from problems at the ranch. He paid the bills, raised the funds, and continued to rescue more animals but had little knowledge of what they required to thrive. He had hired Jerry Owens, a local rancher, to run the place, and assumed that he could do so. Owens repaid his boss's confidence in him by radiating an aura of competence, particularly in relation to his new charge. So, Amory had no idea how unhappy Nim was, sitting alone in his small cage, or how complex the task of caring for him would prove to be.

Owens assumed that Nim, like most new residents, would eventually come around. Unsure of the chimp's boundaries and unaware of how dangerous he could be if he was upset, Owens initially allowed people to get far too close. During his first week in Texas, Nim bit one of his keepers on the hand, badly. If people came too near the bars of his cage, Nim nicked them with his nails or lunged for them as if he wanted to hurt them. Although the staff had picked up a few signs, they had no techniques for safely handling Nim. Thus, he was not only failing to make new friends but earning a reputation for being a mean-spirited chimp who had become disturbed after years of abuse in research facilities. Owens claims to have taken Nim out of the cage for walks, hoping to make a difference in his attitude, only to realize it was a mistake. Nim was skilled at slipping away, and Owens had to resort to a dart gun to get the chimp under control. Rumors about a deranged "talking" chimp at the ranch spread through Murchison. Locals wanted a peek at Nim — from a safe distance. Some thought he was a wizard, some the devil.

Several weeks after Nim's arrival, Bob Ingersoll appeared at the ranch unannounced, in his 1971 Alfa Romeo. Had Amory invited him, Ingersoll would have been waiting for Nim at Black Beauty the day he arrived. But Amory and Ingersoll, already at odds over Nim's final disposition, were not destined for a relationship of mutual respect. Now Ingersoll simply wanted to make sure the chimp was in good hands. By the time Ingersoll parked his car and walked over to Nim's enclosure, Nim was signing, "Bob," "out," "key." Ingersoll says Nim knew the sound of his car and anticipated his arrival. Owens could see they knew each other, but Amory had left strict orders not to let the chimp out under any circumstances. Owens asked Ingersoll to sign a waiver agreeing not to sue if he got hurt. Then Ingersoll spent three uninterrupted hours in the cage with Nim.

Ingersoll made a real difference for Nim. He interpreted for Nim, helped the staff understand him, and taught them some more signs. He explained what the chimp required for basic care, how to amuse him, and the foods he liked best. But Ingersoll was alarmed by the conditions Amory had provided for Nim. Black Beauty had been expanding, rapidly adding acreage, animals, and staff, which made it difficult for Ingersoll to understand why Nim was stashed in a small, dark cage. Chimps were not like the other exotics living at the ranch. The apes required far more attention, which Amory had not understood. Ingersoll had never wanted Nim to go to Black Beauty for precisely this reason. Once he saw the chimp house, he importuned Amory to expand it and to get Nim a companion. Ingersoll explained — to whoever would listen — that chimpanzees lived in social groups. They required the company of one another to survive in captivity; otherwise they became depressed and ill. Some just gave up and died. Nim was a sensitive and gregarious creature who would go steadily downhill in isolation. Besides friends, Nim needed trees to climb (ideally right in his enclosure), fresh air to breathe, lots of sunlight, and a view of the sky.

Amory, used to an adoring public and quite unaccustomed to any complaints concerning Black Beauty, resented Ingersoll's criticisms. If there were any problems at the ranch, Amory was loath to admit to them. Unfortunately, Ingersoll's persistence was more abrasive than persuasive. He continued to pester Amory with phone calls, and when Amory stopped taking them, he wrote letters. He wanted Nim moved to a primate sanctuary, where he would be with other chimps. But Nim was not going anywhere. Amory told Owens not to let Ingersoll into Black Beauty again.

Nim's second visitor was another old friend. Stephanie LaFarge was in the process of reconstructing her life when word of Nim's incarceration at LEMSIP got out. She and WER were divorced, the children were older and more independent, and she had finally earned her doctorate. But the LEMSIP fiasco had forced her to recognize how much of an impact Nim had made on her life and how naive she had been about his future. LaFarge had never had much to do with the animal protection movement, but she found Amory's zeal for mass rescues appealing. She had talked to him during the LEMSIP controversy and they had struck up a relationship. Amory had a scathing view of Project Nim for failing to take into consideration the chimp's long-term welfare. He questioned not only Terrace's role in the experiment but LaFarge's as well. LaFarge herself was coming around to the same view. Now that Nim was safe in Texas, she wanted to see him again, for her own peace of mind. Amory invited her to Texas.

Jenny Lee insisted on making the trip with her mother. During the LEMSIP debacle, she had been away at college, far removed from the protests. But like her mother, she missed Nim and ached to see him. "I thought about him almost every day," she says, thirty years after Nim left her mother's household. "I still do."

When LaFarge and her daughter arrived at Black Beauty, Amory and Marian Probst, his longtime assistant at the Fund's New York office, personally accompanied them to Nim's cage. (Probst and Amory were a team, and she became president of the Fund in 1998, when Amory died.) By this time, Nim had been at Black Beauty for about six months, but he was still unsettled and nervous. LaFarge insisted on going into his cage right away. Probst and Amory were dead set against it and begged her not to. Nim was bigger, no longer her baby. And there were rules at the sanctuary, with "No humans inside the cage" being the most critical one. Jenny too thought her mother was crazy, but she knew that trying to dissuade her from anything once she'd made up her mind was a waste of time. Before anyone could stop her, LaFarge opened the cage door, slipped in, and locked the door

455

behind her.

Amory, Probst, and Lee were frozen with fear as Nim walked up to LaFarge. A few seconds went by during which nothing happened and they even seemed to make a connection. But suddenly Nim grabbed her ankle, pulled her off her feet, and dragged her on her back to a corner of the cage. He stood in front of her, making sure that she could not reach the door to escape. "We thought he was going to kill her," recalls Probst. "Cleveland and I knew that we would not be able to shoot Nim to save Stephanie. We loved him too much." As a reporter in the *Texas Monthly* drily put it, "You would not want Cleveland to be in charge of making a Sophie's Choice between you and any animal."

Amory and Probst went into rescue mode, trying to distract Nim with food and lure him to a different part of the enclosure. They called to him repeatedly, hoping he would leave LaFarge and come over to them. Nim obliged them more readily than they expected, releasing his prisoner. LaFarge crawled out of the cage on her knees, as fast as she could. "Nim let her go, but he was totally in control," Probst recalls.

LaFarge had cuts, bruises, and a sprained ankle, but she bore Nim no grudge. Look-

Tom Martin, Nim, and hash pipe

ing back on the incident she says, "It was the least I owed him." Jenny Lee felt a mixture of emotions. She was furious with her mother for entering the cage and jeopardizing her life — and possibly Nim's life too. And she was stunned by Nim's rage at her mother. "He wanted to kill her," says Lee. "We had no idea." Years later, LaFarge speculates that Nim was angry and knew exactly what he was doing to her. Having abandoned him, she felt that she deserved his rage.

Visitors from Project Nim continued to

drop down on the ranch, somewhat like tornados, leaving swaths of destruction in their wakes. One of the most disastrous incidents occurred when Tom Martin, one of Nim's part-time Delafield keepers, arrived. Martin had lived nearby in Riverdale with his parents and often took Nim home to hang out with them. The whole family knew Nim and enjoyed his visits. On one occasion when Nim was out with Martin he was photographed smoking dope from a hash pipe. The picture was published in *High Times* magazine over a caption that described Nim as a "monkey linguist" who had "invented a special signal — one forefinger to lower lip — meaning, 'Hit me with the ganja, you Babylonian Sodomite!' "

Terrace had fired Martin soon after he had been hired because, in Martin's own words, "I was somewhat nuts." Martin had been diagnosed with bipolar disorder, which, at the time of Nim's rescue by Amory, was not yet under control. But he adored Nim and had become convinced that spending time with the chimp would be a cure-all for his mania. During one of his spells, determined to pay a visit to Nim, Martin boarded a flight for Dallas with all of $20 in his pocket. He was so disruptive on the flight that when he exited the plane he was greeted by three police officers and taken to jail. In his briefcase, Martin had a copy of the Koran, an ounce of pot, and a knife. His incredibly patient wife flew to Dallas and bailed him out of jail. But Martin refused to leave Texas without seeing Nim, so they drove to the ranch. Somehow Martin managed to convince Jerry Owens to let him in Nim's cage. The chimp's shoe fetish had stayed with him, and one of the ranch staffers gave Martin a pair of big boots to wear into the cage so Nim wouldn't destroy his sneakers. Once inside the cage, Nim wanted to pull both boots off Martin's feet, but one of them was stuck. Nim became frustrated, grabbed Martin by the elbow and hurled him up into the air, then bit him. An ambulance was called for Martin, and he was delivered to the closest hospital. Martin's wife wanted to take him home from there, but he insisted on bidding Nim farewell and returned to the ranch with fifteen stitches in his arm and a huge bandage. Once again, Owens let Martin back in the cage, and nothing untoward happened this time. Finally, his wife got Martin on a flight back to New York.

Black Beauty Ranch had been founded only five years before Nim arrived. Amory had no idea how difficult it would be to oversee a sanctuary in Texas from New York City. Once Nim was in residence he realized he had an even bigger challenge, and he needed someone more experienced than Owens to help him meet it. Owens didn't share Amory's radical views about animal rights, nor did he feel any need to improve the animals' quality of life as the ranch expanded.

Amory set about finding a trustworthy ranch manager, one who was knowledgeable about multiple species, had respect for the abused animals in residence, and would be able to provide adequate care for Nim. But Billy Jack Saxon, the man Amory eventually hired to replace Owens, was even worse. Saxon, already working at the ranch, knew the drill and wanted the job; perhaps Amory hired him simply because he was there. Billy Jack was more Texas than Texas, a good ol' boy who drove a big car, had a big belly, and had lots of kids. Amory let him know that if he could cut any corners and save a few dollars, he would be pleased. So Saxon made a deal with a local bread company to take all its leftovers, which he fed to the horses and burros, providing a diet that was inexpensive but unacceptable by most standards. Amory knew about the plan and assumed that his ranch manager, at the very least, knew what animals ate. But worse than the bread, Saxon was breeding his own hogs on the side and driving them to slaughter in the ranch truck, which sported a proud Black Beauty Ranch logo. Amory seemed to be the only person in Murchison who didn't know about it.

Back at the ranch, Nim was bored and lonely. Had Amory spoken at length with any of the folks from Project Nim, the chimp's fascination with locks would not have been a surprise. At Black Beauty, as at his previous places of residence, Nim kept his mind occupied by investigating the ways he could maneuver his way out of his confinement. "Half and Half" now became known as "Houdini," a nickname that had suited him at Delafield also. The first few times Nim escaped, Amory worried that he might run off into the woods and never be seen again. But Nim wasn't interested in the woods. When he got out of his cage, he went to the manager's house, right next door to his enclosure. Typically, he raided the refrigerator, maybe turned on the television, and got into any bed that was available. One time, he sneaked into the house when the Saxons' miniature poodle was home alone; as the story is told at the ranch, the dog came running at Nim, barking hysterically, and Nim grabbed the dog and banged it against the walls over and over, covering the place with blood. It was a brutal death, but Nim wasn't vicious, just frightened. Saxon returned home to a blood-splattered crime scene. He grabbed his dart gun, shot Nim, and then carried him back to his cage. The Saxons had loved their little dog.

Nim repeatedly broke out of his cage to romp through the Saxons' house and all the nearby buildings on the ranch. Since no one had figured out how to handle Nim inside or outside his cage, the jailbreaks, as Lemmon had called them, were a problem. At one point, Amory began to think that Nim needed a house, not a cage. He had the staff fill Nim's cage with furniture, hoping he might feel more at home and less inclined to bust out. But like any self-respecting chimp, Nim destroyed everything in the cage by hurling it at the walls, jumping on it, and tearing it apart.

From this, Amory concluded that the chimp was too wild for a house and too human for a cage — an apt description of most captive-raised chimps. But Amory just had Nim in the wrong cage, in the wrong circumstances. Boredom and species isolation are torture for a chimpanzee. Nim began pulling out his own hair, pacing, and repeatedly displaying the same nervous behaviors seen in zoo animals. The Black Beauty staff, mostly locals in addition to an able Mexican crew, realized that something was wrong. When Amory and Probst finally figured out the problem, "we felt stupid," according to Probst. "We should have realized Nim needed a friend much sooner." By this time, he had been at Black Beauty for more than a year.

Amory turned to Lemmon for help. The two men had parted on good terms, as Amory never wrote a negative word about the IPS director, at least while Lemmon was alive. By 1984, Lemmon had begun selling off all his remaining chimps to LEMSIP or anyone else who would pay for them. He was in the process of closing down IPS for good. His lungs were failing, and Dorothy Lemmon, still residing with her ex-husband, was becoming more depressed over her own health. Lemmon and Dorothy were spending as much time as possible in Costa Rica, where they had built a small house in the jungle, the one place where they spent time alone together, without any outside interference. There were only a few chimps left in Norman by the time Amory called, wanting to find Nim a girlfriend. (Early on, Inger-soll had begged Amory to take Onan, Nim's brother, still stuck at LEMSIP, but Amory had refused. Eventually Onan was secretly slipped out of LEMSIP, via Mahoney, and sent to Primarily Primates instead.)

The timing was ideal. Lemmon, eager to find places for every last one of his chimpan-zees, offered him Sally, a twenty-year-old female who had been at IPS since 1973, the year Nim was born. The two chimps may have met in passing over the years. Sally was born in 1964 somewhere in Africa. Her captors nabbed her for a circus trainer and shipped her off to the United States. After performing for almost a decade, she was retired and given to Lemmon. Known as "the professor" in the circus/rodeo world, Lemmon was one of the few scientists train-ers liked and respected; they found his farm to be far more hospitable than the alterna-tives when they were looking for a place to retire their chimps, and they believed Lem-mon when he swore he would never sell the chimps off to medical researchers. By the time Sally arrived in Norman, this unusu-ally congenial chimp had acquired a variety of acrobatic skills. She walked upright, danced on her toes like a ballerina, and roller-skated. Lemmon believed that his trained chimps — those who had come from the entertainment business — enjoyed showing off their talents. When visitors toured through IPS, Lemmon encouraged the chimps to perform. The most common trick among them was a cigarette gag. The chimps all liked to smoke, but a few put the lit end of the cigarette into their mouths as if they were making a dumb mistake, and then proceeded to take a long deep drag. First-time visitors always gasped, a response that all the chimps found highly amusing.

Lemmon had held Sally back from the first few LEMSIP shipments. He may have had a particular use for her in his behavioral projects, or it is possible that he was especially fond of her. It's also possible that she wasn't a candidate for LEMSIP because, having taken a load of buckshot in her abdomen the day she was captured, she was unable to get pregnant, which may have made her less desirable to the lab. But with the demise of the farm upon him, Lemmon knew that all his chimps would have to go somewhere. When he suggested Sally to Amory, he described her as "easy to manage." He had estimated her value at $50,000 for insurance purposes but offered her to Amory for $5,000, in a bargain-basement deal. Amory agreed to pay the bill after a six-month trial period; if Nim liked Sally, she could stay forever. In a painful bit of irony, which Amory must have noted, he had to sign a contract with Lemmon agreeing that Sally would "not be used for medical or biological purposes which involve chemicals, surgery or other procedures which may be considered painful or injurious to the animal; which may shorten its life or be injurious in any way to its health."

A year after Sally arrived in Texas, Pat Crown, Lemmon's assistant, started to write dunning letters to Amory, reminding him that he had failed to pay the fee for her. Amory put Crown off, pleading poverty, and eventually Lemmon cut Sally's price in half. The Fund paid $2,500 for Sally, and Amory never heard from Lemmon again.

The end of IPS was approaching. In 1985, Dorothy Lemmon surreptitiously purchased a gun and shot herself in the head; her body was found on the floor of her greenhouse. The following year, as Lemmon's health became more precarious, the remaining chimps were sold. Lemmon was hospitalized in Norman with complications from emphysema. He died on January 12, 1986, of congestive heart failure.

Chris Byrne at the Black Beauty Ranch

Sally had seen trouble — what captive chimp hadn't? But she was gregarious, polite, and accustomed to interacting with other animals as well as humans. Sally was "smaller than Nim but with double his charm," wrote Amory. "Unlike Nim," he added, "she didn't grab, bite or try to escape." Sally had far better manners than Nim, and she invited attention from the staff. At twenty years of age — ten years Nim's senior — she was calmer, easier to please, less sneaky, and far less manipulative. During her first weeks at the ranch, she was neither moody nor unhappy. It seemed as if Sally understood that her life was going to improve at Black Beauty. The staff took to her immediately. But to Amory, it was Nim's response that mattered most.

It is hard to say whether or not Lemmon knew that he was sending Amory the ideal match for Nim. The IPS director ordinarily made decisions that benefited himself, not his chimps. But he did know his chimps well, down to the idiosyncrasies of their personalities, and there's no denying that when Sally arrived at Black Beauty, Nim's state of mind underwent an almost instant change for the better. By all accounts, the two chimps were soon inseparable. They may have recognized each other from Norman, giving them a basis for their relationship, but in Texas that relationship grew into a strong, deep bond. Nim refused to leave her side — not that he had anywhere to go had he been so inclined. The chimps still badly needed a larger cage, but sharing his space with Sally was far better for Nim than inhabiting it alone. The cage became "the chimp house," and the gloom that had enveloped it like a black cloud began to dissipate. It was suddenly quite obvious, as Ingersoll had repeatedly told Amory, that chimps needed each other in order to survive.

Nim and Sally played together, huddled closely, groomed each other for hours at a time, and eventually nested together in a loft area at night. Nim taught Sally how to sign "drink," "banana," and "gum," three of the words he used most frequently at the ranch. Nim's physical and psychological closeness with Sally was the much-needed antidote to his depression. For the first time in many years, Nim was settling in, looking content.

Amory, along with Probst, who occasionally accompanied him on visits to the ranch, believed that the two chimps were in love, not unlike humans. "You could see it," Probst insists. "Nim's eyes followed Sally around. If he felt she was unhappy, he would try to figure out what she needed and cheer her up." Nim was jealous when humans came too close to Sally. She belonged to him, and he was possessive of his new friend. He still managed to escape, which remained his signature activity. But now he took Sally by the hand and escorted her out of their cage with him, as if they were going on an excursion. The staff learned that if they could get to Sally and lead her back to the chimp house, Nim would follow at a short distance.

With Nim in good psychological shape, Amory began to feel more confident in Black Beauty's ability to handle chimpanzees and possibly more primates. The ranch received dozens of requests to take in a variety of species. Thousands of retired monkeys from research laboratories, often rhesus macaques, many of whom needed quarantine and special attention, were among the animals waiting for someplace to go. The alternative for them was euthanasia. Eventually, Amory took his first six macaques from the Wisconsin Regional Primate Research Center, and he would continue to accept more (including a group from LEMSIP). Soon, Nim and Sally would be able to watch, or at least hear, a colony of monkeys, a few gibbons, and two mountain lions (Katy and Sergei, from a roadside zoo), in a community of cages built near the chimp house.

Amory was besieged with requests from people who wanted to visit his animals. All the horses and burros, as well as the primates, had stories to be told, and Amory saw no reason to keep the public at a distance. His staff transformed an old green bus into a touristmobile, and on Saturdays groups of people piled onto the vehicle for a tour and the opportunity to ride through acres of rolling fields where hundreds of animals were roaming.

Nim, of course, had a line of visitors, including a number of deaf admirers, waiting to meet the famous chimp and see him sign. Phyllis Frelich, a founding member of the National Theater for the Deaf (best known for her Broadway run in *Children of*

Cleveland Amory's touristmobile

a Lesser God), and her interpreter, Jane MacDonald (also an actor), both fluent in ASL, had read about Nim and always felt a sense of closeness to him. Amory invited them for a visit, but when they arrived at Black Beauty, they were specifically asked not to pressure Nim into signing with them if the chimp wasn't in the mood. "We had just driven a very long way," says Mac-Donald, who had come for the express purpose of signing with Nim and was disappointed. But when they walked over to the chimp house, where Nim and Sally were lounging on a tire swing, Nim voluntarily signed to them, and he seemed thrilled to get a response. He did want to sign.

Nim may have been much happier once Sally arrived, but there continued to be serious problems at the ranch, mostly having to do with the management. Although Amory seemed to be wearing blinders, insisting that all was well in Murchison, the problems could not be ignored forever. Saxon, like Owens before him, did not share Amory's high standards for the care of his rescued animals, and even if he had, there were major challenges to meet. With the large animals being spread out over hundreds of acres, their conditions were difficult to monitor, requiring more effort and vigilance than the small staff could possibly provide. Amory's "Ranch of Dreams," as he called it, had turned into a bit of a nightmare. Two elephants in residence did not have adequate enclosures or diets and were not thriving. The macaques were living in a small cage where fights broke out and they could not easily be separated; the mountain lions barely had room to pace back and forth. And the chimps, Nim and Sally, were still confined to a dismal, woefully inadequate cage.

Amory's eyes were forced open in 1990 when a story about Saxon's hog business finally broke in a local paper. The press smelled hypocrisy and kicked up a storm about the ranch, where animals were supposed to be saved, not bred and eaten. Actually, the slaughtered pigs were not rescues; they belonged to Saxon. But it made no difference. The controversy reached Amory, who told Saxon to close down his hog farm or leave Black Beauty. Saxon chose the latter. From his perspective, managing a multi-species sanctuary must have made pig farming look like a picnic. The next manager would have a completely different and far more humane attitude. Black Beauty was about to become an authentic sanctuary.

Nim had bonded closely with Sally, but he remained aloof from most humans at the ranch, if not occasionally antagonistic. Amory himself could never get near him — and was smart enough not to try. He was so frightened of Nim that once when he was at the ranch during one of Nim's frequent jailbreaks, the Curmudgeon at Large locked himself in the nearest bathroom until Nim had been returned to his cage. But all the fear inspired by Nim was about to dissipate with the arrival of Chris Byrne and Mary de Rosa (now Mary Thull), the couple Amory hired to take over the ranch from the Saxons.

Byrne, a blond Englishman, had true compassion for animals, especially when they had been abused, and years of hands-on experience taking care of them. A colorful character who loved to recount tales from his storied past, he had managed a large horse farm for the Du Pont family in Pennsylvania, handled exotics (with the exception of chimpanzees) on Hollywood movie sets, fought runaway forest fires in California, and traveled all over the world camping out in the wild. There was virtually no country he hadn't seen, river he hadn't crossed, or challenge he considered too great. A mixture of Crocodile Dundee and Brad Pitt, Byrne was a daredevil with an abundance of charm and a genuine touch with animals — and women. Amory hired Byrne as the new manager after one interview, on the day they met. De Rosa, at the time living with Byrne in Dallas, was also eager to be part of the ranch operation, and she moved to Murchison with him.

Byrne had a fresh eye and a perspective quite different from that of the previous managers. He had not grown up in Texas, where livestock is purely a business. Byrne, like Amory, believed the animals at the ranch, all of whom had been abused or become disposable, deserved to thrive, not merely survive.

Nim and Byrne clicked right away, mostly because the new manager respected the chimp and kept his distance at first. He would take the necessary time to get to know Nim.

Byrne identified as an animal advocate, not an activist, but he was more. He knew about animals and what they needed. He was rugged and gentle at the same time, a man who could do anything with his hands — build barns, fix trucks, handle medical emergencies — and would make sure that no animal at the ranch was neglected. Equally important, he and Amory shared an ideological commitment to active rescue. They both wanted to be able to respond quickly when zoos were ready to dump crippled elephants or the BLM rounded up wild mustangs for slaughter. Black Beauty had space, and Byrne wanted to fill it with needy animals. He had contacts in the circus world with owners who were eager to quietly get rid of unwanted animals, often sick or old. But before he could take in more animals, he needed to improve conditions for the ranch's current residents. Amory gave his new manager carte blanche to make the necessary changes.

Byrne discontinued the stale-bread filler on the animals' menu and ordered his own custom blend of grains and nutrients, which he had delivered to the ranch each week. It made an immediate difference for the burros, now joined by an assortment of large animals — Amish draft horses, buffalo, broken-down thoroughbreds — all saved from auctions and slaughterhouses. Amory griped about the bills, counting every penny, but ultimately he respected Byrne's judgment. As word got out that Black Beauty was turning into a well-run sanctuary, Byrne was deluged with requests from rescuers. He convinced Amory to buy more land, fence off new paddocks, and expand the population. Byrne took in two camels from private collections. He also drew up plans for a larger home for Nim and Sally. Finally, they would have more outdoor space and natural light, as well as high perches from which they could get a bird's-eye view of ranch activities to amuse them. Byrne considered the renovation a necessity, but there were so many animals in need of immediate attention — individually tailored diets, medical examinations, one birth control measure or another — that it would be a long time before the renovation got under way.

Not only did Byrne want each animal checked by a vet and on the right diet, but he believed that each one deserved a proper name. Calling them by name was another way to convey his respect for them. Many had only numbers or tattoos, so Byrne named them all, and he never forgot their names. In the process, he gave Sally her last name — Jones. Perhaps he felt that Sally deserved a surname to keep up with Mr. Chimpsky.

Mary de Rosa, who became Mary Byrne when she married Chris on August 24, 1992, at the local courthouse in Athens, Texas, was a professional photographer without much experience with animals, but she took to them quickly, pitching in wherever she was needed. Together, the Byrnes developed an efficient system for feeding the many animals scattered across the huge ranch their individuated diets. Normally almost all of the staff was called upon to do these feedings, which required driving a truck around hundreds of acres. But one Sunday morning, when the Byrnes found themselves alone at the ranch without any help, Chris tended to the usual emergencies — broken fences, sick animals, escapees — while Mary fed the fifteen hundred residents on her own. It took her the entire day. On a more typical day at the ranch, it was Mary's job to watch the bills. As she recalls, "Chris dreamed about buying $100,000 tractors while I worried about whether or not we could afford to buy enough yogurt" — a welcome snack for the chimps and all the other primates.

Nim's jailbreaks could never be entirely prevented, and he continued his old pattern of heading straight for the manager's residence, now occupied by the Byrnes. Bringing Sally Jones with him, he would show up at the front door, as if he thought they had been invited for dinner. Nim on the lam under any circumstances was extremely dangerous, so when the chimps arrived, Chris always made a point of appearing pleased to see them, so that no one, including Mary, would panic. He welcomed them with hugs and treats, and they typically went right for the refrigerator and gorged themselves. Sometimes they even seemed to be trying to comport themselves like good guests. Once when Nim and Sally were sitting on the couch in the living room, Sally got up, opened the nearby sliding door, went outside to defecate, and then returned to the couch. Had she been toilet-trained, she might have used the bathroom.

Unlike previous managers, Chris was loath to use a dart gun, which was the fastest and often preferred method of dealing with a loose chimp. He knew Nim was terrified of guns, and he felt he could prevent Nim from having a fit and hurting someone without having to resort to sedation. The best strategy for keeping Nim calm, he found, was to play along with him until he became bored and more willing to return to his cage.

As unnerving as it was to have the chimps in their home, Mary and Chris did take some pleasure in it, for interacting with them when they were out of their cage was an extraordinary experience. Over time, the Byrnes became more relaxed when the chimps arrived. Once they were drinking beers and watching television and so failed to notice when Nim and Sally wandered out of the living room and began to explore the house. A few minutes later, the Byrnes started searching and found the chimps sitting on the floor in the walk-in closet Chris had built for Mary, trying on her shoes. Nim had never met anyone else with a shoe fetish that rivaled his own; Mary had sixty pairs. The party was over. Mary yelled at them to stop right then, drop the shoes, and get out of her house. Chris was afraid her screams would start a riot; Nim could have destroyed the place in seconds. But he didn't. Nim and Sally just ran out the front door, with Chris close behind them. Once outside, he noticed that his favorite camera was hanging around Nim's neck. Chris put on his most miserable face and cried, "Nim, not my camera, please give it back!" Nim stopped, lifted the camera up to his head, the lens facing his face, and snapped a picture. (The lens cap, however, was still on.) Grinning, he threw the camera on the ground, jumped on it, and finally handed it back to Chris. It was a small price to pay, and Chris was grateful it wasn't any worse. He coaxed the chimps back to their cage with promises of ice cream, as if absolutely nothing had happened.

The next day, Mary went to a local Goodwill shop and bought Nim several pairs of shoes that were large enough for him to squeeze his feet into and that he could call his own — not that he ever gave up his penchant for stealing people's shoes.

In 1993, Sally Jones had a stroke. She made a full recovery but was diagnosed with diabetes, not uncommon in chimpanzees. The disease was manageable, but Sally's health was declining. She had lethargic days when it was an effort for her to move at all. At twenty-nine years old, the former acrobat was overweight and out of shape. Her diabetes had gone undetected for too many years, and there was no room in the cage for her to run and climb. She required a new diet, insulin, blood work, exercise, and regular care — in other words, much more care and attention than she had been getting.

Because Nim became furious when Byrne doted on Sally or gave her any special attention, Byrne knew that if Sally was to get the kind of hands-on care that would help her thrive, it could not come from him. Whenever Byrne entered Nim and Sally's cage to encourage Sally to try her new diet, take her medicine, and play, Nim had to be locked in a separate section of the cage. Each time, he voiced his anger and hurled his body, along with any available objects, at the walls. Then he ran around the small space in a mad frenzy — all normal antics (called "displaying") for a pissed-off chimp. Byrne hoped Mary might be willing to take Sally on. Mary had been around the chimps enough to have already established a positive relationship with both of them. He thought that if Mary performed these ministrations for Sally, it might not bother Nim as much.

Though Mary had often watched her husband work with the chimps, she had never been in the cage with either one of them. Walking into any cage with a chimpanzee, even one as easygoing as Sally, requires courage. Mary was nervous but willing to give it a try. She entered slowly as

Byrne watched from outside, in a spot where he could leap to her rescue and also be seen by Nim; Byrne wanted Nim to feel that he was with him, not Sally. Once inside the cage, Mary stopped and waited for a response from Sally. The chimp looked up, apparently surprised to see Mary there; then she walked right over to her and gave her a hug. Mary never forgot that hug. It was so gracious, so welcoming. Mary is convinced that Sally was trying to make her feel comfortable and put her at ease. From that moment on, there were never any problems between them.

Now they were a foursome. The Byrnes hung out with the chimps, practically double-dating, one couple on the outside of the bars and the other on the inside. Sometimes Chris and Mary set up chairs near the barrier between them. They were close enough that they could reach through the bars and touch the chimps, scratch their backs, hold their hands, or pass them a drink. The Byrnes tried to keep the chimps stimulated, giving them new toys or hiding objects for them to discover on their own (a process called "enrichment" in captive environments).

Various staff members tried to stop by the cage once a day during their spare moments

— which were few, since the staff was small, ranging at different times from about five to ten people, and they were almost always overworked. They were at the job from dawn until dusk, or even all night long if there were sick animals who required their care. One unusually talented and dedicated employee, a young man named Alfredo Govea, made a point of befriending Nim, and they became close. Alfredo often ate his lunch with Nim, sitting on the grass outside Nim's cage.

But even with the best efforts of the Byrnes, and the additional attention from other members of the staff, the chimps had many empty hours to fill. Time can seem endless and often cruel for caged animals.

Nim and Sally did have some diversions in their enclosure: a small television set, rarely watched; a tire swing; a basketball set; and a variety of allegedly indestructible toys. But the chimps mainly passed the time interacting with each other — grooming, cuddling, playing, chasing. When occasional squabbles erupted, their high-pitched screeches could be heard from a distance. Minutes later the couple would make up and hug. Nim was frequently seen signing "sorry" to Sally, who always forgave her close friend.

On his own, Nim spent hours flipping through the pages of old magazines, seeming particularly diverted by images of people. The magazines, which Nim tore to shreds, were swept away at the end of each day and replaced by new ones in the morning. But he did manage to keep two children's books intact — no small accomplishment. His prize possessions, they were carefully tucked away in the loft area of his cage. (WER would have appreciated Nim's affection for books.) During the day, Nim brought the books down from the loft and pored over them intently, as if studying for an exam. One was a *Sesame Street* book with an illustrated section on how to learn ASL. The other was in essence his personal photo album from his New York years, a battered copy of *The Story of Nim: The Chimp Who Learned Language,* published in 1980. In it, dozens of black-and-white photographs of Nim — with Terrace, La-Farge, Petitto, Butler, and a handful of others — tell the story of his childhood (or an idealized version of it) from his infancy to his return to Oklahoma. Nim appears dressed in little-boy clothes, doing household chores, and learning his first signs. The book ends with a photo of Nim and Mac playing together, cage-free, in Oklahoma.

The accompanying text explains that Nim is a chimpanzee, not a human, which was why he had been sent back to IPS.

Byrne understood that Nim had been raised to believe that he *was* human, and he respected Nim's history, although he never encouraged him to sign. No one in Texas learned much ASL, apart from the several words they picked up from Nim. The staff focused on keeping the chimps physically healthy, mentally stimulated, and safely contained, which was a sufficiently time-consuming, complex task. In an effort to improve Nim's diet, which over the years had evolved in response to his cravings for junk foods and sugar, Byrne insisted on weaning the chimp off Coke, his favorite drink. (Nim continued to demand a cup of coffee in the morning and was grumpy if he didn't get it.) When visitors came through Black Beauty with soda cans in their hands, Byrne asked them to throw the cans away. Anyone caught breaking the rule had to turn over their sodas to Nim. It was an odd punishment, given that sodas had been outlawed for both chimps, but the lesson was primarily for the visitors — they were not allowed to tease the chimps with food or drinks, even unintentionally.

Chris Byrne gave Nim his first birthday

party at the ranch. The staff made lemon pies, one of Nim's favorites, and baked a large cake. Someone lit the candles and Nim immediately blew them all out, without missing one, in a single breath, through the bars of his cage. Those present were very moved by his eager participation in this simple ritual. It was one of those powerful moments when an artifact of Nim's unique past surfaced from somewhere deep inside his memory, giving the staff a brief glimpse of his childhood days. Once Byrne saw that Nim had learned to love birthday parties, he made sure that Nim had one every year. "He wasn't like any other animal we had ever seen," Probst says. "He wasn't like an animal."

The romance between Nim and Sally outlived the one between Mary and Chris. Mary loved the animals but not the isolation on the ranch — or Byrne's constant flirtations with other women. Like Amory, Byrne was seductive, and there was no shortage of women who were happy to reciprocate his interest. In 1995, he took off for a conference, and when he returned, Mary had decamped to a hotel in Dallas, taking their little dog, a stray mutt they'd named Shorty, with her. She never returned to the ranch. Although she and Byrne talked on the phone and managed to mend fences, Mary never saw Sally again. "I couldn't just show up one day and then disappear again," she says. "It would have been too hard on us both." Byrne remained committed to Black Beauty.

Four years after her first stroke, Sally had a second one, on March 21, 1997. Byrne rushed her to the hospital, but she died the following day. Nim and Sally had been together for almost ten years. Byrne had finally begun construction on their expanded enclosure, which was two weeks away from completion, but Sally never set foot in it.

The loss of Sally was like a death in the family for the staff. One can only imagine how devastating it was for Nim. "He was inconsolable," wrote Amory. "After Sally was gone, he sat on her bed, refusing to move or eat." Chimps grieve for the dead just as humans do. Once again, Nim sank into a listless sadness as he mourned the loss of his closest companion. But this time there was a deeper understanding of chimpanzees and their emotional needs, and Byrne knew something had to be done to console Nim. The solution came via Nim's old friend, Bob Ingersoll.

Byrne had allowed Ingersoll to visit Nim a few times behind Amory's back, and the two men had struck up a cordial friendship. When Ingersoll heard that Sally had died, he realized that the best way to get Nim through his grief was to supply him with another companion. He called Byrne to offer condolences and to put him in touch with a veterinarian who was looking for places to send dozens of chimpanzees. He knew that Nim would die without a friend. This time, Amory had to agree.

Ironically, the veterinarian was James Mahoney, currently in charge of LEMSIP, but only long enough to preside over its demise. LEMSIP was closing its doors in the aftermath of several animal-rights-related controversies, all legal nightmares, that had proved too much for NYU. One of them had cost Moor-Jankowski his job, though in this case it was he who was doing the whistle-blowing. After charging another NYU researcher with unethical practices, MJ was terminated, and Mahoney was left to dispose of the remaining animals in a short period of time. In the process of closing LEMSIP, NYU had already agreed to sell one hundred chimpanzees to the Coulston Foundation in Alamogordo, New Mexico. (If there were more chimps available, the university didn't seem to know or care.) But Mahoney did not want to send even a single chimp to Coulston, much less a hundred. Activists had spent years trying to close the place down, and numerous lawsuits against it were pending. The Coulston Foundation was known for toxicology experiments that were so hard on the chimps that even some researchers considered them to be inhumane. (Whether they yielded any worthwhile results was also a subject of much debate among the researchers.) Mahoney had seen the facility in New Mexico, and as a result had been moving chimps out of the lab in the dark of night to any nonresearch facility that would take them.

The IPS chimps, regardless of any contract that Lemmon had signed, were not exempt from the deal NYU had made with Coulston, and Mahoney told Ingersoll about it. Ingersoll and Mahoney had first met during the protest around Nim. They were an odd couple, but they had somehow come to respect each other. "Bob could be difficult," says Mahoney. "But there is no one more devoted to chimpanzees." Ingersoll had been helping Mahoney make connections with sanctuaries. But time was running out, so when Byrne called Mahoney to request a female chimp for Nim, Mahoney was eager to oblige. Mahoney, of course, remembered Nim from his brief but well-publicized stay at LEMSIP. The vet had a thirty-three-year-old chimp named Lou-Lou whom he described to Byrne as a "sophisticated girl who was not hysterical." He was confident that she could handle the transition to Murchison and that she would make Nim — whom he recalled as exceptionally intelligent — a suitable companion. But there was one not insignificant catch: Lou-Lou had a friend at LEMSIP named Midge, and Mahoney wanted the ranch to take them both. Midge was an overly sensitive twenty-two-year-old male whom Mahoney feared would fall apart if sent to Coulston. He told Byrne that Black Beauty could not have Lou-Lou unless they agreed to take Midge as well, and he insisted that the chimps would not be an undue burden. Although Midge and Lou-Lou had both been subject to various drug protocols, neither had been used in HIV research, so they did not have to be isolated from other primates or given any special handling.

Ingersoll, of course, encouraged Byrne to agree to Mahoney's terms. Byrne, however, knew that Amory wanted only one chimp. He also knew that if he picked up a phone to discuss the problem with his boss, Amory would tell him, "No way." So Byrne simply said yes on his own. His plan, according to Ingersoll, was to tell Amory that LEMSIP had made a clerical error and sent two chimps to the ranch instead of one. He knew that once at Black Beauty, Midge would be safe. Amory would never send a chimp back to a biomedical lab.

Byrne and Ingersoll were pleased. The sooner the chimps arrived, the better off Nim would be. But they also realized that three was an odd number. The social dynamics between chimps were complicated, and Byrne felt four would make for a better balance. Ingersoll suggested that Byrne make a personal call to Fred Coulston, the head of the foundation, for a chimp. Coulston rarely let go of any animals, especially to the animal protection movement, and getting one for the ranch would be an achievement. Byrne considered the proposition to be a challenge. While Ingersoll sat listening, Byrne picked up the phone and got Coulston himself on the line. This in and of itself was unusual. "In his cool English accent," Ingersoll recalls, "Chris told Fred how lonely Nim was and how the ranch desperately needed a female chimp." Byrne succeeded in charming the notoriously crusty researcher. Coulston agreed to give Byrne a chimp, and in return, Byrne agreed not to say terrible things about Coulston to the press. Byrne didn't have time to talk to the press anyway, so it was a deal he could easily make.

Coulston selected a thirty-five-year-old female named Kitty who had been used as a breeder for more than two decades. Wild-born in Africa and purchased by the research facility at Holloman Air Force Base in 1972, she had been shipped off to Coulston ten years later. Kitty had more than paid her dues. According to Amory, Kitty had given birth to more than a dozen babies, including four sets of twins, and had rarely enjoyed a breath of fresh air. If saving her had been a fluke, it also proved to be Byrne and Ingersoll's greatest achievement together.

Introductions between animals are always a delicate matter. Hoping to make Nim's transition easier, Byrne staggered the arrivals of the three new chimps. Mahoney sent Midge to Texas first. After traveling cross-country for several days in the back of a truck, the chimp arrived on May 14, 1997, appearing somewhat bewildered and disoriented. The loyal veterinarian was at the ranch waiting for Midge, hoping to help him

Kitty

get through the transition. The chimp entered his new cage warily, his eyes glued to Nim. The strangers circled each other, keeping their distance and never touching. But the cage was small, despite Byrne's renovations, and after only a few minutes, the two chimps were somehow back to back, and Nim inadvertently bumped into Midge. "Both of them became very upset," Mahoney recalls. "They immediately had a tumble and Nim bit Midge in the ankle." It was a nasty bite, and Midge was bleeding. Then something completely unexpected occurred. Nim appeared to become remorseful about hurting Midge, which he had not intended to do. He began signing "hug" to Midge, trying to apologize and make friends.

Meanwhile, Byrne was concerned about the wound on Midge's ankle. He wanted to get some antibiotic ointment on it, but Midge, who didn't know sign language or understand that Nim was not a threat, had become so upset that he wouldn't let Byrne or even Mahoney near him. Thinking quickly, Byrne had an inspiration. He called Nim over, put the ointment on Nim's hand, and asked him, in plain English, to put it on Midge's wound. Nim promptly walked over to Midge, slathered the ointment on his ankle, and in doing so broke the ice between them. Mahoney had met thousands of chimpanzees in his life, but he had never seen anything like this. He was deeply impressed by Nim's ability to empathize with Midge and reach out to him. Within the hour, the chimps were hugging.

Kitty arrived on June 3, and the introductions went smoothly. Her first night, she slept in a separate part of the enclosure, cordoned off from Nim and Midge by a metal guillotine door. In the morning, Ingersoll found Nim banging on the door, signing, "hurry," "open," "now." He couldn't wait any longer to meet the beautiful, regal Kitty. A maternal, wise creature, she immediately cottoned to Nim, obviously the dominant male; he allowed her to groom him right away. They would become close, although no other chimp would ever replace Sally in Nim's life.

Lou-Lou, who became Lulu in Texas, slipped into the enclosure on June 17, where she happily found her buddy Midge. Lulu was larger than Kitty but more relaxed and less intense. The group was complete. With their various affinities, tensions, and power trips, they were a family. The other three chimps brought Nim back to life. In the end, Amory gave his blessing to all three newcomers. He had no choice. Byrne often did what he wanted to do at the ranch, without Amory's knowledge. Amory's only leverage with Byrne was the budget. But Amory would have done anything possible to keep Nim content. His misery without Sally had been painful to see.

As the group dynamic established itself, Byrne was required to exercise more control, not less, over the chimps' care. It was easy to upset any one of them, and a domino effect could ripple through the group and last for hours, even days. Byrne wanted them to remain as calm as possible and was particularly concerned when visitors shouted at them and disturbed the group. Amory had welcomed the public to the ranch, where Nim was the prime attraction for most people. But some of the less sensitive visitors would stand in front of Nim's cage, calling out at him to sign, which irked Byrne — and Nim. So Byrne put up a railing that stopped the flow of traffic from getting too close. Visitors had to maintain their distance from the enclosure, out of respect for the chimps' privacy. Nim did enjoy attention, however. When he saw children at the ranch, he often waved them over, eager to meet and touch them through the bars (which he could do if they were given permission to go beyond the railing to approach the cage). He often signed to newcomers, hoping they might understand, but if they failed to respond, he lost interest in them. Kitty, Midge, and Lulu all learned several basic signs from Nim.

Periodically, people from Nim's past continued to show up. Neither Herbert Terrace nor Laura-Ann Petitto ever came, but Joyce Butler visited for several days with her husband and son. She and Nim spent hours talking, signing, and grooming each other through the bars of the cage.

Gradually, Nim assumed a central role at the ranch. He watched the other animals — elephants, giraffes, monkeys, and gibbons — from a captain's walk in his cage as they arrived at the ranch. All the people who worked there, from the cleaners to the feeders to the volunteers, wanted to cultivate relationships with him, and he reciprocated their affection. He formed attachments to many of them, made up signs for their names, and counted on them to stop by and visit every day. He may have lost Sally, but he had three new companions, and he was finally living in a world where he was understood and appreciated. He often gave Byrne a pat on the shoulder, as a friend might do, through the bars of the cage.

Amory continued to visit the ranch in his final years, hobbling on a cane out into the fields, where his animals surrounded him. Of all the animals at the ranch, Amory was most fond of the burros. He died on October 14, 1998, at his home in New York City. He was eighty-one. Amory left behind a thriving ranch and Marian Probst to run it. During his memorial service, his ashes were placed in a salt shaker and tied around the neck of Friendly, one of the first burros rescued from the Grand Canyon. As Friendly ambled about, he scattered the ashes around the ranch. Amory's headstone was put in the ground next to the one for Polar Bear, the famous stray cat he had rescued one Christmas Eve, who became the hero of his bestseller, *The Cat Who Came for Christmas.* The staff at Black Beauty redoubled its efforts in memory of Amory.

On March 10, 2000, Nim was playing on his favorite tire swing, which he used as a lounge chair. A staffer greeted him at 11:15 on her way into the kitchen to get the chimps their morning snack of fresh fruit. (Breakfast had been hours earlier.) Nim anticipated cantaloupe, which he loved, and signed "hurry" as he caught her eye. When she returned ten minutes later with the food, he was crumpled on the floor of his cage, totally still. Kitty was hysterical, jumping up and down and screaming. Byrne ran into the cage, lifted Nim up into his arms, and drove him to the hospital, weeping. "The veterinarians took one look at him and said, 'Cardiac occlusion,' " Probst recalls. Nim was dead. A necropsy done at the South West Primate Hospital confirmed a massive heart attack. His end had been swift.

Kitty grieved for Nim. It would take her months before she began eating again and taking comfort in the other chimps. Byrne, badly shaken by the shock and the loss, kept busy with the other animals. He had been devastated when Amory died, but Nim's death was far more shattering. The chimp was only twenty-six years old. He should have lived for at least another twenty years.

On May 22, a small group gathered for Nim's memorial. The sun was shining, and a few miniature horses and burros wandered among the mourners. Kitty, Midge, and Lulu, just down the path in their enclosure, were strangely quiet. Gibbons sang in the background, and the two camels, Omar and Cairo, hung their heads over a nearby rail as if they were part of the group. Two months had passed, but the sadness remained. Stephanie LaFarge had not been back to the ranch since she had entered Nim's cage and he had thrown her to the floor (while sparing her any serious damage). She flew to Texas for the memorial and wept through it, the only representative from Project Nim.

Byrne led the service, trying to keep the mood upbeat. The others around him were quiet, holding back their emotions, wiping their eyes. Amory *was* Black Beauty — but Nim had become its heartbeat. All the staffers who had come anywhere near the chimp had developed a personal relationship with him — Nim had taken their shoes, played a joke on them, given them an artwork, taught them a sign, or done something else that was unusual and memorable.

Byrne spoke of his profound affection for Nim. He had come to understand that Nim was a chimpanzee — not a human, or an experiment, or a means to anything. Byrne had known Nim for ten years. Each day they had spent time together. Byrne might share his lunch with Nim, or a drink at the end of the day (on opposite sides of the bars). They telegraphed their moods by communicating through their eyes and bodies. Byrne talked to Nim as if he were a person and a friend, and he believed that the chimp understood him. They occasionally signed a few words to each other, although Byrne had often said that sign language was irrelevant to their relationship. From time to time, Byrne believed that their discussions, however they communicated, verged on the philosophical. It was as if Nim was questioning Byrne, asking him over and over, "Why am I here? Why am I locked in a cage?"

Byrne had thought seriously about the answer to that question. He had concluded that Nim was not asking to escape but making a more poignant comment on the injustice of his captivity. Freedom was never an option for Nim, nor was it the answer to his troubles. There can never be any freedom for captive-born chimpanzees. From Byrne's perspective, Nim had come to accept the cage in which he was confined — and protected. "Nim needed his cage," he told the group gathered at the memorial. "It was his house and the only place where he was in control. The problem was keeping the rest of us out."

WHERE THEY ARE NOW

Thomas Bever recently stepped down as head of the linguistics department at the University of Arizona in Tucson. He currently runs the language and cognition laboratory at the university and remains focused on what he describes as the "interface between language and cognition."

Rick Budd finished his master's degree in Oklahoma and moved to Austin, Texas, for law school. He continues to practice law in Austin.

Joyce Butler completed her doctorate at the University of Massachusetts in 1992. She also has an associate's degree as a sign language interpreter. Joyce was the principal of a public school in Stockbridge, Massachusetts, for fifteen years and is currently director of curriculum and instruction for the South Hadley Public Schools. Her husband, Rick Wilcox, is chief of police in Stockbridge. They have three children, one horse, a dog, and three cats.

Chris Byrne died on September 3, 2002, in a freak accident at Black Beauty Ranch. Byrne was checking the animals on a Sunday evening, driving through the ranch's 1,400 acres, as he often did. That evening, he drove his truck into a ravine, apparently to check on a horse; the truck turned over, spilling him out, and rolled over him. Chris's body was found the following morning. He was fifty-two and had been at the ranch for twelve years.

Renee Falitz spent fifteen years as an interpreter for the deaf and then returned to graduate school. She works as a speech/language pathologist in the Miami-Dade school system. Renee shares her home with two Siamese cats.

Roger Fouts remains at Central Washington University in Ellensburg, where he and Deborah Fouts are co-directors of the Chimpanzee and Human Communication Institute. They have co-authored more than one hundred articles on ape language and continue to do research with their chimps.

Washoe died at the Institute on October 30, 2007, after a short illness. She was forty-two. Loulis is alive and well. The Gardners retired three more chimps, Tatu, Dar (Kitty's offspring, born at Coulston), and Moja, to Fouts's custody. (Moja died in 2002 of an unidentified infection.) None has been allowed to breed, as Fouts does not believe that any animal should be born into captivity. His three chimps are not required to work on days when they are not receptive to the demands of research. The public is invited to attend workshops and meet the chimpanzees (for the price of admission), but no one is allowed into the chimp enclosure. Apart from his own research and writing, Fouts is a highly regarded global advocate for chimpanzee protections in the wild and in captivity.

Vera Gatch lives on her farm in Norman, Oklahoma. She continues her work as a psychologist.

Henry Herrmann is still practicing law in Boston. When possible he donates his time to public interest cases.

Robert Ingersoll commutes between San Francisco and Norman, Oklahoma. He is the vice president of Mindy's Memory, a sanctuary in Newcastle, Oklahoma, founded and run by Linda Barcklay. The sanctuary provides housing, care, medical attention, and bucketloads of fresh vegetables and fruits several times a day to a population of recovering research monkeys. Ingersoll assists Barcklay with hands-on care of the animals. He remains married to Belle Ball, a court reporter for the U.S. District Court for the Northern District of California. Belle finally met Nim for the first time at the Black Beauty Ranch. She recently commented that "Bob is going to mourn Nim forever."

Bob Johnson trains analysts and associates at an investment bank in New York City. He lives alone happily in Queens, New York.

Albert LaFarge is a literary agent who lives in Boston. He is married and has two children.

Ann LaFarge was an editor in the publishing industry for almost thirty years. She is now a freelance "book doctor" who divides her time between New York City and Millbrook, New York. She writes a weekly book column for a chain of Hudson Valley newspapers. Ann and Stephanie LaFarge have become close friends.

Annik LaFarge is a well-known editor in the New York publishing world. She is currently the publishing director of Bloomsbury USA.

Louisa LaFarge lives in the San Francisco Bay Area with her two children, ages nine and six. She is studying to be a teacher and is also a competitive swimmer.

Matilda LaFarge lives just outside New York City with her husband and son. She currently works as a publicist for *Consumer Reports.*

Stephanie LaFarge is senior director of counseling services at the American Society for the Prevention of Cruelty to Animals (ASPCA). She has pioneered the use of psychological evaluation and intervention with adults and young people who have been convicted of animal cruelty. Prior to employment at the ASPCA, LaFarge counseled drug addicts at a storefront clinic in Newark, New Jersey, worked with terminally ill children at the Rhode Island Hospital in Providence, and spent ten years as a sex therapist in New York City. She and her award-winning therapy dog, a border collie once slated for euthanasia at the ASPCA shelter, have done animal-assisted therapy in the aftermath of major disasters, including the 9/11 attacks. LaFarge currently lives in the Midwest.

W. E. R. LaFarge moved to Rhode Island, married for a third time, and had one more child. He died on October 27, 1994, of non-Hodgkin's lymphoma. WER's wife subsequently remarried and sold off the LaFarge farm, which had been in the family for generations. A book of WER's poetry, *The Changing and Unchanging Harvest,* was published by Heartwork Press in 1980. WER wrote at least twelve plays, including *Mutation,* which received an OBIE award in 1977. At the time of his death, he was preparing a second collection of poetry for publication and working on a novel titled *Mother Right.*

Heather Lee teaches in a New York City preschool. She is also a dancer and performer who occasionally appears in her father Ralph Lee's theatrical events. Heather is married and has one son.

Jenny Lee is a landscape architect who specializes in zoo environments. She currently works for the Wildlife Conservation Society, based at the Bronx Zoo, and has helped to design exhibits including the Congo Gorilla Forest, Tiger Mountain, and Butterfly Garden. Jenny feels that Nim's impact on her career is somewhat ironic. "Most people who work in zoos have mixed emotions about the animals," she says. "It's a constant struggle for many of us to see them in captivity every day, although we are proud of the exhibits that they live in." Jenny is married and has one daughter. She lives with her family in Hastings-on-Hudson, New York.

Joshua Lee lives with his wife and three children on Puget Sound in Washington State. He is currently the manager and prop artisan of a local cabaret show.

Peter Lemmon is divorced and the father of two children. He still lives in Norman, Oklahoma, in a contemporary house that he designed and built. Peter works as a computer programmer for the Oklahoma Department of Health.

James Mahoney is the author of *Saving*

Molly: A Research Veterinarian's Choices, published by Algonquin Books in 1998. (Molly was a dog that he and his wife rescued while vacationing in Jamaica.) He is considered one of few experts in primate medicine and often travels to sanctuaries and other facilities in Europe, Africa, and the U.S. to assist in the care of the chimpanzees. Mahoney shuns most animal activists and journalists. He believes that behavioral research on animals is more inhumane in the long run than biomedical research.

Roger Mellgren teaches psychology at Indiana University. He and his students are currently assessing "personality relationships between dogs and their owners" in a local animal shelter. Mellgren also does research on two species of sea turtles in their natural habitats.

Jan Moor-Jankowski was fired from LEMSIP in 1995 and locked out of his laboratory. By this time, he had become embroiled in at least two controversies that he believed affected NYU's decision to terminate his position and close down the laboratory. In the first, Moor-Jankowski reported Ron Wood, another NYU researcher doing work on drug addictions with a group of monkeys, to federal authorities; Moor-Jankowski believed that Wood's monkeys were unduly suffering during his cocaine experiments. The second controversy began years earlier, when Moor-Jankowski, the editor of the *Journal of Medical Primatology,* published a letter from Shirley McGreal, the prominent director of the International Primate and Protection League, which attacked the plans of an Austrian pharmaceutical company (Immuno AG) to use wild-born chimpanzees in a new hepatitis study. Unhappy with McGreal's criticism, Immuno responded by filing libel suits against all those involved, including McGreal and Moor-Jankowski. Moor-Jankowski, a firm believer in the First Amendment, argued that regardless of their views, both sides had the right to air their opinions. The case went through the courts for seven years, all the way to the Supreme Court, and eventually, in 1994, Moor-Jankowski prevailed. By this time, he had become a hero to many animal rights activists, which did not make him more appealing to NYU. He died from a stroke on August 27, 2005, at the age of eighty-one.

Chris O'Sullivan earned her doctorate in experimental psychology from OU in 1981. Her current research investigates the nature of sexual violence and is supported with grants from the U.S. Department of Justice. O'Sullivan lives in New York City, where she quietly rescues stray cats and dogs.

Laura-Ann Petitto is director of the Cognitive Neuroscience Laboratory for Language and Child Development at Dartmouth College. She and her husband, Kevin Dunbar, a psychologist who also teaches at Dartmouth, have three daughters. Petitto is an expert on "babbling" and how children acquire language.

Marian Probst turned over the Fund for Animals, and with it the Black Beauty Ranch, to the Humane Society of the United States in 2004, six years after Cleveland Amory's death. D. J. Schubert, a wildlife biologist who was close to Amory and loyal to the Fund, had been managing the ranch for two years, in the aftermath of Byrne's sudden death. Schubert protested the HSUS takeover and was summarily fired. HSUS renamed the ranch the Cleveland Amory Black Beauty Ranch and has no plans to close it down. The new ranch manager, Richard Farinato, completed the plans that Schubert had begun for an expanded chimpanzee enclosure. **Kitty,**

Lulu, and **Midge** are doing fine under the care of keeper Dawna Epperson, who began as a volunteer under Chris Byrne and is now a full-time employee. The chimps enjoy a grassy area, real trees, and far more room outdoors than Nim and Sally ever had. Kitty is forty-five and one of the oldest chimps alive in captivity.

Sue Savage-Rumbaugh is a scientist at the Great Ape Trust (GAT) in Iowa, where she continues to do innovative language and cognition research with a colony of bonobos. Savage-Rumbaugh and her associates (including her husband, Duane Rumbaugh) own the research animals and have full responsibility for all aspects of their care. GAT is a state-of-the-art facility that rivals all other research centers and many sanctuaries. Over the years, Savage-Rumbaugh has co-authored numerous articles and books, including *Kanzi's Primal Language: The Cultural Initiation of Primates into Language* (with Pär Segerdahl and William Fields), published by Palgrave Macmillan in 2005. This book includes a retrospective analysis of Project Nim and of Chomsky's negative impact on early ape language studies. Savage-Rumbaugh is currently the leading light of a small, progressive, global movement of academics who are determined to prove, in undeniable scientific terms, that apes are intelligent animals with the capacity to communicate, learn, create, and generate their own culture. Her bonobos are currently born into a hybrid, interspecies world; from birth, humans and their natural mothers jointly raise them. The bonobos communicate with humans by pointing to individual symbols on a keyboard; the keyboard is printed on paper and laminated in plastic to make it more portable and durable. The bonobos and humans voluntarily carry the sheets to facilitate communication with each other.

Herbert S. Terrace still has an office in Schermerhorn Hall at Columbia University, where he continues to teach psychology. He has two children and recently separated from his wife. The focus of his research, in his own words, "is the evolution of intelligence with specific emphasis on cognitive processes that do not require language." Terrace remains occupied with the mysterious origins of human language and has concluded that it "could only have evolved from ancestors who had already been selected for their ability to share and exchange knowledge non-verbally." He is currently training a group of fourteen rhesus macaques to learn visual sequences by trial and error in a project on cognition and memory. The monkeys learn to tap arbitrary flashing images in a specific order. When they succeed, they are rewarded with bits of monkey chow the size of M&M's. Terrace believes that the monkeys enjoy the work, which he equates with playing video games. (However, the one time I briefly observed them during a trial, this did not appear to be the case.) Each monkey has a name and a small cage inside Columbia's biomedical facility, which is north of the main campus. Terrace's graduate students, as one told me, occasionally make popcorn for them on weekends to cheer them up.

Maurice Temerlin became an expert on the psychology of cult membership. One of his articles, published in the *Cultic Studies Journal,* described the way in which psychotherapists turn their practices into cults. He died on January 30, 1988, at the age of sixty-four, in a tragic skiing accident. **Jane Temerlin** is a social worker living in Portland, Oregon; she co-authored a number of articles with her husband. Their son, **Dr. Steven Temerlin,** is a medical doctor.

Bill Tynan was at last report working for the *Berkshire Eagle,* a newspaper in Pittsfield, Massachusetts. He lives in North Egremont, Massachusetts, with his wife.

Maggie Wheeler (once Jakobson) lives in Los Angeles with her husband and two daughters. She works as an actress in film and television and is best known as "Janice" in the series *Friends.* Maggie frequently tells her children Nim stories. "Just this morning," Maggie reports, "my seven-year-old daughter jumped into my arms and was clinging to my neck — she felt just like Nim."

Carolyn and **Pan** died in LEMSIP. **Wendy** remained at IPS until her death in 1985. **Bruno** was one of the first chimps injected with the hepatitis serum at LEMSIP. He died there, too sick to be moved to a sanctuary. **Booee** escaped LEMSIP and is alive and well at the Wildlife Waystation, a sanctuary in California. Booee remained clear of HIV research, but was infected with hepatitis C. For this reason, he is caged with one female chimpanzee named Jolly, also infected with hepatitis C, and they remain isolated from the other animals at the sanctuary. **Onan** was sent to Primarily

Primates, a sanctuary in Texas, where he died of a heart attack in 1999. **McCarthy (Mac)** was sold to LEMSIP in 1985, near the end of IPS, where he died. **Lilly** was surreptitiously removed from IPS before she could be shipped off to LEMSIP; according to Ingersoll, **Alyse Moore** took Lilly somewhere safe. **Sheba** resides at Chimp Haven, a spacious government-funded sanctuary outside of New Orleans, Louisiana. (The facility was not affected by Hurricane Katrina.) She is twenty-six years old.

NOTES

Prologue

Savage spent most of her days at this research facility, collecting data: Savage's dissertation, titled "Mother-Infant Behavior Among Captive Group-Living Chimpanzees (Pan troglodytes)," won her a Ph.D. from the University of Oklahoma in 1975. The births described in this detailed and fascinating work took place during an eight-month time span from November 1973 to July 1974.

in an early experiment in primate population control: In 1966, Oscar and Pat Konyot, chimp trainers employed by Ringling Brothers, contacted Lemmon for advice on birth control. Their female chimp was becoming pregnant at inopportune times for the circus. Lemmon sent them a two-month supply of Enovid and in a letter advised them to smash up the pills with Tang powder or wine. If the pills worked

(Lemmon had tested them successfully on some of his stump-tailed macaques), he further suggested that they obtain a prescription from their own physician. With his customary humor, Lemmon added, "You don't have to tell him that it is for a chimpanzee."

Introduction

he proceeded to observe and photograph animals around him for 112 days: Candland, *Feral Children and Clever Animals,* 208.

98.7 percent: This figure fluctuates with the progress of genome research and with the particular methodology of the researcher.

can produce any kind of offspring at all: Stephen Mihm, "Human Chimp Hybrids," *New York Times,* December 10, 2006, page unavailable.

the facility moved to Emory University in Atlanta, Georgia, where it remains today: The Yerkes National Primate Research Center of Emory University is one of eight laboratories in the country funded by the government (NIH). There are currently 5,000 rodents and 3,400 primates (squirrel monkeys, rhesus macaques, pigtail macaques, cynomolgus monkeys, chimpanzees, sooty mangabeys, and capuchin monkeys) at Yerkes, all of whom are used in a range of biomedical and behavioral experiments; the medical experiments include research on AIDS, cardiovascular diseases, drug addictions, and transplantation medicine. (Frans de Waal, a primatologist at Emory and the author of many popular books on primate behavior, is the best-known researcher at Yerkes.) Fierce battles between Yerkes researchers and animal advocates — over conditions inside the facility and the ethics of individual research projects — are routine. In a recent skirmish, Yerkes applied for a species permit (from the U.S. Fish and Wildlife Service) to use one hundred sooty mangabeys (a protected endangered species) for a new medical research project; Yerkes also requested permission to euthanize sixty mangabeys currently in the facility and, in return, offered to make annual gifts of $30,000 to a mangabey field research project in Côte d'Ivoire. A coalition of nine animal welfare organizations, represented by counsel, protested these new permits, arguing that using endangered animals for any medical research set a terrible precedent. Jane Goodall, Shirley McGreal, Roger Fouts,

William McGrew, and Mark Bekoff were among the scientists who signed a letter to protest this permit. Yerkes eventually withdrew the request and the publicity died down. However, it later became clear that Yerkes had been informed that sooty mangabeys were about to be downlisted from their endangered status, which would make them eligible for the experiments — without *any* permits. (Whether Yerkes moved this project forward or not is currently unclear.) In May 2007, soon after the dust from this dispute settled, Yerkes received a five-year, $10 million federal grant from the National Institute of Aging for experiments comparing the aging process in humans and chimpanzees. Yerkes hopes to develop a vaccine against Alzheimer's disease. Primate activists argue that there is nothing to be gained from this research — apart from the grants.

spoken in what was described as a "hoarse stage whisper": Noell, *The History of Noell's Ark Gorilla Show*, 147. *The History of Noell's Ark Gorilla Show* is a self-published memoir by Mae Noell, a chimp trainer/breeder based in Tampa, Florida. Noell befriended a number of scientists working in Orange Park at Yerkes and became friendly with the Hayeses while Vicki was residing with them. Noell claimed to hold the world record for chimp births in a privately owned colony — forty-five — and she prided herself on her ability with chimps. (Noell was also friendly with Lemmon and sold him several newborns.) She and Catherine Hayes became friends, and the two women occasionally arranged playdates with their chimps in the afternoons. (Kongo, Noell's pride and joy, performed wrestling matches in roadside circuses with any human brave enough to enter his cage — and willing to pay for the experience of getting badly beaten up by a chimp.) Noell was impressed by Catherine Hayes's control over Vicki and the chimp's ability to whisper several words in her strange voice. They sat at the kitchen table with Vicki and ate snacks together.

The Gardners hypothesized that chimpanzees did not have the same vocal apparatus as humans: An active debate on whether or not chimps and humans have similar vocal boxes persists. A 2003 study by four Japanese scientists (T. Nishimura, A. Mikami, J. Suzuki, and T. Matsuzawa) compared the descent of the larynx in human and chimpanzee infants and found no significant anatomical differences. The authors describe humans and chimps as "morphologically similar" and argue that chimps' inability to make words is not due to any physiological differences between them and humans. This argument was used by Terrace in a recent article on metacognition and the evolution of language to bolster Chomsky's notion of a universal — inherently human — language ability.

"Spiders spin spider webs because they have spider brains": Pinker, *Language Instinct,* 5.

"If we could hear them speak, we might not want to hear what they say": Fudge, *Animal,* 127.

"It's about as likely that an ape will prove to have a language ability": Susana Duncan, "Nim Chimpsky and How He Grew," *New York* magazine, December 3, 1979, 84.

there is abundant evidence that animals can communicate to each other: The question of whether chimpanzees or other nonhuman animals have an actual *language* of their own is endlessly debated. Most scientists believe that they do not. But this seems to be the case largely because no one has been able to prove otherwise. Most research dollars have been spent teaching animals to communicate using one of our languages, such as ASL, in order to further understand the evolution of human language. The pendulum, however, is beginning to swing in the opposite direction. Now we are studying *their* languages. A recent study at Yerkes on chimp-to-chimp communication identified thirty-one distinct manual gestures and eighteen vocal/facial signs. (Certainly, the fact that chimps communicate to each other with gestures and dramatic facial expressions is hardly news to most primatologists.) More interesting, and less well known, is research by Dr. Con Slobodchikoff, a biologist at Northern Arizona University, who is researching the language of prairie dogs. Slobodchikoff studies their vocalizations using videotapes and sonographs that measure the frequencies of the animals' alarm calls. He claims that prairie dogs have their own distinct language, complete with a structure of nouns, verbs, and adjectives. His data show that prairie dogs warn each other when predators are approaching and that they can distinguish between hawks, humans, and coyotes.

Chapter One

Lemmon continued to wear his sandals barefoot but immediately shaved off his goatee — and grew it right back: This anecdote was taken from a history of the OU psychology department, part of a broader history of psychology in Oklahoma, which was commissioned by the Oklahoma Psychological Association (OPA) and edited by Dr. Charles Whipple. While visiting Norman, I received an early draft of this document, which is peppered with personal quotations and vivid anecdotes. But when I recently requested a final draft of the OU history from the OPA I was surprised to find that all sections pertaining to William Lemmon had been deleted from the document. Richard Hess, executive director of the OPA, did not respond to inquiries concerning this editorial decision.

(Three half siblings from their father's first marriage made periodic visits): Kathleen, Butch (William Lemmon III), and Alan were Lemmon's children from his first marriage. Butch was hit by a car in Norman while visiting his father and was killed in 1957. He was thirteen years old. Peter Lemmon believes that his father "never emotionally recovered from the

Ahab and Gene Clark

tragedy."

the newborn chimp would be her first and only child: Lemmon had previously given Gatch a mandrill baboon to keep as a pet. But when Mae arrived, the sibling rivalry became so intense that Gatch feared Lou Lou, the young mandrill, might harm the chimp. Lou Lou was immediately removed from the house. The mandrill was a pet — Mae was a member of the family.

Chapter Two

Carolyn produced her first baby, Ahab, two years after her arrival in Oklahoma: Ahab,

Nim's oldest brother, remained with Carolyn for seventy-six days before Lemmon moved him into a human family to become part of the psychologist's ongoing research. For one reason or another, Ahab was passed along from family to family for two years and then returned to IPS. Lemmon kept him, briefly, in his own house, to maintain Ahab's species isolation while he selected the chimp's next placement. During this time, Gene and Nita Clark contacted Lemmon to offer him an adult female named Mo who was eleven years old. Nita and Gene ran a traveling rodeo show in which their trained chimpanzees performed "trick riding" on the back of a fifty-two-inch-tall Appaloosa pony; their chimps did somersaults, rode standing up on their hind legs, and leapt off and on the moving pony. Gene and his brother Bobby Clark were well-known rodeo clowns, and their names appear in the Rodeo Hall of Fame. Mo, who performed for many years, had originally been purchased from the St. Louis Zoo, but she had become too big and strong to continue on the rodeo circuit. In 1970, Nita and Gene drove up to IPS in a Cadillac pulling Mo in a horse trailer behind them; a baby chimp named Ronnie was sitting in the backseat of the car. Ronnie knew how to start the car himself and roll the windows up and down, which caught Lemmon's attention. As Nita explained in a telephone interview, "All our chimps understood English and Professor Lemmon was really impressed." Lemmon purchased Mo from the Clarks and changed her name to Mona. That day, the Clarks met Ahab and they wanted to purchase him as a companion for Ronnie. But Lemmon held off, unsure of how Ahab would respond to Ronnie. Six months later, after Lemmon had begun acclimating Ahab to other chimps, the Clarks came back to get their new baby. As it turned out, Ahab was not a confident young male. He constantly sucked his thumb and wandered around with a blanket. But he bonded intensely with Nita as they traveled the rodeo circuit, living in motels, moving from town to town. Nita dressed him up for shows but the chimp never left her lap. He was a mama's boy. The Clarks were patient and they loved Ahab. They waited for him to become more self-assured before they put him on the back of their pony. But that day never came. Ahab caught pneumonia and died six years later. (While at IPS, Mona gave birth to three babies — Lilith, Daniel, and Ruth — before her sale to LEMSIP in 1981.)

"Shoot the mother, remove baby": Peterson, *Eating Apes,* 42.

"Lemmon's dominance of Pan": Fouts, *Next of Kin,* 127.

By 1968, Lemmon had five newborn chimps living in human families: They were Pan, Wendy, Mae, Lucy, and Abe/Bruno. A sixth infant, named Emanuel, the first born at IPS, was also about to be placed.

"Noam should be Nim": Terrace, *Nim,* 28.

"teaching them even one sequence is not an easy thing to do": Many scientists have dismissed the intelligence of pigeons — and all other birds. However, their cognitive capabilities did not escape Irene Pepperberg, a research associate at Harvard University and a professor at Brandeis University, who was the first psychologist to begin a language study with African gray parrots. Pepperberg compares their linguistic achievements to those of children, great apes, and marine mammals. Having had the pleasure of meeting Alex, her first parrot, who died on September 6, 2007, at the age of thirty-one, I can assure you that his verbal skills were remarkable by any standards. Alex could identify

fifty different objects, distinguish seven colors, count up to six, and understand concepts including "bigger," "smaller," "same," and "different." (I observed him naming objects and counting them.) Pepperberg's relationship with Griffin and Wart, her two other parrots, is equally complex and fascinating. Her close relationship with each bird informs their working relationships. Alex, referred to as an "avian scholar" in Pepperberg's detailed newsletter on the progress of her research, "was the intellectual equivalent of a five-year-old."

Chapter Three

Nim was trying to breast-feed on her: Human breast-feeding of captive-born chimpanzees is not so unusual today. Recently, two babies were born at the Beijing Zoo; one mother had no milk and the other rejected her baby. So the keepers found human surrogates to breast-feed the babies every three hours until they were a normal weight.

Dr. Lerman happened to have a son who had been born right at the same time as Nim: No detailed studies comparing the development of humans and chimps existed until the recent translation of a memoir by Russian scientist Nadezhda Nikolaevna Ladygina-Kohts. In 1916, Ladygina-Kohts, on her own, purchased a two-year-old chimp and set up a cage for him in her own Moscow home. She named the chimp Joni and proceeded to keep detailed notes on his physical and psychological development. Her motivations appeared to be scientific; however, her methods of discipline, all of which she described in detail without regret, went beyond heartless to cruel. Ladygina-Kohts claimed to be emotionally attached to her chimp, but she referred to him alternately as her "despot" and her "prisoner" and whipped him when he became too obstreperous. Joni died after three years of rough treatment and meager basic care. Several years later, Ladygina-Kohts gave birth to a son, named Roody, and began once again to keep copious notes on his development. The result is probably the first comparative study between human and chimpanzee infants, complete with photographs and the author's personal revelations. Her strange and obsessive diary was translated from Russian into English, edited by Frans de Waal, and published by Oxford University Press, entitled *Infant Chimpanzee and Human Child,* in 2002.

"scientific revolution with religious conse-
quences that occurs once every few hundred
years": Stuart Baur, "First Message from
the Planet of the Apes," *New York* magazine, February 24, 1975, 33.

"It is one thing to explain to a graduate student
why it is important to switch bird number 36
from condition A to condition B for two
weeks": Terrace, *Nim,* 34.

Terrace looked for money and staff to hold the
project together: According to Terrace,
Project Nim received grants from: the
National Institutes of Mental Health, the
Whitehall Foundation, the William T.
Grant Foundation, the Mrs. Cheever
Porter Foundation and the Solomon
Guggenheim Foundation, and approxi-
mately $300,000 was raised. Additional
support came from Columbia University,
Children's Television Workshop, WER La-
Farge, and Terrace.

Chapter Four

As Terrace once told a reporter meeting Nim
for the first time, "Once you get a look at
Nim, it is difficult to take your eyes off him":
Baur, Stuart, "First Message from the
Planet of the Apes," *New York* magazine,
36.

"Nim often used signs at home in more inter-

esting ways": Terrace, *Nim,* 54.

"the same punishment could make matters worse": Terrace, *Nim,* 59.

In a poem called "dear Gleaming Family": The Changing and Unchanging Harvest," W. E. R. LaFarge. California: Heartwork Press, 38.

Chapter Five

The psychologist purchased pocket-size tape recorders for trainers to use: Obviously, Nim's trainers could not take notes while dealing with Nim. Small audio recorders were a good idea, but inevitably Nim became interested in them, and often grabbed and broke them.

"I suggested that someone look into Nim's room to see that he was breathing normally": Terrace, *Nim,* 114.

"Laura was the most effective and influential in establishing methods of teaching Nim to use sign language": Terrace, *Nim,* 69.

Chapter Six

Taking responsibility for even one chimp was more than he felt: Terrace's colleagues — the Gardners, the Rumbaughs, Pepperberg — were all adding animals to their colonies. The Gardners regularly retired chimps (and gave them to Fouts for safekeeping) as they added youngsters to their subsequent experiments. Thus far, Pepperberg has kept all her parrots with the exception of one who demonstrated zero interest in scientific trials. As Pepperberg explained, birds are sentient creatures with different personalities and degrees of intelligence. She knew right away that her new parrot would make a fine pet in a home but would have been a disaster in her language lab. (She found him a good home.) Certainly, birds are smaller and easier to deal with than chimpanzees. But it is not impossible to keep chimps, and those committed to the field — and their chimps — figure out a way to ensure their long-term safety.

The plan remained a fantasy: In *Nim,* Terrace wrote: "I was not the only member of the project who would have to cut back on his contribution to the project" (192). He goes on to explain that his staff, including Butler and Tynan, "made clear that they could no longer continue their yeoman service with Nim." Butler and Tynan were especially infuriated by Terrace's claim that they did not want to continue on with Nim and maintain the momentum of the study. They fought hard to continue the project and wanted to care for Nim.

Valium and Sernalyn: Sernalyn (phencyclidine, PCP, or "angel dust") is an immobilizing agent that is no longer used as an anesthesia for animals as it produced too many harmful side effects. Today, better drugs are available, including ketamine ("Special K"), which is used in combination with other drugs to safely knock animals out for any reason.

Chapter Seven

accompanied the article: W. B. Lemmon and M. L. Allen, "Orgasm in Female Primates," in *American Journal of Primatology,* 1 (1981), 15–34.

called the Pig Barn: Another researcher had put up the building for forty South African pigs acquired for a study on the effect of stress on the heart. The pigs were systematically shocked as their vitals were monitored. In the end, all were slaughtered. Peter Lemmon remembers the smell of the massive barbecue that followed.

When the rod began to buzz, Bruno repeatedly slapped his head in an energetic effort to sign "hat": Fouts, *Next of Kin,* 144.

But there were no cages, so the island was as good as it got for the Norman chimps, and they are standard today at the more spacious chimp sanctuaries: Lemmon was one of the first to build islands for his chimps and monkeys. Carole Noon, the reigning expert on captive chimp behavior and rehabilitation, is founder and director of Save the Chimps, which currently operates a deluxe sanctuary in Florida. In 2002, Noon took over the Coulston Foundation, in Alamogordo, New Mexico (with a grant for $3.7 million from the Arcus Fund), where more than two hundred chimpanzees were living in desolate conditions. In an effort to make some immediate improvements in their quality of life, Noon opened up their cages to the outdoor runs (twenty-four hours a day) and gave them perches; then she carefully introduced chimps to each other, put them all on a decent diet, gave them medical attention, and brought in a staff to show them that not all humans were cruel. (The day I arrived for a tour happened to be Halloween, and one staffer, dressed in a gorilla suit, was running up and down the halls in various buildings to amuse the chimps.) Over the past several years, Noon has been slowly moving chimps to her Florida facility. She plans to eventually move them all. Coulston will then be bulldozed — or completely transformed. Only one other sanctuary in the country rivals Save the Chimps. Chimp Haven in Keithville, Louisiana, was built in 2001, after then-president Bill Clinton passed a law called the Chimpanzee Health, Improvement, Maintenance and Protection (CHIMP) Act, which mandated funding for the lifetime care of those chimpanzees still languishing in prison-like research labs. This was a historic moment: the government realized that these chimps deserved something in return for having given their entire lives to medical research, NASA, and all kinds of other research projects. Chimp Haven won a $40 million contract to build a facility. The chimps currently in residence live in a vast sanctuary setting with many natural elements. However, Chimp Haven was born out of a collaboration between the biomedical industry and the federal government. In the final hour, the pharmaceutical industry demanded the right to reclaim and use the animals for any research deemed necessary, and Clinton capitulated. For this reason, Jane Goodall, Carole Noon, and Roger Fouts, among others, resigned from the Chimp Haven advisory board in protest. More recently, these same advocates are trying to change the legislation to permanently retire the chimps from research.

hanging out on the island with Bruno and his buddy Booee, another signer: Booee was one of the legendary (and favorite) chimps at IPS. He was given to Lemmon in 1970 by Dr. Fredrick Snyder, director of the Laboratory of Clinical Psychobiology at the National Institutes of Mental Health in Bethesda, Maryland. Born in the Bethesda facility, Booee was subject to an experimental split-brain operation that was thought to be a cure for epilepsy. It was not. According to Fouts in *Next of Kin,* a neurosurgeon had "severed his corpus callosum, cutting all the connections between his two cerebral hemispheres." Snyder and his wife, Martha, felt sorry for the chimp and took him home to nurse him back to health. In the process, they fell in love with Booee and did not want to return him to the lab or the care of the neurosurgeon. The research, totally unsuccessful, left Booee with what Fouts described as "two separate brains." Snyder had been to IPS and found it to be an unusually good place for chimpanzees. In a friendly letter to Lemmon, Snyder referred to IPS as "Lemmon's school of orthogenic training for spoiled and wayward chimpanzees." The Snyders desperately wanted to send Booee to Norman and get him as far away from the lab in Bethesda as possible. On March 19, 1970, Snyder wrote to Lemmon: "The gods are whimsical. About six weeks ago the neurosurgeon, Maitlan Baldwin, who controlled the fate of our little chimp, was abruptly felled by a cerebral hemorrhage and died a few days later." Baldwin's successor was quite willing to release Booee, who arrived at IPS a few months later and became a notable star in Fouts's signing program. Booee and Bruno, the same age, were inseparable. Snyder, like others, believed that Lemmon would protect his chimps from biomedical research for the duration of their lives. Bruno and Booee were sold to LEMSIP and shipped off together in 1981.

their first chimp had died at a young age in an accident: In 1963, Lemmon purchased an eight-month-old chimp named Charlie Brown (for $850) from a breeder in Tucson, Arizona. Lee Brooks Thorton sold a variety of exotics, many of which she trapped in her own backyard, along with more common purebred dogs, cats, and large birds. In a letter to Lemmon, she frankly described her operation: "I steal the babies before they are weaned and a

542

pet shop here bottle-feeds them and sells them as pets — or I sell them to museums and zoos." Lemmon appreciated Thorton's ingenuity and shared her fascination with different species. They struck up a casual relationship, as Lemmon did with many backyard breeders. Thorton loved her one and only chimp, but when her husband began taking him out to bars at night to entertain his drinking partners, she felt unable to protect him. Thorton decided to get the chimp out of town and offered him to Lemmon. Pan and Wendy had been in residence for almost two years, and Lemmon was eager to acquire more chimps. To keep Charlie Brown in species isolation, Lemmon gave him to the Temerlins. But one year later, Charlie accidentally hanged himself while twisting his favorite blanket through the bars of his cage to form a hammock. Devastated, the Temerlins decided to get another chimp baby right away. Three weeks later, Lucy was born.

"smashed to the brink of unconsciousness": Temerlin, *Lucy: Growing Up Human,* 49.
"caught the stream of [his] urine": Ibid., 58.
the Temerlins . . . made the agonizing decision to send her to a small chimpanzee rehabilitation program in Africa: In 1969,

Stella Brewer (now Stella Marsden) had founded a small rescue and rehabilitation program in Gambia for orphan chimps who had lost their mothers to poachers; Brewer somehow got hold of the babies before they were sold to medical labs or zoos and raised them herself until they could be safely released into a national park, where she monitored their progress and survival. Her success rate was highest with wild-born chimps who had not felt the touch of human hands. Brewer accepted Lucy (and her companion chimp Marion) into the program.

Chapter Nine

Vanessa, a young, gregarious chimp out for a stroll with Gary Shapiro: Dr. Gary Shapiro is a leading expert on orangutans. He cofounded the Orangutan Foundation International and served as vice president from 1986 to 2004; he remains actively involved in ape conservation.

(Lemmon sold Sheba, when she was still an infant, to the Columbus Zoo): Sheba, now twenty-six years old, was recently sent to Chimp Haven in Louisiana. But her future is subject to a complex legal battle between scientists, animal advocates, and Ohio State University. Ironically, Sheba

was lucky to have ended up at the zoo rather than at a biomedical lab. At the zoo, her surrogate mother, a woman named Marsha King, took good care of her for two years and subsequently convinced the zoo to release Sheba to a scientist doing innovative — and noninvasive — research on animal cognition. For almost three decades, Dr. Sarah (Sally) Boysen has studied how chimpanzees learn. Eventually, Boysen put together a group of seven chimpanzees (including Sarah, Premack's famous chimp), who resided in her lab, which was affiliated with OSU, where she has been a professor of psychology for more than two decades. Boysen's work has been published in academic journals and covered in television documentaries; Sheba is also the subject of a children's book called *Sheba the Chimp and Skylar.* (Skylar, her pal, is a basset hound who kept her company in the lab.) In a familiar story that is reminiscent of the debacle between Lemmon and OU, financial tensions between Boysen and OSU over the funding for her lab finally resulted in a disaster: OSU locked Boysen out of her lab and arranged to move all her chimps to Primarily Primates, a sanctuary in Texas. Whether the sanctuary is an appropriate place for Boysen's chimps — or any others — is now a legal question. According to several chimp experts, Primarily Primates had gone *way* downhill, and the more than five hundred animals in residence were living in miserable conditions. Two of Boysen's chimps died soon after they arrived in Texas. The others, including Sheba, were recently moved to Chimp Haven, a sanctuary in Louisiana. As I write, several lawsuits are pending and Sheba's final disposition remains unclear.

"Most scientists tend to think of chimps as large white rats to be experimented on. We look at them more as colleagues": Ed Zuckerman, "You Talking to Me?" *Rolling Stone,* June 16, 1977, 47.

No one was surprised when she demonstrated that humans interrupted the chimps far more often than the reverse: Chris O'Sullivan, Roger S. Fouts, Mark E. Hannum, and Katie Schneider, "Chimpanzee Conversations: Language Cognition and Theory," in *Language Development,* vol. 2: *Language, Thought, and Culture,* ed. Stan Kuczaj (N.J.: Lawrence Erlbaum, 1982), 397–428.

Other experiments focused on how Nim's social context affected his ability and willing-

ness to sign: Chris O'Sullivan and C. P. Yeager, "Communicative Context and Linguistic Competence: The Effects of Social Setting on a Chimpanzee's Conversational Skill," in *Teaching Sign Language to Chimpanzees,* eds. R. Allen Gardner, Beatrix Gardner, and Thomas E. Van Cantfort (Albany: State University of New York Press, 1989), 269–79.

"would always miss Nim": Terrace, *Nim,* 234.

Chapter Ten

"whether or not chimpanzees would transmit sign language across generations": Fouts, *Next of Kin,* 417.

"had doubts about the ethics of taking the infant from its natural mother . . . and delivering him to the questionable affections of Washoe": Linden, *Silent Partners,* 75.

But now that it suited his own purposes, he was apparently willing to do the same: In retrospect, there is no doubt that Loulis was far better off with Fouts than he would have been remaining at Yerkes or IPS. Fouts saved his life.

His vocabulary was "pure drill," Terrace told the New York Times. *"Language still stands as an important definition of the human species":* Dava Sobel, "Researcher Challenges Conclusion That Apes Can Learn Language," *New York Times,* October 21, 1979.

"you'd have to conclude that they don't have language either": Sobel, ibid.

"Then we watch them like a hawk to see which signs are transferred": author and title unavailable, *Dallas Morning News,* December 10, 1979.

Blum estimated that in the early 1980s, forty thousand primates (monkeys and apes) were living in laboratories: Today, it is estimated that approximately thirteen hundred chimps remain in research laboratories. This number does not include those chimps living in sanctuaries, in zoos, with trainers who work in the entertainment industry, or in private homes. Results from a census of captive chimps in America taken by the Great Ape Project (GAP) were published in 2003. At that time, there were "3,100 captive great apes spread across 37 states, including a staggering 1,280 in biomedical research." This census was intended as a "snapshot in time." But the results, published by GAP, offer far more than a snapshot. Essays by leading activists and primatologists (Jane Goodall, Marc Bekoff, Roger Fouts, Francine Patterson, Birute Galdikas, Peter Singer) offer analysis and history, while

548

charts listing the animals by name, gender, species, location, and place of origin provide slim but affecting profiles of each and every captive ape.

Chapter Eleven

"the chemistry of pregnancy": Blum, *Monkey Wars,* 171.

"There is nothing fortress-like about LEMSIP": Ibid., 168.

at LEMSIP, primates, especially chimpanzees, were considered optimal surrogates for vaccine studies: LEMSIP would conduct hepatitis trials for many years until Moor-Jankowski succeeded in developing a vaccine for hepatitis B. Subsequently, the lab moved into AIDS research, a boondoggle in terms of cash flow but a dismal failure for researchers because HIV does not kill chimps. It is now widely believed that chimpanzees are not ideal surrogates for humans. Much of the biomedical research done on chimps has proved to be completely spurious, and anti-vivisectionists question whether we could have developed the hepatitis vaccine some other way. New research protocols that bypass research on live animals (or greatly reduce their numbers), using tissue samples, computerized data, and so forth, have been developed. Using any animal for toxicity studies, cosmetic research, or other experiments not deemed critical to human survival is considered unethical by many researchers. Using chimpanzees for *any* medical research is currently controversial and already illegal in several countries.

"Terrace himself says this chimpanzee is only a mimic": "New York Day by Day," *New York Times,* June 8, 1982.

"Just because he can't create a sentence doesn't mean he should be subject to these tests": Ibid.

"Do animals suffer needlessly?": Robert Reinhold, "Do Two Research Chimps Want to Retire?" *New York Times,* June 10, 1982.

the depression that resulted from their isolation from their peers, was even more excruciating: In 1997, Dr. Mahoney sent fifteen LEMSIP chimpanzees to the Fauna Foundation in Montreal, Canada, founded and run by Gloria Grow and her husband, Dr. Richard Allen. Many from this group were positive for HIV/AIDS and hepatitis; they were also suffering from severe emotional problems that turned their rehabilitation into a serious challenge. The chimps required medical attention and as much tender loving care as they would allow;

they were frightened, frenzied, traumatized, and dangerous. Grow traveled to LEMSIP to meet them and made the decision to take them all. The alternatives for the chimps were further incarceration in another medical facility — or euthanasia. The feisty Canadian rescuer then faced legal battles over permits to bring them safely to Canada, where they would remain. The next hurdle was raising the funds to build a chimp house — and then building it. The Fauna Foundation has grown over the years into a choice spot for retired chimps. Grow continues to devote her life to her colony (twelve of the original LEMSIP chimps are still living) and has become an advocate for the liberation of all chimps in biomedical facilities.

Fouts, for whatever reasons, was reluctant to speak out initially: Years later, Fouts kicked into action and got some results. In 1995, he visited Booee in LEMSIP for a *20/20* segment with Hugh Downs on the plight of signing chimps still stuck in biomedical labs. After thirteen years in LEMSIP, Booee recognized Fouts and signed enthusiastically to him. Fouts was brokenhearted, but determined to rescue the chimps. His moving reunion with Booee was aired on television, and once again the public demanded that LEMSIP release the signing chimps; five months later, Dr. Mahoney arranged for Booee and eight other chimps to be transferred to the Wildlife Waystation, a sanctuary in California where they were permanently retired from research. Booee had been infected with hepatitis, but he was not sick when Roger and Deborah Fouts visited him later that year in California. Once again, the sweet chimp greeted his old friends with joy.

"— you are fucking crazy!": Two decades later, Steven Wise, another Boston attorney once described as "one of the pistons of the animal rights movement," coined the phrase "animal personhood" and made a cogent argument that some — not all — animals deserved legal protections in court. In his book *Rattling the Cage,* Wise suggests that obvious distinctions can be made between, for instance, insects and chimpanzees. There is no longer any doubt that the latter (along with bonobos, elephants, parrots, dolphins, orangutans, and gorillas) are sentient — they feel pain and are self-aware — creatures. Therefore they deserve basic rights, including protection from harm.

Wise argues that until the courts recognize that chimps have "personhood," they cannot be legally protected. Advocates are watching a recent case in Austria. Paula Stibbe petitioned the court to become the legal guardian of Hiasl, a twenty-six-year-old chimpanzee living in a local sanctuary that may soon close down; should this happen, Stibbe wants to protect the chimp from being sent off to a biomedical laboratory. On April 24, 2007, the judge rejected Stibbe's request because, as the Associated Press reported, "Hiasl didn't meet two key tests: He is neither mentally impaired nor in an emergency." The case has been appealed.

Chapter Twelve

"Dining with Cleveland is like going to a party": Carol Flake, source unavailable.

When HSUS refused to take a public position against hunting: Amory often used humor as a weapon. In one of his commentaries on the *Today* show, he announced the formation of a new club called "The Hunt-the-Hunters Hunt Club." Describing its philosophy, he explained that club members treat hunters the same way that hunters treat animals: "We shoot them for their own good."

As a reporter in the Texas Monthly drily put it, "You would not want Cleveland to be in charge of making a Sophie's Choice between you and any animal": Michael Blumenthal, "Wild Kingdom," Texas Monthly, January 1999, 54.

The picture was published in High Times: High Times, September 1979, vol 49, 121.

Chapter Thirteen

Sally was "smaller than Nim but with double his charm": Amory, Ranch of Dreams, 192.

Amory hired Byrne as the new manager after one interview: D. J. Schubert, a wildlife biologist working for the Fund, originally found Byrne in Dallas. Amory asked Schubert to spy on him for a few days in Dallas, check out his house and lifestyle, to see if he appeared to be as good as Schubert believed he was. Byrne checked out. Then Amory flew to Dallas to meet him over lunch.

Byrne took in two camels from private collections: According to a primatologist currently employed at the Bronx Zoo, there are more tigers in private collections in the United States than there are in the wild. This amazing statistic makes a clear comment on the disappearing wild. It is difficult to collect data on exotic animals in private collections. Some of them, no doubt, survive in captivity far longer than they would in the wild. But many are sold off to canned hunts, where hunters pay to shoot specific species at virtually point-blank range.

The Story of Nim: The Chimp Who Learned Language: The book is by Anna Michel, with photos by Susan Kuklin and Herbert Terrace.

"He was inconsolable": Amory, *Ranch of Dreams,* 201.

confirmed a massive heart attack: Nim had an enlarged heart and an EKG done two years before his death indicated potential heart problems. He was not on any medication or treatment protocol. His brother Onan had the same condition and had died six months earlier at Primarily Primates.

BIBLIOGRAPHY

Amory, Cleveland. *Ranch of Dreams.* New York: Penguin, 1997.

Baker, Steve. *Picturing the Beast: Animals, Identity, and Representation.* Urbana: University of Illinois Press, 1993.

Bekoff, Mark. *The Emotional Lives of Animals: A Leading Scientist Explores Animal Sorrow, Joy, and Empathy — and Why They Matter.* Novato, Calif.: New World Library, 2007.

Blum, Deborah. *Monkey Wars.* New York: Oxford University Press, 1994.

Boyd, William. *Brazzaville Beach.* New York: William Morrow, 1991.

—————. *Love at Goon Park: Harry Harlow and the Science of Affection.* Cambridge, Mass.: Perseus, 2003.

Boysen, Sarah. *Sheba the Chimp and Skylar.* New York: Scholastic, 1991.

Brewer, Stella. *The Chimps of Mt. Asserik.*

New York: Alfred A. Knopf, 1978.

Candland, Douglas Keith. *Feral Children and Clever Animals: Reflections on Human Nature.* New York: Oxford University Press, 1993.

Crist, Eileen. *Images of Animals: Anthropomorphism and the Animal Mind.* Philadelphia: Temple University Press, 1999.

Daston, Lorraine, and Gregg Mitman, editors. *Thinking with Animals: New Perspectives on Anthropomorphism.* New York: Columbia University Press, 2005.

Fossey, Dian. *Gorillas in the Mist.* Boston: Houghton Mifflin, 1983.

Fouts, Roger, with Stephen Turkel Mills. *Next of Kin: What Chimpanzees Have Taught Me About Who We Are.* New York: William Morrow, 1997.

Fudge, Erica. *Animal.* London: Reaktion Books, 2002.

Gardner, R. Allen, Beatrix T. Gardner, and Thomas E. Van Cantfort. *Teaching Sign Language to Chimpanzees.* Albany: State University of New York Press, 1989.

Goodall, Jane. *Reason for Hope: A Spiritual Journey.* New York: Warner Books, 1999.

Grandin, Temple. *Animals in Translation: Using the Mysteries of Autism to Decode*

Animal Behavior. New York: Scribner, 2005.

Greek, C. Ray, and Jean Swingle Greek. *Specious Science: How Genetics and Evolution Reveal Why Medical Research on Animals Harms Humans.* New York: Continuum, 2002.

Griffin, Donald. *The Animal Mind: Beyond Cognition to Consciousness.* Chicago: University of Chicago Press, 2001.

Hahn, Emily. *Eve and the Apes.* New York: Weidenfeld and Nicolson, 1988.

———. *On the Side of the Apes.* New York: Thomas Y. Crowell, 1971.

Haraway, Donna. *The Haraway Reader.* New York: Routledge, 2004.

———. *Primate Visions: Gender, Race, and Nature in the World of Modern Science.* New York: Routledge, 1989.

Hauser, Marc D. *Wild Minds: What Animals Really Think.* New York: Henry Holt, 2000.

Kete, Kathleen. *The Beast in the Boudoir: Pet Keeping in Nineteenth-Century Paris.* Berkeley: University of California Press, 1994.

Kuczaj, Stan, editor. *Language Development,* vol. 2: *Language, Thought, and Culture.* Hillsdale, N.J.: Lawrence Erlbaum, 1982.

Ladygina-Kohts, N. N. *Infant Chimpanzee and Human Child: A Classic 1935 Comparative Study of Ape Emotions and Intelligence.* New York: Oxford University Press, 2002.

Linden, Eugene. *Apes, Men, and Language.* New York: E. P. Dutton, 1975.

———. *Silent Partners: The Legacy of the Ape Language Experiments.* New York: Ballantine Books, 1987.

Mahoney, James. *Saving Molly: A Research Veterinarian's Choices.* Chapel Hill, N.C.: Algonquin Books, 1998.

Marks, Jonathan. *What It Means to Be 98% Chimpanzee: Apes, People, and Their Genes.* Berkeley: University of California Press, 2002.

Marshall, Julie Hoffman. *Making Burros Fly: Cleveland Amory.* Boulder, Colo.: Johnson Books, 2006.

Noell, Anna Mae. *The History of Noell's Ark Gorilla Show.* Tarpon Springs, Fla.: Noell's Ark, 1979.

Pepperberg, Irene Maxine. *The Alex Studies: Cognitive and Communicative Abilities of Grey Parrots.* Cambridge, Mass.: Harvard University Press, 1999.

Peterson, Dale. *Eating Apes.* Berkeley: University of California Press, 2003.

Pinker, Steven. *The Language Instinct: How*

the Mind Creates Language. New York: William Morrow, 1994.

Ritvo, Harriet. *The Animal Estate: The English and Other Creatures in the Victorian Age.* Cambridge, Mass.: Harvard University Press, 1987.

Rothfels, Nigel, editor. *Representing Animals.* Bloomington: Indiana University Press, 2002.

Rudicille, Deborah. *The Scalpel and the Butterfly: The War Between Animal Research and Animal Protection.* New York: Farrar, Straus and Giroux, 2000.

Sapolsky, Robert M. *Monkeyluv: And Other Essays on Our Lives as Animals.* New York: Scribner, 2005.

———. *A Primate's Memoir.* New York: Scribner, 2001.

———. *The Trouble with Testosterone.* New York: Touchstone, 1997.

Savage-Rumbaugh, Sue, and Roger Levin. *Kanzi: The Ape at the Brink of the Human Mind.* New York: John Wiley and Sons, 1994.

Segerdahl, Pär, William Fields, and Sue Savage-Rumbaugh. *Kanzi's Primal Language: The Cultural Initiation of Primates into Language.* New York: Palgrave Macmillan, 2005.

Singer, Peter. *Ethics into Action: Henry Spira and the Animal Rights Movement.* New York: Rowman and Littlefield, 1998.

――― (foreword). *The Great Ape Project Census: Recognition for the Uncounted.* Portland, Oreg.: Great Ape Project Books, 2003.

Slater, Lauren. *Opening Skinner's Box: Great Psychological Experiments of the Twentieth Century.* New York: W. W. Norton, 2004.

Smith, Vince. *A Chimp in the Family: The True Story of Two Infants — One Human and One Chimpanzee — Growing Up Together.* New York: Marlowe and Company, 2004.

Stallwood, Kim W., editor. *Speaking Out for Animals.* New York: Lantern Books, 2001.

Strum, Shirley C. *Almost Human: A Journey into the World of Baboons.* New York: Random House, 1987.

Temerlin, Maurice K. *Lucy: Growing Up Human: A Chimpanzee Daughter in a Psychologist's Family.* Palo Alto, Calif.: Science and Behavior Books, 1975.

Terrace, Herbert S. *Nim: A Chimpanzee Who Learned Sign Language.* New York: Alfred A. Knopf, 1979.

Terrace, Herbert S., and Janet Metcalfe, editors. *The Missing Link in Cognition:*

Origins of Self-Reflective Consciousness. New York: Oxford University Press, 2004.

Waal, Frans de. *The Ape and the Sushi Master: Cultural Reflections of a Primatologist.* New York: Basic Books, 2001.

————. *Chimpanzee Politics: Power and Sex Among Apes.* New York: Harper and Row, 1982.

Wallman, Joel. *Aping Language.* Cambridge: Cambridge University Press, 1982.

Washburn, David A., and Duane M. Rumbaugh, editors. *Primate Perspectives on Behavior and Cognition.* Washington, D.C.: American Psychological Association, 2006.

Wise, Steven M. *Drawing the Line.* Cambridge, Mass.: Perseus Books, 2002.

————. *Rattling the Cage: Towards Legal Rights for Animals.* Cambridge, Mass.: Perseus Books, 2000.

Wolfe, Cary. *Animal Rites: American Culture, the Discourse of Species, and Posthumanist Theory.* Chicago: University of Chicago Press, 2003.

ACKNOWLEDGMENTS

Stephanie LaFarge embraced this project from day one. She remained generous with her time and thoughts until the bitter end. She also introduced me to her extended family — the Lees and the LaFarges. Their willingness to talk about their simian sibling and a complicated chapter of their adolescent lives made this a better book. Jenny Lee, especially, made Nim come alive each time we spoke. Ann LaFarge also shared memories from a difficult time in her life. Early on, I went to see Herbert Terrace at Columbia University; he was initially surprised by my interest in Nim, but willing to talk. I thank him for not turning me away.

Dozens of graduate students gravitated toward Project Nim. Joyce Butler, Renee Falitz, Bob Johnson, Bill Tynan, Susan Quinby, and Mary Wambach all helped me to understand Project Nim — and Nim. I am grateful to them for giving an outsider the inside story.

On an early research trip to Norman, I met Robert Ingersoll, whose assistance has been invaluable. Peter Lemmon kindly invited me to see the Institute for Primate Studies right before the farm was sold, providing me with a memorable glimpse of the old pink house on the hill. IPS suddenly became real.

During the initial research phase of this book, I had much to learn about chimpanzees, research laboratories, sanctuaries, and the people who dedicate their lives to primates. Carole Noon, a leading expert on the rehabilitation of ex-research chimps, allowed me to spend a few days at the Coulston Foundation in Alamogordo not long after she took over the facility. That visit, albeit brief, was an eye-opener. It wasn't LEMSIP, but it was close. I am grateful to Noon for giving me access to this hidden world.

D. J. Schubert welcomed me to the Black Beauty Ranch and was eager to answer questions and assist me with this project. At Black Beauty, I spent time with Kitty, Lulu, and Midge, Nim's three chimpanzee companions. Schubert gave me free rein to observe the animals twenty-four hours a day, which was a rare and extraordinary op-

portunity. At Black Beauty, Dawna Epperson took me under her wing and shared her
insights into the primates in her care. No
one is closer to Kitty, Midge, and Lulu;
Dawna is their "mother."

For invaluable research assistance, their
time, and all kinds of support, I want to
thank Harry and Gigi Benson, Lois Bloom,
Chadwick Bovee, Carol Ann Germain, Jane
Isay, Barrie Olson, John Pollock, Marian
Probst, Bambi Schieffelin, Ann Watkins (my
travel companion to Texas), Lee Watt, and
my sister, Lindy Hess. Many other close
friends — you know who you are — offered
counsel over the years I was working on this
book. I especially want to thank Michael
Singer and Ruth Reichl for the night they
told me, unequivocally, that I had to write
Nim's story. *Nim Chimpsky* crystallized at
that very moment.

Sarah Lazin, my agent and close friend,
took on this unusual project with great
enthusiasm. Without her blessing, I would
never have become Nim's biographer. I can
never thank her enough. She sent my proposal to Beth Rashbaum at Bantam, where
I have had a charmed experience. Meghan
Keenan, Beth's assistant, took every opportunity to help me turn this book into a
reality. Virginia Norey, an animal lover

herself, designed a genuinely beautiful book. As for Beth, I have wanted to work with her for many years. Her sharp mind, insistence on excellence, and willingness to polish every word until it shines — turned *Nim Chimpsky* into a readable book. Unlike myself, Beth never lost her sense of direction as she followed Nim from New York to Texas. I also had the pleasure of watching her fall in love with Nim. She is, by any definition, a great editor.

Last, but never least, my husband, Peter Biskind, listened to countless stories about Nim and read multiple drafts of this book. His influence is pervasive and invaluable. Peter never fails me.

PHOTO CREDITS AND PERMISSIONS